THE CRIME OF ALL CRIMES

The Crime of All Crimes

Toward a Criminology of Genocide

Nicole Rafter

NEW YORK UNIVERSITY PRESS

New York and London

NEW YORK UNIVERSITY PRESS
New York and London
www.nyupress.org

References to Internet websites (URLs) were accurate at the time of writing. Neither the author nor New York University Press is responsible for URLs that may have expired or changed since the manuscript was prepared.

ISBN: 978-1-4798-5948-1

For Library of Congress Cataloging-in-Publication data, please contact the Library of Congress.

New York University Press books are printed on acid-free paper, and their binding materials are chosen for strength and durability. We strive to use environmentally responsible suppliers and materials to the greatest extent possible in publishing our books.

Manufactured in the United States of America

10 9 8 7 6 5 4 3 2 1

Also available as an ebook

For my beloved friend Susan Erony, who has spent much of her life painting images of genocide,

and in memory of another dear friend, Christine Margaret Alder, of Melbourne, Australia, 1950–2015

CONTENTS

ILLUSTRATIONS

This book was born in a specific time and place—and as quite a surprise to me. I had gone to Linz, Austria, on a Fulbright Fellowship to teach at Johannes Kepler University. I soon discovered that Linz was Adolf Hitler's hometown. He was born nearby; he went to grade school in a gloomy, abandoned building a few blocks behind my apartment; and his mother's house was still standing on the other side of the Danube. I walked to it across the grandiose Nibelungen Bridge, named and designed by Hitler as the entrance to what he intended to be his mausoleum. From my fifth-floor window above the Hauptplatz, I looked down on the balcony from which Hitler announced Germany's annexation of Austria—an occasion for wild celebration by most of Linz's inhabitants—though not, of course, for its Jews, most of whom were dead within the week or deported to Dachau.

A few years before I moved to Linz, the European Union had chosen the city as a "cultural capital," giving it prize money to encourage cultural development and tourism. Some of the funds went to an artists' project that identified locations of events from the Nazi period and then stenciled, in white paint, brief descriptions on the pavement:

April 1945; 8 Marienstrasse. Anton A. is departmental head of the city administration and criticizes the execution of two female "Eastern workers" for the theft of milk as being inhuman. He is sentenced to death and shot.

1943. 20 Lederergasse. The teacher Hermine L. writes a number of letters that were critical of the regime to her brother Walter who is a soldier stationed in Vienna. Both were sentenced to death and executed.

Everywhere I turned, I was brought up short by reminders of the Third Reich. I passed Adolf Eichmann's apartment on my way to the market. A few kilometers down the Danube was Hartheim Castle, where mentally disabled inhabitants of the region, considered threats to the purity of Aryan "blood," were "euthanized" in one of the first gas chambers. In the other direction lay the Mauthausen concentration camp, for extermination through labor. Reaching out from Mauthausen like tentacles were the cold, dank tunnels of the Gusen and Ebensee underground camps, where skeletal prisoners produced munitions, airplanes, and V-2 rockets until they died and were tossed on the heaps of corpses in the corridors.

I had gone to Linz planning to write a history of criminology and ended up beginning a book on genocide. Although I had no ambition to add to the history of Linz or the Nazi system, I was transfixed by Hartheim Castle, associated as it was with the mentally disabled, a population whose criminalization I had been writing about for decades. For years after I returned to the United States, I corresponded with Cathrin Dorner, the docent who had given me my tour of Hartheim, questioning her about the layout of the institution, its history, and her experience of working so close to a gas chamber. Eventually I chose the Nazis' efforts to exterminate the mentally disabled for in-depth treatment in this book. I was nearly finished with the book's final chapter when I discovered that the great-grandfather of one of my Austrian students had died in the Hartheim gas chamber.

* * *

Raphael Lemkin, the Polish specialist in international law who coined the word "genocide," founded modern genocide research before and during World War II by studying the Armenian and Ukrainian genocides and the rules imposed by the Nazis on occupied countries. After World War II, Lemkin continued research on genocide; after his death in 1959, this work was continued by historians and sociologists such as Leo Kuper, Helen Fein, and Raul Hilberg. Many early students of genocide were Jews; some had been born in Europe and lived through the Holocaust. Holocaust studies slowly expanded, remaining a field in its own right while also branching off into genocide studies. Stimulated by the atrocities in Rwanda and the former Yugoslavia, genocide studies exploded in the 1990s, spreading to new fields and drawing in researchers with no direct connection to the Holocaust. This book is part of that expansion.

One of my biggest problems in writing this book was simply keeping abreast of the flood of journal articles, monographs, edited collections, and government reports on genocide. I asked Google Scholar to keep me updated on all publications concerned with genocide, which resulted in an almost daily list. (I grew to dread opening it, for each new source that I added to my working bibliography slowed my writing process.) Genocide studies today is truly a crowded, multidisciplinary field—but it has seldom dealt with genocide as a crime. A few criminologists have already written about genocide; with them, I aim at adding criminology to the interdisciplinary mix.

* * *

I could not have produced this book without the help of numerous friends and colleagues. Graduate students gave generously of their insights and time, especially members of my Crimes against Humanity seminars. Laura Siller, mobilizing undergraduate Jocelyn Griffin to assist her, organized my data using the NVIVO program—and lit up my office with the sparks of her ideas. Jeff Botto, another graduate student, prepared appendix A and my graph of twentieth-century genocides. My doctoral student Kristin Bell-Gerke, with whom I coauthored an essay on gender and genocide, read and commented astutely on the entire manuscript—parts of it several times. I was helped greatly by Katharina Neissl, whom I first met as a student in Linz and whom I lured to Northeastern University's graduate program. The books Katharina and her family have given me greatly expanded my library on Linz and National Socialism in Austria. My former graduate student Chad Posick, now at Georgia Southern University, also commented on the entire book and discussed new ideas with me. Andrew Baranauskas, a current Northeastern gradute student, helped me prepare the Index.

Colleagues at the School of Criminology and Criminal Justice, Northeastern University, were enormously supportive. I want to thank in particular Dean Chet Britt, who helped me get started, Katya Bochkovar, Carlos Cuevas, Kevin Drakulich, the always tough and always helpful Amy Farrell, Natasha Frost, Jack McDevitt (who also helped me get started), Jacob Stowell, Brandon Welsh, and Greg Zimmerman. Yves Hyacinthe and others in Northeastern's Interlibrary Loan office provided a lifeline to distant journals and books.

Colleagues elsewhere who contributed include Johann Bacher of Johannes Kepler University; Michelle Brown of the University of Tennessee; Cathrin Dorner of the Hartheim Castle Memorial Site; Abbott Gleason of Brown University; Vannessa Hearman of the University of Sydney, who helped with photographs of the Pancasila Monument; Shadd Maruna, now of Rutgers University–Newark; Annie Pohlman, University of Queensland, to whom I turned often for help with the Indonesian genocide; Annika van Baar of VU University, Amsterdam; Geoff Ward of the University of California–Irvine; Sandra Walklate of the University of Liverpool; and Per J. Ystehede of the University of Oslo. During the early stages of this book, Susanne Karstedt, now of Griffith University, shared her work on genocide, mass atrocities, and violent societies. Hollie Nyseth Brehm of Ohio State University read and commented on much of the manuscript; I profited especially from her in-depth knowledge of the Rwandan genocide, which she shared most generously. Near the end of the writing (or so I thought), I received a fourteen-page, single-spaced critique of the manuscript from Andrew Woolford of the University of Manitoba; it slowed me down, but the book is much the stronger for this generous, close reading and discussion of key issues.

Once again I received expert guidance from colleagues at NYU Press, most significantly my superb editor, Ilene Kalish. This is the third book on which I have worked with Ilene, and my admiration grows with each volume. Others at NYU Press who helped get my manuscript into print included Caelyn Cobb, Dorothea Stillman Halliday, and Andrew Katz. I also appreciate the help of the press's anonymous reviewers of the manuscript.

Henry Ferrini and the Gloucester Writing Center gave me a peaceful break for writing by the ocean. My computer-savvy friend Christine Bowker took over the job of finding the illustrations and getting them in shape for publication, work that would have taken me weeks to do on my own—and that, in truth, I could not have done on my own. Without Chris's long hours of help and her patience, this book would have no illustrations. My old friend Susan Erony, who knows genocide from the inside, helped me through psychologically hard times even when I did not mention them. Other friends and family contributed as well: Victor Swenson, Judith Yarnall, Sunali Goonesekera, Alex Hahn, Sarah Hahn, and above all my husband, Robert Hahn, who edited every chapter and endured hours of genocide talk that he might have preferred to skip.

1

Genocide, Criminology, and Evolution of the "Crime of Crimes"

The Katyn Forest Genocide, 1940

In the spring of 1940, 22,000 citizens of Poland—mainly officers of the Polish army, police officers, and prominent intellectuals—were systematically executed by members of Josef Stalin's secret police, the NKVD, in what became known as the Katyn Forest Massacre. The mass slaughter began as soon as the ground, near the camps where the prisoners were held in western Russia, was soft enough to dig pits for the bodies. Due to the great secrecy of the massacre, no one knows exactly where all of these men (and one woman—a second lieutenant) were killed, although skeletal remains show that most were executed with a shot to the back of the neck that went up through the brain and out the skull near the eyes. Eyewitnesses later reported that many victims had been shot in a soundproofed basement room by a NKVD executioner wearing a butcher's apron, hat, and long gloves—to protect himself from blood and spattering brains. He was able to kill about 250 Poles a night. Their bodies were then buried in neat rows, one on top of another, in mass graves; one grave site, in the northwest Soviet Union, was in the Katyn (pronounced KA-tin) Forest, which gave the massacre its name.[1]

Few of the victims suspected what lay in store for them, for the Soviets had beguiled their prisoners with rumors of release. Some left their prison camps to the music of marching bands; apparently the Soviets were helping celebrate their release. Others were given typhus shots as though to protect them on their journey home. They did not realize that Stalin and his Politburo had condemned them to death; nor did anyone in Poland know about their fate. Their families were hurriedly deported to the far north, where many of them died from hunger or the cold. The prisoners' disappearance was a mystery that the entire Polish nation struggled to solve for the next fifty years. This was a secret genocide.

Because the victims of the event seem so different from those of the Holocaust—the popular template for genocide—many who read about the Katyn Forest Massacre might be reluctant to term it a genocide. Yet it fits the United Nations' definition of genocide as an act "committed with intent to destroy, in whole or in part, a national, ethnical, racial or religious group, as such"—meaning as a group with those characteristics.[2] The Soviet Union had recently annexed the eastern half of Poland; Stalin planned to incorporate the land into the Soviet Union, erasing that part of Poland entirely or turning it into a satellite state. Yet, because his plans were unknown, when the Soviets captured a large number of Poles—army officers, reservists, professors, lawyers, engineers, and artists who recently had been mobilized into the Polish army—the bewildered prisoners barely resisted, for they had no idea that they were at war. Nevertheless, when spies later secretly interrogated them in the prison camps, they insisted on their loyalty to Poland. Stalin and his Politburo, certain that these Polish patriots, if freed, would resist the Soviet takeover of their country, eventually condemned them to death.[3]

"Stalin was a pioneer of national mass murder," writes the historian Timothy Snyder, "and the Poles were the preeminent victims among the Soviet nationalities."[4] The Soviets mistrusted these particular Poles for reasons of ethnicity, nationality, social class (they were educated "bourgeoisie"), and politics. Their removal from Poland and later liquidation was, as Snyder puts it, "a kind of decapitation of Polish society."[5]

But although the Katyn Forest Massacre meets the UN's first criterion for genocide—it was intended to destroy, "in whole or in part," a national group—it differs in so many respects from the Holocaust that even genocide scholars rarely mention it.

Goals of This Book

The omission of the Katyn Forest Massacre from discussions of genocide—common but unfounded—leads directly to a central question of this book: What do genocides look like? Do most or all of them in fact resemble the Holocaust? If not, what—if anything—do genocides have in common? I devote much of the book to answering this question. A second key question asks how genocides have evolved over time. But let me begin by explaining what I hope to accomplish in this book. My goals are

- to identify the changing contours of genocide across the twentieth century through comparative study of eight genocides;
- to draw conclusions about the causes of genocide on the basis of comparisons of these eight disparate genocides; and
- to probe the ways in which criminology might contribute to better understanding of the crime of genocide.

I have structured the research to examine genocide as a generic phenomenon—comparing genocides to see if typical patterns appear—and to investigate genocide as a crime. The book is based on a unique data set: detailed comparative information about eight diverse genocides committed throughout the world and throughout the twentieth century. Its approach is that of comparative criminology.

As an exploratory study, this one is not designed to promote a major new theory about genocide or to back one of the many theories already in play—although it does confirm some earlier theoretical positions and disconfirm others. Above all, the study's value lies in its effort to apply a rigorous, systematic methodology—comparative criminology—to genocide in order to determine what the phenomenon "looks like." While historians have produced invaluable studies of single genocides, little agreement has as yet been reached about how social science might be used to compare events of this type. Until recently, most "comparative" studies of genocide were edited collections of chapters on individual genocides with introductions that generalize across the examples but do so intuitively and unsystematically.[6] This is changing today with the publication of truly comparative studies that do much to illuminate the nature of genocide.[7] Moreover, quantitative research on genocide is surging ahead.[8] Although the present study is only minimally quantitative, its systematic character helps establish more reliable conclusions about the nature of genocide than edited "comparative" collections were able to reach.

It seems strange that few people have tried to apply criminology to genocide, given that genocide is first and foremost a crime and that criminology, broadly defined to include methods and explanations from sociology, psychology, history, and other fields, offers rich possibilities for improving our grasp of genocide.[9] I try to see how far criminology can carry us toward better comprehension of this type of atrocity.

The prospects might seem dim, given that many criminologists focus on street crime and that criminology is largely a product of the Global North, whereas most genocides, until recently, were thought to have occurred elsewhere. Nonetheless, I want to see how well criminological methods and theories apply elsewhere, including to the Global South and the world's most serious crime. Moreover, a new generation of scholars is insisting that colonial genocides occurred in both the United States and Canada, atrocities against indigenous peoples that can no longer be dismissed just because they do not conform to the Holocaust template or easily fit with the UN's definition of genocide.[10] These scholars are leading the way toward a powerful new understanding of the crime of genocide.

It may also seem strange that I, in particular, think criminology is up to these tasks or can be trusted to accomplish them without causing serious harm. In "Criminology's Darkest Hour," I wrote about criminology's role in the Nazi genocides, during which explanations of crime were adapted to eugenic ends and used to justify the extermination of not only criminals but also Jews, "Gypsies," homosexuals, and other "asocials."[11] In *Creating Born Criminals*, I wrote about eugenic criminology, a movement (ca. 1870–1940) in the United States and elsewhere that criminalized people with mental disabilities and established eugenic prisons in which so-called feeble-minded criminals could be held for life.[12] One outcome was the US Supreme Court's infamous *Buck v. Bell* decision, in which Justice Oliver Wendell Holmes, Jr., allowed forced sterilization of people deemed feeble-minded; otherwise, Holmes reasoned, their "degenerate offspring" would end up as killers.[13]

However, the eugenics movement has passed, and I have grown less doubtful of criminology's potential. Over decades of thinking about criminology, I have found it a flexible tool for addressing all sorts of social problems. And genocide *is* a crime, albeit one that until recently most criminologists ignored. Moreover, criminology has always been deeply engaged with politics and social justice. I wrote this book because I think criminology can improve understandings of the very complex phenomenon of genocide.

A Changing Crime in a Changing World

There was a time, not so long ago, when genocide seemed to have remained fairly static over time as a type of event. The model was set by a biblical story in the book of Numbers, in which Moses sends the Israelites to war against the Midianites. When the Israelites had slain all the males and captured their women, children, and flocks, they returned to Moses, expecting praise for their efforts. But to their surprise, he was furious: "Have ye saved all the women alive? . . . Kill every male among the little ones, and kill every woman that hath known man by lying with him. But all the women children, that have not known a man by lying with him, keep alive for yourselves."[14] In this telling (we might call it the biblical model), genocide begins with a leader who orders his soldiers to destroy all males in the targeted group while permitting them to pillage and keep surviving women (at least the virgins) and female children for themselves as slaves or other chattel.

For some people, the biblical model remains a dominant image of genocide, and in some respects, that image is correct. One consistent characteristic is that genocides rarely, if ever, result in total destruction of the victim population—even all of its men. Of the Poles in the Russian prison camps, about 395 survived the Katyn Forest Massacre, approximately 100 of whom were probably informants.[15] One who was spared was the nephew of a Soviet film director. Another, who was wanted for interrogation by the NKVD, was led to the forest but pulled back; he ended up teaching economics in Canada.[16] There are always some survivors who live to tell their tale. In twentieth-century genocides, as in the war on the Midianites, moreover, wholesale theft of property is common and may even be a central aim of the slaughter. And in more recent genocides, the victors often continue to evince great interest in the captured women's sexuality, although they are more likely to rape than to kidnap and assimilate the virgins.

In the academic world, static models of genocide were abandoned as Holocaust scholars adopted the idea of genocide as a *process*. There followed stage models and, with them, sensitivity to internal dynamics in genocidal events.[17] But scholars produced few broad overviews that might give a sense of changes over time in genocide itself—not in individual genocidal events but in the phenomenon per se—until the criminologist Susanne Karstedt began writing about the evolution of genocide.[18] Even then, the changes remained difficult to detect because genocides differ so much among themselves.

In what follows, I identify and try to explain some of these changes. Next I identify changes in *responses* to genocide over time, and I conclude this section by noting how the *study* of genocide has changed in recent years.

Genocide Is Changing

The crime itself is evolving. From the arrival of the Spanish in the New World and well into the twentieth century, genocides often were precipitated by colonialism, with its hunger for land, physical resources, and the labor of the indigenous population.[19] Later (and into the present) genocide was often linked to decolonization and efforts by postcolonial states to establish themselves as homogeneous nations. During the first half of the twentieth century, the crime tended to be committed by nation-states against other states. Both colonialist and interstate genocides drew on imperialism, nationalism, and grand ideologies of race and ethnicity to justify their atrocities. These justifications were still used to rationalize genocides at the end of the twentieth century, but they had lost their former power. Today, as Karstedt writes, contemporary genocides and other mass atrocities "typically occur beneath the level of the nation-state and independently of its boundaries. They evolve in the environment, social formation and the complex actor configurations of 'extremely violent societies.' . . . Diverse groups of perpetrators participate for a multitude of reasons, ranging from state government forces to militias. . . . Perpetrators are located beyond borders, and recruited across borders."[20] One of the most prominent changes, then, is the fluidity and localization of recent genocides. That genocides now tend to be committed *within* a country, often as part of a civil war, helps explain why the pace of genocide picked up in the second half of the twentieth century. Genocide was simply not as big or costly an enterprise as it often had been in the past.

The location of genocides and their frequency by global location also changed over the twentieth century (fig. 1.1). Genocides in Asia declined; there was but one genocide in Europe (in the former Yugo-

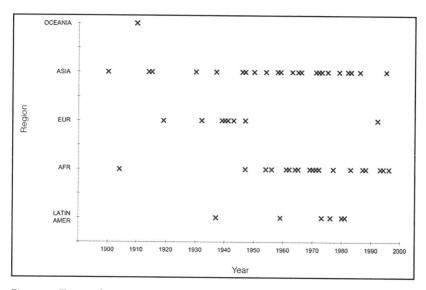

Figure 1.1. Twentieth-century genocides by location and frequency. *Note*: This figure does not include cultural genocides.

slavia) after the middle of the twentieth century; and genocide in Latin America started to die out with the end of the Cold War, which was fought by proxy in countries like Guatemala. In contrast, Africa—which had little genocide through the mid-twentieth century—was thereafter beset by atrocities of this type. Many occurred in Central Africa, where they were tied to ethnic conflicts (especially between Hutu and Tutsi; see appendix A) and where the struggles flowed back and forth across borders.[21] Victims and offenders sometimes exchanged roles in the process. "While genocide scholars routinely place people into categories such as 'victim,' 'perpetrator,' or 'bystander,'" one research team observes, "these categories are not mutually exclusive in reality. Rather, a Rwandan may have killed a neighbor and saved the life of another neighbor, perhaps within the course of a single day."[22] In early twenty-first-century struggles in Central Africa, warring parties grabbed for whatever resources were available; some sold illegally seized goods such as diamonds and precious metals to organized crime groups, which supplied them with weapons in return.

Some political analysts have attempted to explain the global shift of genocide to Central Africa by arguing that globalization stimulated atrocities in this area. When one looks at the embeddedness of the conflicts in international networks such as those of arms sales and illegal trading, globalization may indeed seem to have been a culprit. However, globalization coincided with declines in genocide elsewhere and may even have encouraged them.[23] So the role of globalization is at best unclear, and in any case, one needs to consider globalization in the context of ongoing regional conflicts.[24] The most plausible explanation of the global shift in genocide is ethnic conflicts—themselves rooted in the racism of colonization—in newly forming (or re-forming) African states.

Is the rate of genocide increasing, or do states and other large-scale groups, perhaps constrained by the growth of humanitarian law since the mid-twentieth century, resort less frequently to mass atrocities today than in the past? A number of scholars claim that genocide is declining, a position reinforced by the high-profile erudition of Steven Pinker, the Harvard University psychologist, in his 2011 book *The Better Angels of Our Nature: Why Violence Has Declined.*[25] This is a comforting message, but if anything, the genocide scholar Robert Melson argues, genocides have increased in frequency since the breakup of the Soviet Union and emergence of the "third world."[26] My data (fig. 1.1) point to the same conclusion—a conclusion reinforced by the tendency of twenty-first-century genocides to simmer under the radar as prolonged and episodic struggles among paramilitary groups in weak states and, thus, perhaps, to be invisible to those who are tallying genocides.[27] I return to this issue later, when I discuss the political scientist Kathryn Sikkink's identification of a "justice cascade" that may have started deterring genocides the world over. Scholars should be able to reach a definite conclusion in this debate in another few years.

Among the notable changes in genocide over time is the apparent increase in the use of mass rape as an instrument of genocide, although it is hard to know whether the increase is real or simply a byproduct of greater awareness and poor records on earlier atrocities. In any case, there is less abduction of women and children today than in earlier periods, no doubt because slavery is now outlawed. Another change—although this impression is harder to prove—is that genocide today involves less deliberate dehumanization than in earlier decades. At the very least, there seems to be a falling off from the high-water mark of systematic victim degradation set by the Nazis, even though the decrease is ragged and broken by ugly exceptions. A final change is the spread in worldwide recognition of genocide as crime.

Responses to Genocide Are Changing

"Who, after all, speaks today of the annihilation of the Armenians?" Adolf Hitler asked, announcing his decision to commit genocide against the Poles and trying, at the same time, to reassure his military.[28] Hitler expected history to grant the Nazis impunity—freedom to commit genocide without consequences—and his expectation was not unfounded: at the time (1939), no group had ever been brought to trial and punished for genocide. But in the aftermath of World War II, nations mobilized to bring the Nazis to justice, and the Nuremberg trials of Nazi leaders marked the beginning of the end for impunity—at least for high-level perpetrators. Those who defeated the perpetrators tended to treat themselves to victor's justice, even when they, too, had arguably committed atrocities.

It was not easy, however, to persuade nations to give up their traditional sovereignty—their autonomy and independence to do as they pleased, even if what pleased them was genocide. The world had to wait until the early 1990s for the next international challenges to impunity, which came from the United Nations in the form of two special courts, the International Criminal Tribunal for the former Yugoslavia (May 1993) and the International Criminal Tribunal for Rwanda (November 1994), both established in response to conflicts that looked genocidal. Today, among those who are most concerned with human rights, *everyone* remembers the annihilation of the Armenians.

Another change in responses to genocide came with the 2002 establishment of the International Criminal Court, a court of last resort with jurisdiction over genocide, crimes against humanity, war crimes, and the crime of aggression.[29] As of January 2015, 123 countries had ratified or acceded to its establishing document, the Rome Statute, which defines and prohibits these crimes. (The United States, reluctant to cede sovereignty, is not one of them.) Establishment of the International Criminal Court breathed new life into the global trend of holding leaders criminally accountable for human rights violations.[30]

One of the most visible signs of that trend is the transitional justice movement—judicial and nonjudicial measures to redress massive human rights abuses and improve accountability, survivor support, and the building of democratic institutions. The transitional justice movement includes truth commission officials, genocide prosecution teams, NGOs (nongovernmental organizations such as Human Rights Watch), academics, and local judges (such as those of Rwanda's informal *gacaca* courts). Extending far beyond formal criminal justice, its goals range from helping survivors of genocidal rape to putting shattered nations back together.[31] The transitional justice movement is something new under the sun.

Changes in response to genocide have been made apparent through reportage and media, notably through treatment in film. Some of the earliest footage of the Holocaust, shot as Russian and Western troops opened up Nazi concentration and death camps, has been unearthed, processed, analyzed, and included in documentaries such as Alain Resnais's monumental *Night and Fog* (1955).[32] More recent contributions to this genre include films about genocides such as the Katyn Forest Massacre (*Katyn*, 2007, made by Andrzej Wajda, the great Polish director whose father was one of the victims) and the French genocide against Algerians (*The Battle of Algiers*, 1966, Gillo Pontecorvo's shocking movie). Genocide films both reflect and promote a worldwide consciousness of genocide that did not exist a generation or two ago.[33]

Another change is the emergence of genocide tourism, which raises public consciousness through creating memorials—not simply monuments but transformations of genocide sites into places where visitors can see what happened, mourn, and struggle to understand. Nazi concentration and death camps are now well-established tourist sites, with Auschwitz, Buchenwald, Dachau, and others visited by millions of people a year, many of them German. (One scholar estimates that "as many people now visit Holocaust memorials every year as died during the Holocaust itself.")[34] Cambodia has established a "dark tourism" site at Tuol Sleng, the torture and extermination prison in Phnom Penh, and Rwanda is hoping to become a destination where tourists can visit its Memorial Centre and study its genocide. Such memorials are a byproduct of globalization. They are one of the most powerful of recent changes in the treatment of genocide because they are points where genocide narratives—those of victims, torturers, commandants, slaughterers, survivors, and bystanders—can converge. Even Katyn now has its monument, though it is hard to get to.[35]

In a sign of the changing response to genocide in recent years, former president Bill Clinton traveled to Rwanda to apologize for not having done more to prevent the genocide there. "All over the world," he said, "there were people like me sitting in offices, day after day after day, who did not fully appreciate the depth and the speed with which you were being engulfed by this unimaginable terror."[36] Clinton had a lot to apologize for: timely action might have prevented the genocide entirely, and the lack of action possibly intensified the genocide by signaling that no one cared;[37] but nonetheless, Clinton did, voluntarily, publicly apologize. The contrast of his apology with Hitler's cavalier self-exculpation— "Who, after all, speaks today of the annihilation of the Armenians?"—is a measure of the changes in attitudes toward genocide over the past seventy years. Even the Soviets—albeit much more grudgingly—in 1990 apologized to the Poles for the Katyn tragedy.

The Study of Genocide Is Changing

The foremost change in response to genocide came in 1948, when the United Nations condemned genocide as an international crime and gave it a legal definition. The UN's Genocide Convention was a milestone of the greatest significance in the struggle to protect human rights, and the UN's definition of genocide in terms of "acts committed with intent to destroy . . . a national, ethnical, racial or religious group, as such" remains the norm in international law. However, the UN's definition omits the *political* groups that are often targeted during genocide.[38] Activists and academics alike often informally change the original phrase to read "a national, ethnical, racial, religious, *or political* group," but eventually a more formal change may be needed. Meanwhile, the definition of genocide is widely debated. In chapter 7, I argue that, given the frequency and horror of genocidal rape, it is unconscionable to exclude women from the protected groups. However, instead of advocating the addition of "women" to the list of groups protected against genocide, I argue that the list itself should be deleted in favor of a definition that protects *all* groups harmed by genocide, including groups victimized by colonial genocides. Meanwhile, I base this study only on attempted group exterminations that meet the UN's definition of genocide, modified to include attempted extermination of political groups.

Today, more people are studying genocide than at any time in the past, and more of them live outside the countries, the United States and the United Kingdom, that long dominated genocide studies. Historical and anthropological studies based on painstaking archival and field research, including publication of a massive and definitive volume of Katyn documents,[39] continue to be crucial. They form the bedrock of genocide studies. Today, however, scholars from other disciplines—and even these same disciplines of history and anthropology—use these foundational studies as secondary literature and build on them.[40] Indeed, this approach is typical of what the genocide scholar Scott Straus calls second-generation research on genocide.[41] The focus of scholarship is also changing. Today scholars concentrate less on the decision making of leaders and macro-structural background conditions such as race and ethnicity and more on micro variables such as friendship networks and subtle interactions between leaders. For instance, in a study of the Srebrenica massacre during the Bosnian civil war, the sociologist Stefan Klusemann shows that the atrocity "emerged from short-run shifts in emotions over a period of a day" as the Serbian commander General Mladić established dominance over the UN peacekeepers.[42] Psychology and social psychology, which used to play prominent roles in the theoretical literature on victims and perpetrators, have to some extent been eclipsed by political interpretations. In chapter 5, however, I show that we still must rely on psychology and social psychology to answer the crucial, perennial question about perpetrators: How could they do it?

Another interpretive change is the shift away from obedience to authority as a major explanation in genocide studies. In earlier decades, obedience to authority was used to account for the behavior of subordinate killers and, sometimes, victims who seemed to act against their own self-interest. Enthusiasm for the obedience explanation was stoked in the 1960s by a confluence of high-profile events. First, in 1960, Israel put Adolf Eichmann, the architect of the Final Solution, on trial. Not long after Eichmann's spectacular trial (he testified from a glass booth that protected him from assassination) and execution, the political theorist Hannah Arendt published *Eichmann in Jerusalem: A Report on the Banality of Evil*, a controversial work that stressed what she saw as the

unimaginative, bureaucratic, and almost automaton-like nature of Eichmann's behavior. Shortly thereafter, the psychologist Stanley Milgram
published the first article on his obedience experiments, "Some Conditions of Obedience and Disobedience to Authority," following it up a decade later with *Obedience to Authority: An Experimental View*. Milgram
seemed to prove that the majority of people would, like the Eichmann
portrayed by Arendt, be willing to harm others, even severely, if they
were instructed to do so by an authority figure.[43]

However, the Australian psychologist Gina Perry has now exposed
Milgram as, if not a fraud, at least an imprecise scientist who found what
he wanted to find.[44] "Milgram's obedience experiments," Perry writes,
"are as misunderstood as they are famous. This is partly because of Milgram's presentation of his findings—his downplaying of contradictions
and inconsistencies—and partly because it was the heart-attack variation [in which the subjects shocked the make-believe "learner" until his
screams fell silent] that was embraced by the popular media, magnified and reinforced into a powerful story."[45] Obedience to authority—
once an almost ubiquitous explanation for why men (and some women)
would kill during genocides—no longer seems automatically plausible
as an account of perpetrators' behavior. This is a significant substantive
change in the study of genocide.

Another change is the introduction of new types of scholarship. One
of the most unusual is use of aircraft and satellite photography, which
reveals shifts in earth formations and vegetation. An early example of
this type of research emerged—partly by happy accident—in the Katyn
case. After the massacre, Poles whose relatives and friends had vanished
were desperate to find out what had happened. Meanwhile, the Germans
and Soviets, now battling each other across Poland and into western
Russia, did their best to hide or fabricate the truth of the massacre. In
1943, when the Germans controlled the Katyn Forest territory, a wolf
carrying a human bone led to discovery of a mass grave. The Germans
staged an elaborate propaganda event at the gravesite to demonstrate
that the Soviets were responsible for the slaughter. The Soviets retaliated
with denials that threw the blame on the Germans. The struggle over the
truth continued while US and British officials withheld evidence that
implicated their Soviet allies, and Poles vainly petitioned the Soviets for
documents related to the victims' capture and death.

Figure 1.2. Mass grave at Katyn, Russia, 1943. During World War II, when the Germans discovered a burial pit in Russia's Katyn Forest, they blamed the massacre on the Russians. The Russians, in turn, blamed it on the Germans. This propaganda battle continued for five decades until the Russians finally admitted their guilt.

In 1990, a Polish American investigator discovered German aerial reconnaissance photographs taken during World War II; these images, spanning the period 1941–1944, demonstrated that the area of the mass graves had not been disturbed during the German occupation—and that thus the Germans could not have been responsible for the genocide. The photographs indicated, moreover, that the area *had* been disturbed before the Germans' arrival, thus implicating the Soviets. Further, they showed Soviets bulldozing some of the graves and removing what seemed to be bodies (thus suggesting a Soviet cover-up).[46] Discovery of these photographs coincided with dissolution of the Soviet Union and the policy of greater openness known as *glasnost*. The Russian leader Mikhail Gorbachev finally admitted Soviet responsibility for the genocide.[47]

More recently, in Rwanda, aircraft and satellite photography has been used to discover changes in agriculture before and after the genocide.[48] Although in this case there was no question about whether genocide had occurred or who was responsible, the photographs did show a severe die-off in vegetation after the genocide, highlighting the need for investigators to gauge environmental as well as human damage when calculating the toll of such events. In a study of the Cambodian genocide, the Yale University Genocide Studies Program uses layers of digital maps to show sites hit by US bombing sorties in the disruptive lead-up to the genocide as well as the location of Khmer Rouge prisons and mass graves.[49] Such geographical tools are leading the way to a new generation of methods for studying genocide.[50]

The most radical recent challenge to the study of genocide began with the idea of cultural genocide—destruction of a group by depriving it of access to its land, traditions, history, and values, not necessarily through physical violence but more slowly, as with the "stolen generations" of Australian Aboriginal and Torres Strait Islander children who were forcibly removed from their families by government agencies and church missions. Indigenous children in Canada and the United States also went through experiences that were designed to assimilate them into a "superior" culture and that were destructive in fact (if perhaps not in intent) of their own culture.[51] In 2015, a Canadian commission concluded that the country's former policy of forcibly removing aboriginal children from their homes and sending them to boarding schools "can best be described as 'cultural genocide.'"[52]

Some scholars have tried to fit cultural genocide into the UN definition of genocide, while others go well beyond that to argue that understandings of genocide must fit themselves to the destructive realities of colonialism. The Canadian sociologist Andrew Woolford, for instance, writes that he is not interested in proving "a Canadian Aboriginal genocide against the UNCG [UN definition] standard or any other; instead, [he wants] to (a) establish that the designation of 'cultural genocide' is too qualified and imprecise for understanding Canadian Aboriginal experiences of colonialism, and (b) argue that re-reading and opening certain components of the UNCG through an engagement with Canadian Aboriginal experiences and understandings of group identity, destruction, and intent provides a clearer path to discerning the nature of genocide in Canada."[53] Not all specialists in colonial genocide go so far as Woolford, but there is no denying that he and others pose a strong challenge to traditional ways of conceiving genocide. They also pose a challenge to North Americans who think that genocides are events that happen elsewhere.

Criminology has now become part of the new generation of genocide studies (I review its contributions in chapter 9). Criminology was slow to get involved partly due to its traditional concern with street crime but, above all, because criminologists (like most other people) tend to frame crime as behavior that is criminalized by the government. In criminology—as the critics Alette Smeulers and Roelof Haveman point out—"the *state* determines what is punishable, hence what has to be considered as crime. War crimes, crimes against humanity and genocide are outside the scope of such a definition. . . . The fact that [in genocide] states are suddenly the perpetrators and no longer merely the authorities who try to prevent and punish crime, turns the theoretical framework of criminologists upside down."[54]

Genocide requires a drastic reframing of ideas about justice and inversion of the usual realities. In state-sponsored genocides, the state often defines a certain group as criminal; but in doing so, it *itself* becomes the genocidal criminal, and the criminalized group becomes the victim. Agents of the state charged with maintaining order and restoring justice become agents of terror. For criminologists used to explaining juvenile delinquency or sentencing disparities, it is disorienting to confront a crime that turns basic assumptions inside out.

A Criminological Approach to Genocide

To understand what criminology has to contribute to the study of genocide, one needs only to recognize the nature of the field. Criminology—the study of crime—is a porous, "rendezvous" field that incorporates aspects of anthropology, history, law, political science, psychology, sociology, and other disciplines, depending on the problem at hand.[55] It should thus be able to contribute richly to understanding genocide—its precursors, causes, dynamics, and successes at mass victimization. Specialists in gangs have long tried to pick apart the relationship of the individual offender to the group, which is also a key issue in genocide studies and in prosecutions that attempt to sort out individual from group responsibility. Victimologists have investigated victim vulnerability and bystander dynamics; feminist criminologists have developed theories about mass rape. Neutralization theory enables criminologists to understand how perpetrators (individuals, groups, and states) deal with guilt; brutalization research illuminates the consequences of killing.

Criminology also has much to learn—testing current theories, formulating new ones, expanding its reach and relevance—from studying genocide.

In this book, I try a new approach to genocide research—comparative criminology—that combines historical with sociological methods. My research design involved three steps. First, I chose a sample of eight genocides; second, I developed case-study questions to analyze the genocides in detail; and third, I used the software program NVIVO to make comparisons across the cases for each of my questions.

I began by compiling a list of genocides that occurred between 1900 and 2000. Genocides before 1900 are poorly documented,[56] at least in the degree of detail I needed, but a great deal of scholarly attention has been focused on the first two genocides of the twentieth century, those of the Herero (an African tribe destroyed by a German colonial army, 1904–1907) and the Armenians (an ethnic group almost eradicated by Ottoman Turks, 1915–1923). Thus, 1900 seemed a good year to begin. The year 2000 provided a cutoff by rounding off the era often termed "the century of genocide." My time frame, therefore, is the period 1900 to 2000.

To compile the list of twentieth-century genocides, I used the *Dictionary of Genocide*, the *Encyclopedia of Genocide and Crimes against Humanity*, Genocide Watch's list of genocides, politicides, and other mass murders since 1945, Barbara Harff's work on genocide and political mass murder, and other works (appendix A). Although these sources use varying definitions of genocide, I wanted a comprehensive list of events that authorities consider to have been genocides during the twentieth century. I ended up with a list of sixty-five instances of genocide.[57]

Next I selected my sample. I limited the number of case studies to eight after determining that eight was the maximum number I could treat in a book of this length while covering each case in sufficient breadth and depth. I also limited my selection to cases that fit the definition of genocide as a crime committed with the intent to destroy a national, ethnic, racial, religious, or political group. (This is a modified version of the UN definition; it adds the category "political" to the list of protected groups.) Then I used the following criteria for selecting the final eight cases:

- Degree of documentation
- Variety in type (colonial, racial, ethnic, political, etc.)
- Chronological and geographical spread
- Proportionality (cases reflecting the frequency of genocides over time in various regions of the world)

To determine proportionality, I tallied the frequency with which the genocides listed in appendix A occurred in regions of the world. The tally indicated that my final sample should include two examples from Africa, two from Asia, and one each from the Middle East, Central/South America, Europe, and Eurasia.[58] In order to include Katyn—which seemed particularly important in terms of the second criterion, variety of type—I decided to omit a Eurasian example and include two from Europe instead. (This variety-of-type approach is known as "least similar case" comparison.) The eight cases I finally selected are shown in table 1.1.

Table 1.1. Eight Genocide Case Studies

Genocide	Dates	Region
1. Herero genocide	1904–1907	Africa I
2. Armenian genocide	1915–1923	Middle East
3. Nazi genocide of the disabled	1939–1945	Europe I
4. Katyn Forest Massacre	1940	Europe II
5. Indonesian genocide	1965–1966	Asia I
6. Cambodian genocide	1975–1979	Asia II
7. Guatemalan genocide	1981–1983	Central/South America
8. Rwandan genocide	1994	Africa II

A word on my selection of the Nazi genocide of the disabled: Although for many people the Holocaust is always the prime example of genocide, I do not cover it here because it is exhaustively treated elsewhere. However, I did want to include an aspect of the Nazi genocide in my study. The Nazis' genocidal ambitions extended far beyond Jews to include Bolsheviks, communists, criminals, homosexuals, Jehovah's Witnesses, Romani, Slavs, socialists, and tramps; they further included the physically abnormal, epileptic, "feeble-minded," and mentally ill, groups I combine under the rubric "disabled." To demonstrate the extent of the Nazis' program of slaughter and to follow up on my long-standing interest in the history of eugenics and mentally disabled people, I decided to use the Nazi genocide of the disabled for one of my cases. The disabled constituted a political group in that the Nazis intended to destroy them to excise abnormalities from the German "blood"—its gene pool. The Nazis were trying to reconstitute the German state as a social

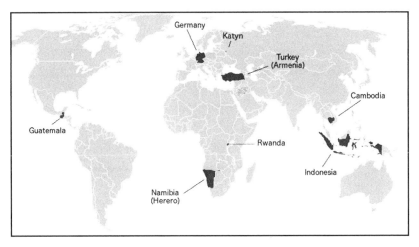

Figure 1.3. Locations of genocides discussed in depth in this book.

and putatively biological organism. In a sense, this was also a racial and national genocide in that the Nazis wanted to get rid of a group that they viewed as a foreign body within their country, a racial threat to the German nation. As it happens, this genocide included thousands of Jews, first those in public and private hospitals and later Jewish prisoners in concentration camps.[59] Moreover, the Nazis' "euthanasia" program for the disabled turned out to be a training program and trial run for the Final Solution to "the Jewish problem."

In statistical terms, mine is a nonprobability, purposive (or judgment) sample, meaning cases were chosen because I judged them to be useful for specific purposes. It is also to some degree a convenience sample: one of my criteria was degree of documentation, and I steered clear of cases on which little primary research had been published. The sample is also a quasi-stratified sample, since I aimed at including cases that would reflect the frequency of genocides over time in various regions of the world.

Would eight different examples have led to different conclusions in this book? While that is certainly possible—every nonprobability sample is by definition subject to bias—many of my conclusions are seconded by genocide scholars who use very different methods. If anything, my method encourages a misleading impression of homogeneity among genocides, for it seeks commonalities, paring away marked differences in favor of generalities. My writing strategy of mixing the stories of specific genocides with conclusions about genocide in general aims at finding a balance between the individual and the general case, the idiosyncratic and the average. But to test my conclusions, this study would need to be replicated using other examples. Note that my list of twentieth-century genocides (appendix A) was compiled from sources that do not include cultural genocides, and thus I have no examples of these in my sample. If I did, some of my conclusions would almost certainly be different. But this is a sample of genocides defined very closely to the UN's standard (identical to it, in fact, aside from the addition of "political" to the list of protected groups).

In sum, using a modified version of the UN's definition of genocide, I drew a sample of eight genocides covering the period 1900–2000 and including examples from around the world, with examples roughly proportionate to the number of genocides experienced by global regions and spread out, in terms of their starting dates, over the entire period. Then I compared the cases across multiple dimensions, using a series of case-study questions (appendix B). The comparative method, as the historian Peter Baldwin writes, "serves primarily to separate the important from the incidental"[60]—what is idiosyncratic to a specific genocide from what is generic to these events en masse—and thus helps answer the first of my key questions: What are the crucial characteristics and components that genocides have in common?[61] The comparative method can also help explain the causes of large-scale social phenomena.[62]

The Layout

Chapter 2 presents summaries of all eight cases; each subsequent chapter relates the full story of one or more of the genocides in the sample. The order in which the genocides are discussed is not chronological but thematic. I have organized the book partly to explore the causes of genocide on the macro (structural), meso (group), and micro (individual) levels; genocide scholars and criminologists alike have shown a strong interest in learning how events "work" interactively at these three levels. This part of the analysis begins in chapter 3 with the macro approach, moving on to group-level explanations in chapter 4 and to individual-level explanations in chapter 5. To some extent, this organization follows changes over time in research on genocide—a trajectory that began with structural explanations but now has expanded to include meso-level theory (here I emphasize sociological explanations) and micro-level work. I also show how these various explanatory levels interpenetrate.

In chapter 2, I lay the groundwork for what follows by explaining how genocide differs from other types of crime—not only street-level offenses and organized crime but also other atrocity crimes. I present capsule summaries of the eight genocides in my sample and profiles (derived from my sample) of genocide's perpetrators and victims. By way of introduction, I present two leading but opposing theories on the nature of genocide—those of Benjamin Valentino and Christian Gerlach—and explain why Gerlach's less top-down, more chaotic and multipronged model better describes the genocides in my sample.

I begin chapter 3, on macro factors, with a detailed examination of the growing tensions in Southwest Africa that led to the Herero genocide of 1904, in which an indigenous tribe started what it knew would be a suicidal war against German soldiers and settlers. This example is particularly interesting in that the victims *began* the war, which means they were perpetrators as well. I then look at other genocides, identifying six structural factors that best predict the onset of genocide: war, state failure, ethnic or racial polarization, colonialism, ideology (which overlaps with other macro factors such as colonialism), and impunity. I also explain why I reject two other macro factors—regime type and poverty—as risk factors for genocide. In conclusion, I propose that we start speaking of states with a "genocidal propensity," just as we speak of individual criminals with a propensity to reoffend.

In chapter 4, I focus on the group level and the emotions of genocidal groups. One of the first stages in genocide is the reframing of identities, a process that entails a chain of emotions. Perpetrators start the process by reframing the identities of those who are to become victims; in doing so, they also recast their own identities, thus changing the emotional valences of both groups. I illustrate this reframing process with the Indonesian genocide of 1965–1966. Then, applying Randall Collins's sociological theory of violence to genocide, I show how his idea of turning points in individual cases of violent behavior also helps explain the emotional dynamics of these large-scale events. I further discuss the emotional tone of genocide in terms of Collins's contrast between "hot" and "cold" violence.

Chapter 5 analyzes the genocidal process on the micro level, from the standpoint of the individual offender. Here I tackle the "How could they do it?" question by proposing a sequence that I call "splitting." Splitting, a psychological process that takes place in the minds of perpetrators, starts with moral disengagement, moves through a shutdown of the capacity to feel empathy, and ends with objectification of the victims. Once victims seem like objects rather than other humans, it is relatively easy to torture and kill them. I apply this analysis to the Cambodian genocide of 1975–1979. Toward the end of the chapter, to further answer the "How could they do it?" question, I examine perpetrators' rational motives (opportunities for looting, fear, and so on)—as opposed to their psychological experiences of splitting.

In genocide, the planners often mobilize gangs or militias to carry out the slaughter. I call these groups "genocidal organizations." Chapter 6 opens with narratives of two genocides that involved mobilization of a genocidal organization: the Armenian genocide of 1915–1923 and the Nazi genocide of the disabled, 1939–1945. These organizations, however, were quite different in character, as were those of other genocidal organizations in my sample; I spend time identifying their commonalities and comparing them with organized crime groups. In this chapter, I also discuss another tool in genocidists' arsenal, the creation of what the philosopher Giorgio Agamben calls the "state of exception."[63] Authorities create states of exception by suspending laws that prohibit certain actions, thus assuring genocidists that they will be safe from punishment.

Chapter 7 turns to the issue of genocidal rape, which a criminological team has aptly dubbed "state rape."[64] In the past, rape was often seen as a spoil of war; today, mass rape is being used as a tool of genocide itself—a means to break down the victim group's capacity to resist and, later, to reconstitute itself. Genocidal rape is a means used by perpetrators to achieve their aim of reconstituting a society.[65] I illustrate these effects with the Rwandan genocide of 1994 before discussing the recent role—and limitations—of international law in the definition and prosecution of genocidal rape.

All genocides end, but we know little about the processes that lead to their termination. In chapter 8, I differentiate genocides by the ways in which they conclude and compare these endings with ways in which ordinary offenders desist from crime. Then I relate the story of the Guatemalan genocide of 1981–1983 to explore difficulties in pinning end dates on genocides, explaining why 1983 is used as the end date in the Guatemalan case despite subsequent violence and discussing how the country's genocidal history feeds into its later high rates of violent crime. The chapter's final section, on reverberations of genocide through generations, speaks to the ways in which genocides linger on, festering without healing. Here I examine survivors' continuing sense of injustice and the personal and political emptiness that genocide leaves in its wake.

In chapter 9, I summarize what I have found about the typical patterns of twentieth-century genocide and how the crime evolved over time. I also discuss the conclusions that can be drawn from criminological research on the prevention and deterrence of genocide. I am not so naïve as to think that deterrence and prevention—even when they work in tandem, as they often do today—will halt genocide entirely; rather, I hope we can discover ways to slow the eruption of new genocides. There is reason to believe that criminology can have some impact on the occurrence of genocide, just as it can lower levels of street-level crime. In conclusion, I identify ways in which criminology can best contribute to genocide studies in the future.

2

What Kind of a Crime Is Genocide?

Capsule Summaries of Eight Genocides

Genocide, a violation of the rights to life, liberty, and security, is the worst form of violence among humans. It can be short (just several weeks for the Katyn Forest Massacre) or long, as with what Samuel Totten argues was the "genocide by attrition" of the Nubian people.[1] It can be secret or ostentatiously public. In contrast to war, which kills soldiers, genocide kills civilians. Genocide is an international crime, meaning that nations throughout the world have agreed the act is wrong and should be punished by them collectively in a demonstration of global condemnation. To meet the United Nations' definition, genocide must be intentional at both the group and the individual level, although intentions can be inferred from actions and do not need to be documented. Genocide may or may not involve ethnic cleansing. It can be mass murder, even if the "mass" of the target group is small and even if some of its members survive; but murder need not occur at all, according to specialists in colonial genocide, although victims certainly do die.[2] Genocide is the destruction of a culture, leading to ruin of its language, rhythms of life, customs regarding courtship and marriage, architecture, crafts, livelihoods, politics, religions, and relationship to the land and to nature.[3] Thus, it is social as well as physical death. Further, it is social death in the sense that (in the words of Claudia Card) "victims are stripped as members of the target group of the social identities that gave meaning to their lives and that would ordinarily also have given meaning to their deaths."[4] Genocide is a violent way of reorganizing society.[5] It is the supreme form of state-organized crime.[6] Genocide is also a gendered event: typically those who engage in combat are men, fighting according to their group's definitions of masculinity, while those who die later—sexually violated and perhaps incorporated into the victor group—tend to be women. Genocide is the destruction of one group by another.[7] It is the destruction of a group "as such"—not because of its actions but because of its characteristics, the traits that make it a group in the first place.

Defining Genocide

The term "genocide" enables us to name the unnamable, to speak of the unspeakable. We owe the word to the lawyer and human rights activist Raphael Lemkin. Born in Poland and fluent in multiple languages, Lemkin had a broad historical view that enabled him to perceive commonalities between the Turks' extermination of the Armenians and the Nazis' extermination of multiple groups during World War II. Wounded and on the run from the Nazis, Lemkin (who was Jewish) moved from one law faculty to another, ending up in the United States but never finding a true home. He coined the word for which he is famous in 1944 by combining a Greek noun, *genos*, meaning "group," with a Latin suffix, *-cide*, meaning "kill."[8] He also—and it is no small "also"—helped draft the United Nations Genocide Convention.

The legal definition of genocide appears in article 2 of the United Nations' Convention on the Prevention and Punishment of Genocide (UNCG):

> Genocide means any of the following acts committed with intent to destroy, in whole or in part, a national, ethnical, racial or religious group, as such:

> (a) Killing members of the group;
> (b) Causing serious bodily or mental harm to members of the group;
> (c) Deliberately inflicting on the group conditions of life calculated to bring about its physical destruction in whole or in part;
> (d) Imposing measures intended to prevent births within the group;
> (e) Forcibly transferring children of the group to another group.[9]

The key word "group" appears no fewer than six times in this short definition. Also noteworthy is the fact that subsections b through e allow for genocides that involve not killing but group destruction through other means. The definition falls short of fully expressing Lemkin's concept of genocide; his was a more "capacious definition" that focused less on killings and included political, cultural, and social destruction.[10] Indeed, the final definition fell well short of an earlier UN resolution defining genocide in terms of "denial of the right of existence of entire human groups," including "racial, religious, political and other groups" and "great losses to humanity in the form of cultural and other contributions."[11] The definition finally approved by the United Nations was the product of debates, negotiations, and defensive maneuvers among many countries.[12]

Lemkin played a crucial role in ratification of the Genocide Convention of 1948. Living alone in New York City, with little money to support himself, Lemkin ceaselessly lobbied for ratification, thereby seriously undermining his health. "In his rush to persuade delegates to support" the treaty, Samantha Power writes, "he frequently fainted from hunger. . . . Perennially sleepless, he often wandered the streets at night. A *New York Post* reporter described him as growing 'paler, thinner and shabbier' as the months passed. He seemed determined to stay in perpetual motion."[13] The UNCG entered into force in 1951, but the United States did not ratify it until 1988—critics worried that it might infringe on US sovereignty—and then only after being shamed by Senator William Proxmire, who over nineteen years delivered 3,211 speeches urging ratification by Congress.

The UNCG failed to include political groups in its final list of potential genocide victims (national, ethnic, racial, and religious groups). In fact, many of the delegates who drafted the UNCG wanted to include political groups among the protected categories, only to be thwarted by others who feared that their countries could be accused of political mass murders of their own.[14] Some genocide scholars get around this omission by using the term "politicide" to refer to the genocide of politically defined groups; others operate as if "and political groups" had been added to the UN's list of protected groups.[15] Cultural genocide, which Lemkin himself had considered a crucial part of the concept, was similarly omitted by the UNCG, and it too is sometimes informally added, occasionally under the heading of "ethnocide." Yet other genocide scholars devise their own definitions, reasoning that in the mid-twentieth century, when the UNCG was written, people tended to conceive of groups in essentialist terms, thinking of religion, race, ethnicity, and nationality as relatively fixed attributes that people are born with, rather than regarding them (as we tend to do today) as constructed categories that are fluid and to some degree changeable.[16] But despite ongoing definitional disagreements, the UNCG remains the international legal definition of genocide, and its core idea remains intact: genocide is a crime against a group.

Because a "group" has no set size, the group destroyed by genocide may be large or small. Severe intentional damage to a small tribe could be genocidal, for instance, even if the group were one-hundredth as large as the Jewish population wiped out by the Nazis during World War II. Indeed, even if the group were one-thousandth as large, the genocide charge might stick if the group were small to begin with—say the Yanomami tribe, which lives in the Amazon rain forest and numbers just 20,000 in all. Aggressors have been charged with genocide against the Yanomami and other small tribes such as the Herero and Namaqua of Southwest Africa.[17] The seriousness of the criminal charge has little to do with the size of the population or number of dead bodies. Indeed, the UNCG does not require dead bodies at all; reflecting this latitude, some current proposals call for including systematic rape and cultural genocide within the formal definition of genocide,[18] while others, as noted earlier, advocate changing the definition to accommodate colonial genocide. Further, the victim group need not be entirely destroyed for the crime to be genocide; the UN's definition explicitly states that aggressors need have only the *intent* to destroy the victim group "in whole or in part."

"Genocide is a social construction," William Gamson declared in a presidential address to the American Sociological Association, meaning not that one can conjure genocide out of thin air but that application of the term depends on a "cultural contest . . . over who is the 'we,' to whom specific moral obligations apply, and who is the 'they,' to whom they do not."[19] His meaning is made clear by the Katyn Forest Massacre: after the event, Germany and Russia spent half a century trying to construct each other as the murderers. The label of genocide is a powerful political construction that often is applied only through lengthy, arduous framing processes. Although labels of genocide may be based on reality—the Russians really did exterminate the Poles at Katyn—their application usually depends on victor's justice: the side that wins gets to define who

committed the crimes, and it rarely recognizes its own genocidal behavior. Guilty groups often react to condemnation with campaigns to
reconstruct themselves through genocide denial.

In *Genocide as Social Practice*, the social historian Daniel Feierstein
writes of genocide as a "technology of power" and "form of social engineering that creates, destroys, or reorganizes relationships within a given
society."[20] This is a particularly useful way of looking at genocide, for
it gives meaning to the us-versus-them divisions (Aryans versus Jews,
Russians versus Poles, Hutu versus Tutsi) that characterize genocidal
thinking and helps explain the tremendous energy that genocidists often
pour into the project of constructing their enemy as a group that must
be destroyed. They want to reorganize their society and need to begin
by demonizing "them." Echoing Feierstein, another scholar describes
mass violence as "demographic surgery."[21] The notion of genocide as
a technology of power and social engineering—as a way of excising an
unwanted population or part of it—also helps explain why, during some
genocides, women belonging to the enemy group are raped on a massive
scale. Genocidal rape destroys the victim group's capacity to regenerate
itself, physically and culturally, thus ensuring that the society will be
permanently reorganized to exclude "them."

Feierstein argues that it is unfair for the UNCG to focus on some categories and not others (such as political groups and women). "Any new
legal definition of genocide will need to include the principle of equality before the law—a principle currently violated by the 1948 Genocide
Convention, which protects some groups and not others."[22] Feierstein
proposes a new definition of genocide as *the execution of a large-scale
and systematic plan with the intention of destroying a human group as
such in whole or in part.*[23] This clear and flexible definition, retaining
the core of the UNCG's meaning while pruning away its problematic
passages, is the best of recent proposals to improve on the UN's definition. One advantage is that it seems to accommodate the demand of
colonial genocide theorists for inclusion of slow, piecemeal processes
that may not be overtly murderous but are just as destructive of a group
as the gas chambers of Auschwitz. Yet it is unlikely that the definitional
debates will end with Feierstein's proposal, and meanwhile, the UN's
definition is firmly entrenched in law.

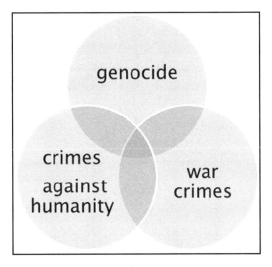

Figure 2.1. Relationship of the three atrocity crimes.

Another useful way to think about genocide is as an "atrocity crime," a term proposed by David Scheffer, a human rights activist and former US ambassador at large for war crimes issues, who defines "atrocity" as "a basket of particularly heinous crimes."[24] The main items in that basket are war crimes (essentially, murder of prisoners of war, rape and murder of civilians, and conscription of child soldiers), crimes against humanity (murder, enslavement, torture, rape, and other inhumane acts committed as part of a widespread or systematic attack against civilian populations), and genocide.[25] All three atrocity crimes violate human rights, and they can overlap, as shown in figure 2.1. (Thus, a wartime attempt to destroy a racial or ethnic group might be adjudged genocide, a war crime, or a crime against humanity, depending on the circumstances.) Scheffer proposed the category "atrocity crimes" because he recognized a need for a single term that would simplify and clarify discussions of genocide and related crimes.[26] Scheffer's analysis thus provides us with a helpful further answer to this chapter's basic question, What kind of a crime is genocide?

In what follows, I first provide capsule summaries of the eight genocides in my sample (longer descriptions appear in the chapters that follow). Then, using the dataset I compiled through answers to my case-study questions, I compare these events in order to provide preliminary answers to the question of the nature of genocide. The last section of this chapter uses the capsule summaries and findings based on my sample to test two major theories of twentieth-century mass murder: those of the American political scientist Benjamin Valentino (2004) and the Swiss historian Christian Gerlach (2010). Throughout, I come at the central question—What kind of a crime is genocide?—from different directions and using different types of information.

Capsule Summaries of Eight Genocides

Short summaries can make historical events seems simple, clear, and unidirectional, whereas the events themselves are usually complex, chaotic, and blurry in their significance. On the other hand, summaries provide convenient starting points.

1. The Herero Genocide, 1904–1907

The Herero (pronounced Heh-RER-oh), a tribe living in what is today Namibia, in Southwest Africa, were colonized in the late nineteenth century by Germany. In 1904, the Herero rose up against their German oppressors, knowing full well that they would lose but preferring rebellion to a failure to challenge the slow death of their people and culture. The leader of the German army went so far as to issue a written order of extermination—one of the rare written authorizations of genocide. Of the roughly 80,000 Herero in the colony before the rebellion, by 1911, only 15,000 remained. Their culture had been obliterated, and survivors became laborers—virtual slaves—for white settlers.

Retrospectively, it is clear that for Germans in Southwest Africa, the end of the genocide was more of a pause than a termination. The influence of the Herero genocide, far from dying with its victims, grew stronger over time, spilling into the Armenian genocide of 1915 and the Nazi genocide that began just thirty years later. Although the German influence was small in the Armenian case (German military advisers encouraged the Turks to get rid of their Armenian neighbors),[27] at home, the African genocide offered Germans an example for the future, providing, in the words of one historian, "ideas, methods, and a lexicon that Nazi leaders borrowed and expanded."[28]

The origins of the German concentration camp can be traced to the Herero genocide, as can the beginning of German studies in eugenics, the idea that humans can be improved by better "breeding." In 1908, Eugen Fischer, who later became the chief authority on eugenics in the Third Reich and a significant influence on Hitler, traveled to Southwest Africa to conduct racial research on the "hybrid" offspring of white men and black women. (The hybrids, Fischer concluded, were inferior to pure whites and should not be allowed to reproduce.)[29] The Herero genocide—an example of racial cleansing of a territory—helped habituate some Germans to the idea that it is legitimate to exterminate people who stand in the way of national aspirations.

2. The Armenian Genocide, 1915–1923

The Armenians, an ethnic group who had lived for thousands of years on land that eventually became part of the Ottoman Empire (and, later still, Turkey), were incorporated into the Ottoman Empire as second-class citizens. Starting in the late nineteenth century, they suffered a series of massive massacres at the hands of the Ottomans, who raped Armenian women, killed entire families, stole their property, and burned their villages. In retrospect, these massacres can be seen as a long and frightful prelude to genocide.

In the early twentieth century, as the Ottoman Empire disintegrated, a reformist "Young Turk" coalition took over, ousting the sultan and starting the process of transforming "Ottomans" into more modern "Turks." However, a conservative triumvirate, the Committee for Union and Progress, seized power, endorsing a nationalist Turkey-for-the-Turks movement. Across the newly forming country of Turkey, this triumvirate established a shadowy Special Organization (the unit's name in translation) prepared to plunder and kill.

On the night of April 24, 1915, the Turks rounded up Armenian leaders and intellectuals in Constantinople. Elsewhere in Turkey, particularly in the east, where most Armenians lived, members of the Special Organization marched Armenian men out of their villages to be shot. It evicted women, children, and the elderly from their homes and forced them on a death march south into the Mesopotamian and Syrian deserts. Armenians were butchered, burned alive, and shoved off boats into lakes and rivers. They were whipped, bludgeoned, and left by the roadside to starve or die of thirst. The Special Organization encouraged amnestied convicts and Kurdish bandits to rape and pillage the deportees; some sold young girls into sexual slavery or forced them into harems. One million or more Armenians died. Today, Turkey still refuses to acknowledge these events as genocide.

3. The Nazi Genocide of the Disabled, 1939–1945

Hitler's eugenics program flowed from his conviction that by eliminating undesirables from the German population, he could improve the purity and power of its Aryan "stock." His "euthanasia" program was anticipated by the Nazi laws of 1933 mandating sterilization of people with mental and physical disorders. In autumn of 1939, the children's "euthanasia" program began—a secret project run by a small group of physicians who agreed to murder disabled children whom they deemed genetically inferior. (I use quotation marks to indicate that the so-called euthanasia or "easy death" program actually had nothing to do with mercy killing. It was a political program aimed at changing the nature of the state, which the Nazis conceived of as a social and biological organism.) The program expanded to cover mentally disabled youths, chronically ill adults, the blind, the deaf, and residents of old-age homes and almshouses; later still, it expanded again to cover criminals and other "asocials." The program became known as Aktion T4, after the address of its Berlin headquarters, number 4 Tiergartenstrasse.

As the T4 program grew, its medical directors looked for more efficient means than poison and starvation to kill the disabled. In the winter of 1939–1940, they conducted their first experiment with carbon monoxide gas; it worked so well that six "euthanasia" killing centers were established throughout Germany and Austria. As the war continued, German troops used firearms to mow down disabled patients in Poland and Russia, while T4 doctors went into concentration camps to select sick and disabled prisoners, especially Jews, for gassing. All told, 750,000 people may have been killed in this genocide. It is difficult to arrive at a total, partly for definitional reasons; as the historian Robert Proctor explains, "for Nazi physicians no sharp line divided the destruction of the racially inferior and the mentally or physically defective."[30]

4. The Katyn Forest Massacre, 1940

Due to Stalin's secret plan to annex eastern Poland, the borders between Poland and western Russia were unsettled and unclear in 1939 when Soviet soldiers invaded and rounded up about 22,000 members of the Polish army and intelligentsia, imprisoning them in three camps in western Russia. The Poles, unaware of Stalin's annexation plan, offered but slight resistance. Spies in the prison camps, interrogating the Poles about their attitudes toward Poland and Russia, discovered that most were avid patriots—just the kind of Polish nationalists who, if released, would resist the Soviet takeover. Thus, Stalin signed orders for their liquidation and the deportation of their families (about 61,000 relatives in all) to Kazakhstan, where many died of hunger and disease. In early spring of 1940, the prisoners were shot, one by one, and buried in pits in the nearby Katyn Forest and other sites. The soil preserved the bodies so well that diaries, medals, and other objects subsequently made it possible to identify disinterred victims.

Later in World War II, when the Germans invaded the Soviet Union, they discovered the burial pits, which they tried to use as anti-Soviet propaganda, reporting with great fanfare that the Soviets had butchered thousands of Poles. The Soviets in turn held the Germans responsible for the executions, and so it went, back and forth, until 1990, when Mikhail Gorbachev, the Soviet president, admitted his country's guilt. The victims' disappearance, and their relatives' inability to learn the truth about their fates, became a central issue in twentieth-century Poland, making of Katyn a wound that could not heal.[31]

That all but one of the Katyn victims was male makes the massacre important when thinking about the relationship of gender to genocide. Moreover, the secrecy of this genocide and the long political drama following discovery of the bodies illustrate how diverse the phenomenon of genocide can be. And yet, despite the idiosyncrasies of the Katyn mass murder, it should, as the historian Norman Naimark puts it, "be considered one of the most unambiguous cases of genocide in the history of the twentieth century."[32]

5. The Indonesian Genocide, 1965–1966

In the early 1960s, Indonesia was home to the largest communist party in Southeast Asia, the Partai Komunis Indonesia, or PKI. The president, Sukarno, tried to balance the demands of the left-wing PKI, the right-wing Partai Nasionalis Indonesia (PNI), and a group of Islamic parties. However, on September 30, 1965, an attempted coup, apparently sponsored by the PKI, left six army generals dead. Immediately, the then-obscure Major General Suharto quelled the disturbance, pushed Sukarno aside, and encouraged a national bloodbath against communists in what was an almost purely political genocide. Six months later, half a million Indonesians lay dead, with thousands more in jail on suspicion of leftist sympathies. According to two historians of this genocide, "These mass murders belong to the worst counter-revolutionary acts of violence of the twentieth century. . . . The killings of 1965–1966 established a new regime of fear which the New Order [Suharto's rule] used . . . to repress nearly every form of protest. At the same time, however, the murders were completely banned from history writing. The official history books state that in September 1965, Suharto promptly thwarted a communist coup."[33] Indeed, people were afraid to mention the genocide even within their own families.

While it is clear that Suharto's army encouraged the killings of communists and their associates, it remains difficult to identify perpetrators and victims in Indonesia, a country fragmented by geography (thousands of islands), language (over 250 tongues), ethnicity (over 300 groups), and religious differences. One authority on the genocide argues that its "ferocity" was "a product of local factors. . . . No central set of events encapsulates the massacres as a whole; the killings were scattered in time and space, and whatever we know about one massacre only dimly illuminates the others."[34] Its chaos and the near incomprehensibility of individuals' motives for slaughtering relatives and friends make this genocide a close fit with Christian Gerlach's theory of "extremely violent societies," discussed later in this chapter.

6. The Cambodian Genocide, 1975–1979

Twenty-five percent of the Cambodian population (two million people) died during the Khmer Rouge regime headed by the revolutionary communist leader Pol Pot.[35] In the background lay a century of French colonial rule and nearly a decade of bombing by the United States, both of which primed the population for the anti-imperialist, Maoist rhetoric of Pol Pot and his Khmer Rouge ("red Cambodian") guerrilla movement. After a five-year civil war, Pol Pot's forces toppled the US-backed government of Lon Nol and began, with astonishing speed, to reorganize the country into a huge network of collective farms.

Cities were emptied, families broken up, and large segments of the population forcibly relocated (some more than once) to satisfy production quotas at the collective farms. On these farms, where rations were inadequate and work hours long, cadres—members of the Khmer Rouge—might punish even slight breakdowns in discipline (such as complaining of being tired) with death. Tens of thousands of Cambodians also died of starvation or disease. Pol Pot engineered the slaughter of Cambodia's educated and professional classes on the theory that they would oppose communism, and in addition he exterminated its Buddhist monks and several ethnic minorities. (His targeting of ethnic and religious groups makes this mass murder fit the UN's definition of genocide.) The most striking aspect of this genocide was the way its leaders—both in Pol Pot's headquarters and on the rural farms—destroyed the Cambodian people. Even vague suspicions of disloyalty led to immediate death or incarceration in the infamous S-21 prison (also known as Tuol Sleng) for torture followed by execution. Invasion by Vietnam ended Pol Pot's dictatorship, but a remnant of the brutal regime retained its UN seat and continued to receive US aid for another decade.

Although the Khmer Rouge did attempt to exterminate some ethnic and religious minorities, their largest target was other Cambodians; most victims were targeted for neither race, ethnicity, nationality, nor religion but because they were suspected of political disloyalty by the cold and paranoid Pol Pot. In sharp contrast to the deportations of the Armenian genocide, in this case, those who were accused of being enemies of the state remained geographically internal, trapped, easy prey to Pol Pot's lethal suspicions. In contrast to the Indonesian genocide, the

Cambodian genocide was tightly organized, run by a centralized government with a stranglehold on its near-helpless populace.

7. The Guatemalan Genocide, 1981–1983

This genocide occurred in the middle of a long civil war (1962–1996) between a right-wing military, generously supported by the US government, and a loose coalition of leftist guerrillas and impoverished Maya, members of the original indigenous population. It was a genocide waged against a group defined on ethnic, racial, and political grounds. The Maya, who had ruled what is now Guatemala before the sixteenth-century Spanish conquest, had darker skin than the country's oligarchs did, a difference used to justify the racism of the conquistadores' descendants. The Maya were not necessarily leftists, but they too were struggling for civil and human rights against an oppressive, deeply conservative government that was in league with wealthy landowners. They were sometimes aided by the Catholic Church as well as leftist guerrillas, but neither source of support could effectively oppose the Guatemalan army, whose generals ran the country.

The genocide coincided roughly with the dictatorship of José Efraín Ríos Montt (1982–1983), who waged systematic, racist attacks on the Maya on the grounds that they supported a communist takeover of the government. Cold warriors in the US bought into this belief (some would call it an oversimplification, others a fabrication), training Guatemalan soldiers in its School for the Americas and lending help through the CIA and Green Berets. Guatemalan paramilitaries attacked over 600 Mayan villages, destroying them, raping the women (sometimes for days on end), smashing infants against walls, burying people alive. (Sometimes, the paramilitary groups included Maya who had been forced to join so-called civil defense patrols.) The genocide ended with the overthrow of Ríos Montt in 1983 and the start of a somewhat less oppressive period in Guatemalan politics.

It is difficult to find reliable estimates of the number of Maya who died as a result of the genocide. It seems likely that well over 100,000 were killed and at least 150,000 were forced to flee to Mexico.[36] The struggles behind this genocide were part of a larger movement in Central and South America to throw off the legacy of colonialism and resist the US injection of Cold War policies into local, often indigenous, efforts to achieve political equality and secure human rights.

8. The Rwandan Genocide, 1994

In about 100 days—from early April through mid-July 1994—extremist Hutu in Rwanda systematically murdered over one million people, both moderate Hutu and Tutsi, and raped an estimated 250,000 women.[37] The goal was to exterminate Rwandan Tutsi entirely.

In the precolonial period, members of the Tutsi and Hutu tribes reportedly lived together with little strain, but tensions grew when German and Belgian colonialists intensified caste distinctions, using older differentiations to construct the Tutsi as superior because more European in appearance. A Hutu uprising of 1959 began the process through which Rwandan Hutu gained the upper hand. Although there was considerable violence against Tutsi in the period leading up to the genocide, Hutu President Juvénal Habyarimana at least pretended to be moving toward greater democracy. His death in a plane crash—possibly engineered by more extremist Hutu, possibly by Tutsi opponents—triggered the genocide. Hutu extremists had lists of the country's Tutsi, whom their militias proceeded to drive into public spaces such as crossroads, schools, and churches and then hack to death with machetes. They also systematically raped Tutsi women. This was a carefully planned and well-coordinated genocide. The journalist Philip Gourevitch writes, "The dead of Rwanda accumulated at nearly three times the rate of Jewish dead during the Holocaust. It was the most efficient mass killing since the atomic bombings of Hiroshima and Nagasaki."[38]

The Rwandan genocide was remarkable for the refusal by the United Nations and United States to take simple steps to stop the violence. Nearly two million refugees fled into neighboring countries. The slaughter ended with the arrival in the capital of the Rwandan Patriotic Front (RPF), Tutsi soldiers from Uganda who had been fighting a civil war with Rwandan Hutu during the genocide and who now formed a new government under the RPF leader, Paul Kagame. By November 1994, the UN Security Council had established an international criminal tribunal to bring justice to surviving Rwandans, and although progress was slow, expensive, and bloody (some witnesses and their families were murdered), over five dozen genocidists were convicted. The court's first conviction, decided half a century after the UN defined genocide, was the first- ever judgment by an international court on a charge of genocide. This same trial established that rape is a crime of genocide when committed with intent to destroy a group.

What Does Genocide Look Like? Preliminary Findings

Historical comparisons uncover parallels among these eight genocides, revealing the core characteristics of the crime. What characterizes the genocides in this sample?

All eight genocides occurred during a period of upheaval or outright war. The Herero genocide began when the tribe attacked German colonizers. The Armenian genocide took place during World War I, in which Turkey fought on the losing side; Turkey had also recently lost a war in the Balkans and was engaged, again losing, in a war with Russia. In Nazi Germany, Hitler waited to begin the "euthanasia" killings until he started World War II, which he expected to distract Germans from the murders of disabled children in their midst.[39] In the Katyn case, Stalin was at war—initially undeclared—with Poland. Indonesia was not technically at war during the 1965–1966 genocide, but it was in close to a state of civil war, with the new military leader, Suharto, determined to wipe out communists; moreover, the genocide was accompanied by small local massacres and deadly neighborhood disputes.[40] The Indonesian genocide, one author writes, was merely "the most dramatic in [a] long series of destructive events."[41]

In Cambodia, genocide began just after the Khmer Rouge won its long war against the previous regime. The Guatemalan genocide became synonymous with the army's war against insurgents and Mayan highlanders. Here, however, there was no perfect polarization, with Maya at one end as victims and the right-wing army at the other as perpetrators, for some Maya worked for the army in civil defense patrols that ravaged Mayan villages, and the army's avowed target was not Maya per se but rather insurgents living in the highlands with support from the Maya. In Rwanda, genocide was practically synonymous with a war between the Hutu government's army and the invading Rwandan Patriotic Front of Tutsi. But as in Guatemala, the genocide did not involve a perfect opposition, here of Tutsi victims and Hutu perpetrators, for some moderate Hutu did not join the murderous Hutu Power movement and thus died alongside Tutsi. Moreover, a 2014 video released by the British Broadcasting Corporation charged that Rwanda's long-term president, Paul Kagame, the man credited with liberating Rwanda from Hutu Power and ending the genocide, helped cause the plane crash that triggered the genocide. In this revisionist story, Kagame saw the assassination of his predecessor, Habyarimana, as the only way to come to power and save Rwanda from the Hutu Power faction. The man who stopped the genocide also started it.[42] These charges, if they stick, will change thinking about the identities of victims and perpetrators in this genocide. But there will be no denying that at the time of the genocide, Rwanda was in a state of breakdown.

These eight cases fully support the often-made claim of a close association of war and genocide.[43] Genocide tends to occur when a nation or other group has just started a war, is in the middle of one, or has just been victorious. The leaders of genocide are often leaders of the war as well. An advantage of having eight cases, however, is that they lead us away from the narrative structure set by the Holocaust—Hitler started a war and then committed genocides—and enable us to identify new narratives in which, for instance, genocide and war start simultaneously, as in Rwanda.[44]

Perpetrator Profiles

In six of the eight cases, the leaders used a special force of some kind to carry out the genocide. In the Herero case, the special force consisted simply of the German troops stationed in Southwest Africa. In the dying Ottoman Empire, leaders created what they termed a Special Organization to carry out the Armenian genocide. Hitler mobilized a secret Reich Committee of physicians to run his "euthanasia" program, while Katyn victims were dispatched by specially trained executioners who could kill hundreds of men a night. During the Indonesian genocide, although there was a great deal of localized and uncontrolled violence, Suharto's army mobilized militias to help destroy communists. No specific killing organization was mobilized during the Cambodian or Guatemalan genocides, but in Rwanda, Hutu extremists armed and trained a militia, the Interahamwe, that helped lead the genocide.

All eight of the genocides involved some sort of "cleansing" (meaning perpetrator efforts to purify a territory or group by excising part of the population), although the cleansing did not always involve race or ethnicity. In the Herero case, the general who issued the extermination order intended to cleanse Southwest Africa of its native inhabitants. The Turks cleansed their country of Armenians in a clear-cut example of ethnic cleansing. In the Nazi case in my sample, the "cleansed" people were defined by neither race nor ethnicity but disability—and their supposedly bad genes. Katyn was a case of both ethnic and social class cleansing (the Russians regarded the captured Poles as "bourgeois"),[45] while the Cambodian genocide involved attempted elimination of ethnic Vietnamese, Chinese, Cham, and Thai residents of the country, together with Buddhist monks. However, the majority of those who were "cleansed" during the Cambodian genocide were simply other Cambodians. In Indonesia, Suharto wanted to cleanse the country of communists, who constituted neither an ethnic nor racial but a political group.[46] The Guatemalan army sought to excise the Maya, or at any rate a significant portion of them, while Rwanda's Hutu Power group wanted to eliminate ethnic Tutsi. Genocidal cleansing, then, is a flexible term covering the elimination of not only racial and ethnic groups but also supposedly biological, social class, religious, and political groups.[47]

A final characteristic shared by perpetrators in these eight cases was impunity—confidence that they would suffer no consequences for their genocide. In Southwest Africa, the Germans almost wiped a native tribe off the face of the earth while stealing its land; in return, they lost nothing while gaining a colony and acquiring experience in committing genocide. The Turks, in return for uprooting and killing over one million Armenians, got the victims' homes and other property; some even appropriated Armenian women as concubines. (After the genocide, Turkey instituted legal proceedings in which the three principal leaders of the genocide, who had fled, were tried in absentia and condemned to death; today, in a complete reversal, Turkey refuses even to admit that the genocide occurred.) Similarly, at the end of World War II, some physicians involved in the T4 program were hanged; but most evaded punishment. In both Turkey and Germany, many of those who were involved in the genocides went on to live and work openly.[48]

The Katyn killers were never brought to trial. In Indonesia, for decades after the genocide, people did not even dare speak about what Suharto and his supporters had done. Impunity ruled in Cambodia as well until 2007, when the last remaining Khmer Rouge leaders, now elderly and infirm, were arrested. Similarly, in Guatemala, Ríos Montt enjoyed impunity for decades, and although he was eventually tried and convicted of genocide, the conviction was overturned by an appeals court in 2013. Rwandan genocidists killed with impunity, fully expecting no punishment; but they were wrong. The UN established its International Criminal Tribunal for Rwanda shortly after the genocide, and by the end of 2012, seventy-five cases had been prosecuted, with sixty-five findings of guilty and ten acquittals. Rwandan courts, in their own proceedings, executed twenty-two people and sentenced large numbers of young men to prison; additionally, community *gacaca* or dispute-settlement courts handled close to two million cases.[49] The Rwanda example, together with other successful prosecutions of atrocity crimes during the late twentieth and early twenty-first centuries, indicates that we have reached a point where genocidists cannot count on impunity, although if they are sufficiently powerful, they will no doubt continue to find ways to evade responsibility.

* * *

In answer to the question What kind of a crime is genocide? my dataset thus enables me to compile a group portrait of perpetrators of genocides that involve mass violence. They commit their deeds during wars and periods of upheaval, when people are highly agitated and their actions are least likely to attract attention. So closely linked are war and genocide that those who lead one often lead the other. Moreover, these leaders are likely to mobilize genocidal organizations—militias and secret support networks—to help with the killing. Genocides frequently involve some kind of "cleansing," be it ethnic, genetic, political, racial, religious, or social class. And historically, genocidists have not needed to worry about consequences. In these respects, most of my cases roughly resemble the Holocaust, although they played out very differently.

Victim Profiles

My dataset also enables me to compile a profile of genocides' victims. *What did the target groups in this sample have in common?*

In seven of the eight cases, the genocide took place in territory where victims and perpetrators both lived. The exception is Katyn, in which the genocide occurred in Russian territory, where the Poles were transported after capture. Otherwise, victims were murdered in their own country, where they lived alongside the killers. Because they were weaker and (in all eight cases) less aggressive than the perpetrators, they were easy targets as well as close to hand.

While all eight genocides occurred during a period of upheaval or outright war, it is still important to ask whether the victims and perpetrators belonged to the conflicting groups. Surprisingly, in just one case, that of the Herero, were victims and perpetrators in actual physical conflict. In a second case, Guatemala, the Mayan victims were in conflict with the army only insofar as they were aiding the insurgents, the ostensible target of the army's attacks. However, the true targets of the Guatemalan army were the Maya per se, irrespective of their relationship with insurgents, as shown by the following account of a typical highland massacre:

> On the day the massacres took place, perpetrators arrived on foot early so as to gather a maximum number of villagers in their homes. Access to the communities was controlled or blocked, soldiers carrying out house-to-house searches and gathering community members in one place. Victims were then immobilized using ropes, rendered completely defenceless, to be tortured and mutilated. When the killings began, firearms were always used and victims were both men and women, young and old. Victims' bodies were often left where they fell, to be preyed upon by animals or otherwise desecrated. . . . Finally, their simple dwellings, built with great effort with materials often carried over kilometres of mountain paths, were set ablaze and the communities utterly destroyed.[50]

In the other cases in my sample, too, there was little or no conflict between victims and perpetrators on the eve of the genocide. In Germany, mentally and physically disabled people were hardly planning to clash with the Nazis. Before the Armenian genocide, Armenians had started demanding more rights, and some sided with Russia in a war against Turkey; but within Turkey, they were not in physical conflict with Turks except when attacked. The Katyn prisoners did not even understand why they had been taken prisoner—and indeed wrote Moscow a letter to ask: "Are we recognized as prisoners of war? If so, we request that we be treated in a manner consistent with norms recognized by all states governing the treatment of prisoners of war. . . . If we are convicts, we request that we be informed of the crimes for which we have been deprived of our freedom. . . . If we are internees, then please provide an explanation of why we were robbed of our freedom, especially as we were seized on Polish territory."[51] In Indonesia, Suharto's takeover was triggered by an alleged communist coup attempt, but even if this allegation was true, very few communists could have known about it. Geoffrey Robinson, an authority on the Indonesian genocide, explains that one can hardly say that the communist party and its opponents were in conflict at that time: "In 1965, on the eve of the October coup, groupings with diametrically opposed political, economic, and class interests controlled different elements of the state apparatus, such as the military, the police, the bureaucracy, and the executive. The coup provided the pretext and the opportunity for the consolidation of the political power of one grouping, led by the PNI, at the expense of the other, the PKI and its allies."[52] In Cambodia, both "sides" were Cambodians, and most of those who died were not enemies of Pol Pot but victims of his paranoia and unrealistic production quotas for rice. Some were killed because they were too weak to keep up with work demands; others "confessed" to undermining his regime only under torture. In my final case, Rwanda, most Tutsi were not in conflict with Hutu Power; rather, the central conflict lay between the invading army, the Rwandan Patriotic Front, and Hutu Power extremists.

Aside from the Herero case, then, genocidists in my sample attacked relatively peaceable, unsuspecting, or helpless opponents. This explains why genocide victims are so often caught by surprise and unable to defend themselves. It also shows how genocide differs from war: in war, two armed sides clash, but in genocide, one side does not go to war. (Even in Rwanda, the Rwandan Patriotic Front invaded only to stop the genocide—or so the traditional story goes. If it is proved that President

Paul Kagame had a hand in the killing of his predecessor, then Rwanda proves an exception to the rule.) These circumstances fit the model of one kind of confrontation in the sociologist Randall Collins's well-known typology of violence, in which offenders find a weak victim to attack.[53] Collins does not cover genocide, but he does identify this pattern of the strong attacking the weak in a wide range of other situations—including domestic violence, bullying, mugging, and police and military confrontations—in which tension builds until the opponent is discovered to be weak or helpless, at which point the stronger party's fear and tension are unleashed "into ferocious attack."[54] In rough outline, this emotional pattern fits most of the genocides I studied.

Were the victims negatively labeled? In all cases, they were. In some instances, the negative label was based on race or ethnicity—for the Herero, "baboons"; for the Armenians, "infidels"; for the disabled, "degenerates" and "useless eaters"; for the Katyn soldiers, "counterrevolutionaries," "bourgeois 'lords,'" and, simply, "Polish," which had negative overtones for Russians. Mayan victims were characterized as "lazy, vicious, conformist, distrustful, reluctant to be civilized, and abusive,"[55] terms that merged with the supposed inferiority indicated by their dark skins. Tutsi were labeled with various animal and insect epithets, most notably "cockroaches."[56] In other cases, the negative labels were based on perceived political views or status: victims of the Cambodian genocide were labeled "enemies of the people" or "'new' people," meaning city people who were by definition less worthy than rural peasants; and victims in the Indonesian genocide were labeled "atheists," "traitors," and (if they were female) "Gerwani whores," meaning communist women who seduced the murdered generals at the moment of the attempted coup. (An amazing number of Indonesian women were accused of this sin, although the coup involved only half a dozen generals and was executed in secret.) In one case, that of disabled people in Nazi Germany, the labels—"degenerate," "useless eaters"—derived from their supposed lowly status in a hierarchy of human worthiness. Negative labeling is a step in the dehumanization process that often accompanies genocide.

Was there an absence of guardian groups that might have protected the victims? The answer is yes in all cases. Even Rwanda, which had about 2,500 UN peacekeepers and diplomats at the time the genocide began,[57] was essentially abandoned. "The desertion of Rwanda by the

UN force was Hutu Power's greatest diplomatic victory," writes the journalist Philip Gourevitch, "and it can be credited almost single-handedly to the United States."[58] However, without denying that the United Nations, the United States, and other countries did almost nothing to stop this particular genocide, one can still note that halting genocide is very difficult when the perpetrators fear no consequences.[59] In the Armenian case, for instance, a large group of vociferous, fervent advocates, composed of missionaries, teachers, diplomats, and other foreigners living in Turkey, gave their all to stop the carnage, and when they failed, they documented the atrocities, writing moving narratives that brought the massacres to the attention of high officials abroad and raising large sums of money for "the starving Armenians" (as the victims were often called). Not only did the Turks shut down the organizations of those who tried to help; they "refused the offers of assistance from foreign countries, even subsequently threatening legal proceedings against people and institutions accused of wishing to assist" the Armenians.[60] It is hard to stop a group that has decided on genocide from carrying out its plan *if* the attackers believe they can act with impunity. Guardians, even when they are present, are nearly powerless to prevent genocide unless they are well armed and determined.

At this point, readers with a criminological background will be thinking of the "routine activity" theory of crime, which analyzes predatory street crime in terms of not the characteristics of offenders but the circumstances in which these acts occur. These circumstances, according to routine activity theory, include (1) motivated offenders, (2) suitable targets, and (3) the absence of capable guardians against a violation.[61] This spatial or ecological theory aims at explaining the location, type, and quantity of illegal acts: in areas where there are potential offenders and unprotected targets, the theory argues, crime rates are relatively high. Routine activity theory fits well with my victim profiles in that, in genocide as in predatory street crime, motivated offenders cross paths with "suitable" or weak targets who lack effective guardians.

Routine activity theory does not go very far in explaining genocide, however, because—although the victim groups are often weak, unprepared, and poorly guarded—genocidal offender groups seek them out very deliberately and with specific motives, such as ethnic hatred. Genocide is more than convergence in space of predatory offenders and suitable targets. However, the theory works better to explain victimization of *individuals* during genocide, for some are killed simply because they are not well hidden or otherwise protected. The theory also points to ways to reduce genocide: increase the resistance of potential targets by strengthening them and improving their guardianship.

What were the long-term consequences of the genocide for the victim groups? For the genocides in this sample, total destruction was the result in two cases, those of the Herero and German people with disabilities. As a tribe, the Herero were demolished, and although individual members survived, they were reduced to slaving for whites. Of the German disabled, few remained in 1945; but more appeared in later generations as a result of the genetic abnormalities and environmental toxins that cause disabilities in all populations. The tens of thousands of disabled people poisoned, starved, and gassed to satisfy Hitler's fantasies about purifying Aryan "blood" have been almost forgotten. The Armenians lost physical aspects of their cultural heritage, including land, churches, and sacred texts; however, they did manage to establish a small state of their own after World War I. In the postgenocidal periods in Indonesia, Mayan areas of Guatemalan, and Rwanda, these places suffered from—among many other severe problems—sex imbalances in the general population: with large proportions of the men dead, the burden of supporting and raising children fell on the women. In Rwanda, those difficulties were compounded for women coping with sexual violation and mutilation; moreover, many women were stigmatized by rape and giving birth to rapists' children.

Survivors also suffer from grief over the loss of family, acquaintances, and their way of life; one predictable result is an increase in mental and physical problems. Poles were so tormented by not knowing the truth about the missing men that their grief became a central theme in twentieth-century Polish history.[62] For Rwandans as for other victims, genocide was economically disastrous. For a while, Rwanda became "the poorest country on earth, with an average income of eight dollars a year."[63] Individual victims of most of these genocides have few memorials. One of the hardest truths of genocide is that people truly disappear, slipping beneath the surface of memory.

* * *

In sum, victims of this sample's genocides resemble those of the Holocaust in key respects, despite the marked differences among the genocides. They were mainly attacked in their own country, where they lived alongside the perpetrators. (Of course, the Nazis went on to commit genocide in other countries as well; here I am thinking of the initial attacks on German Jews.) Although perpetrators embarked on genocide while fighting one foe or another, these conflicts usually had little directly to do with the victims-to-be; thus, victims were caught off guard. (Rwanda's Tutsi were an exception; they knew what was coming, for it was being broadcast daily from the Hutu Power radio station.) In nearly all cases, the perpetrators negatively labeled the victims with terms based on race, ethnicity, political views or status, or alleged genetic inferiority. Victims lacked guardians who could have protected them from attack. For those who die in genocide, one long-term consequence is that most of them vanish from the historical record; for those who survive, the consequence can be a life of suffering and even ostracism. Victims of ordinary crimes usually have at least a hope of justice; but for victims of genocide, justice is often an impossibility.

I elaborate on these findings as the book goes on, but first I flesh out my answer to this chapter's main question about the nature of genocide by drawing on a very different source of information: analyses of twentieth-century mass murder. I will compare the theories of Benjamin Valentino and Christian Gerlach,[64] supplementing them with new work on the broader dynamics of genocide.

Who Runs a Genocide? Is Anyone in Charge Here?
Of Course Someone Is in Charge: The Valentino Model

In *Final Solutions*, the political scientist Benjamin Valentino argues that mass killing is "an instrumental policy—a brutal strategy designed to accomplish leaders' most important ideological or political objectives and counter what they see as their most dangerous threats."[65] Mass killing is a matter of rational choice by the perpetrator group's leaders. In this view, "mass killing does not require widespread, active public support, only passivity or indifference" on the part of the populace.[66] Valentino's book covers a broad swath of mass killings, not only genocide but any intentional killing of a massive number of noncombatants—"at least fifty thousand intentional deaths over the course of five or fewer years."[67] (Thus, he includes, for example, the Allies' bombings of Germany and Japan during World War II; but he has to exclude genocides against small groups.) Valentino's primary interest is in the *cause* of mass killings. After considering and rejecting several other theories, he endorses the instrumentalist perspective in which the "specific goals and strategies of high political and military leaders, not . . . broad social or political factors," are the primary causes of mass killing.[68]

A great virtue of Valentino's theory is that it encourages us to see genocidal decisions from the perspectives of those who made them and to recognize why they felt mass murder was their best alternative. Moreover, most genocides in my sample support Valentino's theory—or seem to at first glance. Five of the events—the genocides of the Herero, Germans with disabilities, Polish soldiers at Katyn, Cambodians during the Khmer Rouge regime, and Guatemalan Maya—occurred when strong rulers made extermination decisions, either all at once (as happened when Stalin signed the order for the Katyn executions) or sequentially (as happened whenever Pol Pot or his henchmen authorized more killings). These genocides were, at least in part, top-down events, set in motion to achieve leaders' instrumental objectives.

Valentino's thesis holds up less well in my three other cases—the genocides in Turkish Armenia, Indonesia, and Rwanda. In the Armenian case, the Turks' 1915 decision to rid their country of Armenians, although it undoubtedly had instrumental aims, can also be seen as the culmination of a series of massacres that had begun in the late nineteenth century and gone unpunished. Moreover, when the Turkish Committee for Union and Progress decided on deportation and extermination, it was to some extent scapegoating Armenians for a host of grave problems it could not handle, especially the 1915 loss of a key battle against Russia.[69] In Indonesia, even before genocide began in 1965, the military had widely violated human rights, and many people expected some sort of governmental cataclysm.[70] Despite the strength of the Indonesian communist party, or perhaps because of it, many Indonesians feared some sort of military violence, which was probably in the offing irrespective of the coup attempt that precipitated the genocide. For Rwandan Tutsi in 1994, as for Armenians victimized decades earlier, the genocide was the culminating blow in a series of massacres, in this case five recent bloodbaths that Hutu had carried out with impunity.[71] The country's instability cannot be understood outside the context of regional chaos and historical competition between Hutu and Tutsi.

Moreover, even the five cases that seem to offer the best support for Valentino's theory call for an explanation that goes beyond strategic interests, for every one of these events was embedded in a situation of extreme violence, if not of war itself. Such violent contexts provide a corrective to Valentino's theory in crucial ways. An analogy might help: in US cities with problems of gang violence, gang leaders may give the signal for killings or fights to begin; but they would have no power to act if they did not live in social situations in which violence is a route to power. To understand gang violence—and diminish it—one must study both the leaders' decisions *and* the contexts in which they occur. A further and exceptionally helpful corrective comes from the Swiss historian Christian Gerlach and his concept of "extremely violent societies."

No One Is in Charge: The Gerlach Model

In *Extremely Violent Societies*, Gerlach rejects the traditional genocide model, which he associates with Valentino. This model distorts our understanding of mass violence, he writes, because it boils multicausal events down to a single cause, the instrumentalist policies of leaders.[72] This model "restricts the analysis" to certain types of events—genocides—which even genocide scholars cannot define with precision.[73] Moreover, the traditional model suggests that causation must relate to the UN's definitional categories of ethnicity, religion, race, and nationality, attributes that it treats as givens rather than the social and historical constructions that they in fact are. And the traditional approach encourages a search for a single kind of intent (a commander in chief making a decision to exterminate, for example), whereas in genocide and other forms of mass violence, intention is in fact spread across a wide range of decision makers who make various kinds of decisions.[74]

How, then, *does* Gerlach define "extremely violent societies"? In them, he writes,

- Violence goes "in different directions," targets "diverse groups," and takes "various forms."
- Violence is generated by a number of institutions and social groups, not just the state and its leaders.
- Motives for violence are complex, as are the links between planning and the execution of plans (here again Gerlach explicitly contradicts Valentino).
- Extreme violence is "a temporary process," for "societies are not extremely violent in principle or by character."
- Violence is often committed by "coalitions for violence," meaning "fairly unstable alliances between social groups with overall diverging political goals." (In the Armenian genocide, for instance, the Committee for Union and Progress forged alliances with Kurds and amnestied criminals, encouraging them to kill and pillage Armenians along the deportation routes; each group in the coalition had different reasons for joining the alliance.) Violence ebbs when the political interests of the main groups in the coalition begin to diverge.[75]

In brief, Gerlach contends that "mass violence originates from complex processes deeply rooted in the society in which they happen or by which they are generated; they are not merely based on state policies."[76] Moreover, they involve a great many people: "Whether in Cambodia or Indonesia, . . . we notice a broad, socially diverse—though by no means universal—participation in violence."[77]

Gerlach's description of mass violence is supported by the examples in my sample—strongly so. This may not be immediately apparent from reading the short summaries, earlier, from which Gerlach might recoil as examples of the "traditional genocide model." Later in this book, however, I show just how multicausal these events were, how coalitions formed and dissolved during them, and how they targeted various groups in various ways. (The Nazi genocides illustrates this point: Hitler aimed at the disappearance of multiple groups, not just Jews; and various sets of executioners—including, in the case of the disabled, physicians and nurses—furthered his aims for reasons of their own, one of them professional advancement.) In all eight genocides, violence flowed from a range of sources, not just the state, and ensnared large numbers of participants. Even the Katyn Forest Massacre, so stark in its outlines, looks complex when one locates it in the context of World War II and acknowledges that it was caused by numerous factors over and beyond Stalin lifting his pen on March 5, 1940, to sign a death warrant.

Gerlach's critique does not completely invalidate Valentino's theory—genocide is after all a crime of groups, all groups have leaders, and leaders of genocidal groups are by definition intimately involved in mass violence. But it does show that we need to supplement Valentino's relatively traditional approach with more recent historiography and with a global perspective. Gerlach pushes us beyond unidimensional stereotypes of victims, perpetrators, and bystanders to see that in some genocides, victims, perpetrators, and bystanders trade roles. (Who were the perpetrators in the Herero case, in which the tribe started the war, and who were the victims? If the charges against Rwanda's President Kagame are true, does that make him a genocide perpetrator as well as a savior of the victims?) Gerlach's concept of extremely violent societies alerts us to the possibility that forms of violence may interact (as when Hitler waited to start World War II before commencing "euthanasia" of the handicapped). And Gerlach's insistence on considering multiple forms of violence, not just killing, encourages us to look at a fuller spectrum of genocidal violence, including systematic rape and forced removal of indigenous children from their homes to prison-like "boarding" schools.

The Broader Dynamics of Genocide

Work by the criminologist Susanne Karstedt provides an up-to-date picture of genocide in the early twenty-first century. Karstedt builds on Gerlach's work but takes a longer, evolutionary view of the dynamics of mass violence.[78] Genocide and other forms of mass violence, she argues, are "embedded in trajectories of long-term conflict."[79] "Extreme violence does not spread indiscriminately across a region or country but rather is highly structured through channels, contagion and networks."[80] Karstedt introduces the metaphor of "waves" of mass violence that sometimes peak in genocide but also involve other sorts of atrocity as the waves surge and ebb. Moreover, she pictures these waves circling the globe, peaking here as they subside there.[81] (I have found similar "waves"; see figure 1.1 and the accompanying analysis in chapter 1.)

Like Gerlach, Karstedt rejects efforts to make simplistic distinctions among perpetrators, bystanders, collaborators, and victims.[82] Such typologies do not work, she argues, because mass violence is so often embedded in regional problems that cause actors to switch roles. "Mass violence and genocide need to be understood in terms of their connectivity within the international system."[83] As an example, Karstedt uses the Guatemalan genocide of the early 1980s, which was not only embedded in ongoing regional and Cold War politics but also involved deep ambiguities in the roles of the Maya, who were both victims and, in the case of those in civil defense patrols, genocidists. One implication of embeddedness is that "race and ethnicity are not necessarily main drivers of mass atrocities," as much of traditional genocide research maintains, "but rather one in a reservoir of . . . motives of perpetrator groups, including economic as well as political aims and security concerns."[84]

Drawing on the criminological concept of "hot spots" or concentrations of crime, Karstedt conceives of hot spots of genocide and mass atrocity that "migrate" around the globe. Central America became a hot spot during the Cold War, for example, due to the confluence of guerrilla insurgents and US-funded counterinsurgencies.[85] More recently, mass violence left Central and Latin American countries behind for the new hot spot of Central Africa, where battling ethnic groups pushed one another across borders and linked up with local groups that then increased the heat. "All spatial analyses of extreme violence and mass atrocities," Karstedt concludes, "confirm that they are highly concentrated at hot spots, as are violence and crime generally."[86]

What Kind of a Crime, Then, Is Genocide?

Genocide has been called unthinkable, inconceivable; people recoil even from imagining it. But truth be told, magnitude aside, genocide is similar in many ways to ordinary violent crime and can be profitably studied in the ways that ordinary violent crime is studied. As the criminologist Hollie Nyseth Brehm and her colleagues have shown in relation to Rwanda, in genocide as in street crime, the perpetrators—at least those who do the actual killing—tend to be men between the ages of eighteen and forty-five.[87] My data suggest that this demographic is typical: across genocides, the perpetrators are young or middle-aged men hot for a fight;[88] they are bullies who pick on the weak. Victims, too, bear similarities: in genocide as in street-level violent crime, they are often defenseless, and they may be subjected to hate speech.[89] Genocide, like street crime, involves multiple types of violence, and its form and occurrence are deeply rooted in local circumstances. Indeed, both kinds of event are even similar in tending to occur in hot spots. The difference lies in genocide's magnitude and intent to destroy a *group*. To note these similarities is not to minimize the horror of genocide, which is without doubt the worst crime in the human repertoire. However, the parallels enable us to apply criminological concepts and research to genocide.

These criminological advantages, however, are far outweighed by what is currently the biggest obstacle to answering the What kind of a crime is it? question. That is the vexing definitional problem. The UN Convention limits genocide to acts intended to destroy national, ethnic, racial, or religious groups. Restive scholars have pushed beyond these confines to focus as well on acts and processes intended to destroy political, cultural, and indigenous groups, as such. The increasingly poor fit between the UNCG and genocide scholarship matters because knowledge matters, and it needs the firm foundation that a settled definition can bring. In addition, and far more consequentially, the world continues to witness acts intended to destroy groups that do not fit the UN's definition. If we really care about the protection of groups as such—for their group characteristics—it is necessary to broaden the UN definition. Otherwise, these acts cannot be prosecuted as crimes.[90]

This problem has grown more acute since the establishment of the International Criminal Court, which began functioning in 2002. The establishing legislation—the Rome Statute—gives the ICC authority to prosecute genocide, but it merely repeats the original definition of genocide, without a word of change. True, the Rome Statute does define crimes against humanity so as to enable aspects of genocide to be prosecuted under this heading. But then they are crimes against humanity— not genocide. If we value the concept that Raphael Lemkin named and fought to see enacted in international law, we need to push for a new answer to the question, What kind of a crime is genocide? One good possibility, as I suggested earlier, is Feierstein's formulation: genocide is "the execution of a large-scale and systematic plan with the intention of destroying a human group as such in whole or in part."[91] However, this is not the legal definition, and the legal definition is unlikely to change in the foreseeable future.

3

The Big Picture: The Macro Dynamics of Genocide

The Herero Genocide, 1904–1907

The twentieth century—a period during which the world was convulsed by at least sixty-five genocides—is deservedly (if perhaps incorrectly) known as "the century of genocide."[1] The pace of these cataclysmic events started slowly in the early decades but picked up in midcentury, peaked during the period 1961–1980, and subsided slightly toward the century's end (figure 1.1). Over fifty million people died in twentieth-century genocides, while millions more were maimed, physically and psychologically, and whole cultures were obliterated.[2]

What caused these genocides, and what made them so common in the twentieth century? What can we learn from studying these atrocities that might make the twenty-first century less wasteful, and woeful, in terms of human lives, culture, and resources?

To answer those questions, one approach is to examine so-called macro factors, meaning, first and foremost, circumstances associated with the state. These can be structural circumstances—such as economic conditions and types of government—that might help explain why states have resorted to genocide. Other macro factors that might conceivably affect genocide are contextual in nature, such as state instability, war, and the ruling elite's endorsement of an ideology such as communism or anticommunism; still others have to do with population characteristics, such as ethnic or racial polarization. As these remarks suggest, macro factors usually work at the state level and may be roughly equivalent to the state itself, although they make themselves felt at the group and individual levels. I also treat impunity—exemption from punishment—as a macro factor, conceiving of it as a risk factor in its own right, part of a political culture. For example, as chapter 6 explains in more detail, during genocides, heads of state will often create a "state of exception" to ordinary laws governing crime and punishments.[3] But I also conceive of impunity as a by-product of other macro factors such as state instability and wartime conditions. Macro factors are risk factors that *may* increase the likelihood of genocide but do not always do so. They are circumstances that set the scene in which genocide takes place; they paint the background, creating the tensions and establishing the mood of menace that often precedes genocide. This chapter shows how macro factors may lead to genocide and how they interact dynamically with one another.

Comparative criminology—the approach I use in this book—looks for commonalities among phenomena across time and space. It helps reveal the underlying causes of events. In this case, I compare eight phenomena—genocides—by looking to see which specific macro factors appear most often. For instance, I take the macro factor of state failure and compare the eight examples to see how often they were accompanied by state disintegration. Then I follow the same procedure with another macro factor such as war, while also asking if war occurred more or less frequently than state failure; if more frequently, I conclude that war is a greater risk factor for genocides in this sample than state failure is. I also ask if state failure and war, interacting dynamically with each other, increase the risk of genocide.

In what follows, I use comparative criminology to examine the relationship to genocide of six macro variables: colonialism, war, state instability and failure, ethnic or racial polarization, ideology (which is not easy to separate from other macro factors such as colonialism), and impunity. (I focus on macro factors that proved important to most or all of my eight examples. However, later in the chapter, I explain why I reject two other macro factors—regime type and poverty—that other scholars have identified as important causes of genocide.)[4]

I open with the Herero genocide, giving a fuller account of that event than earlier. After identifying macro factors in this genocide, I discuss macro factors in the other genocides in my sample. My main conclusion is that war and genocidists' confidence in impunity are key risk factors for genocide. Other factors, too, are highly associated with genocide, but in my sample, war and the expectation of impunity *always* are.

In the chapter's final section, I propose combining the risk factors most highly associated with genocide into the concept of a "genocidal propensity," analogous to the concept of "criminal propensity" that criminologists use to assess an offender's dangerousness and likelihood of re-offending. Knowing that a state (or other kind of collectivity, such as an ethnic group) has a genocidal propensity means that we can work ahead to prevent genocide from occurring. The macro factors discussed in this chapter have important implications for the prevention of genocide.

The Herero Genocide

The Herero, a seminomadic confederation of tribes in Southwest Africa, lived in the area now called Namibia; they grazed herds of cattle on communal lands that they did not think of as private property. (The Herero's conflict with Germany also involved the Nama tribe. I omit that part of the history here for the sake of simplicity, but the omission changes neither the story's outlines nor the analysis.)[5] The Herero's was a nonstate society: while they thought in terms of communal territory, they did not conceive of the territory as the basis for a nation or state. As one tribesman later explained, "Under the Herero law the ground belonged to the tribe in common and not even the chief could sell or dispose of it. He could give people permission to live on the land. . . . Land was never sold to Germans or anyone else. We did not have any idea of such a thing."[6]

Before the early 1880s, when colonization by Germany began, the Herero's tribal confederation consisted of over 80,000 people.[7] By 1903, shortly before the Herero decided to wage war against the Germans, the white population of the colony had reached about 5,000. One historian explains, "The majority of the settlers were cattle ranchers. The rise of the white cattlemen took place concurrently with the decline of the Herero herdsmen. That proud tribe suffered the torments of Job in the last years of the old century and the first years of the new."[8] The Herero's decline in power was accompanied by population loss. A typhus epidemic killed perhaps 10,000 of them.[9] In addition, their cattle were struck by a viral epidemic, rinderpest, which killed 80–90 percent of their herds. (The Germans, who had a vaccine for their cattle, suffered less from the infection.) To make matters worse, white men bought up the Herero's best land and purchased their cattle under a usurious credit system: when Herero could not make their credit payments, ranchers took more of their cattle. In addition, the ranchers would give the Herero small items like fire starters, and not money, in exchange for cattle.

To the Herero, it became increasingly clear that their land, power, and wealth were seeping away while the Germans' fortunes were growing.

Appropriation and despoliation of the Herero's grazing land was a major cause of their uprising. The introduction of railroads broke up their grazing lands. The Germans had already built one railroad to the south; then they started work on another that would cut through the center of Herero territory. The railroad company, according to the historian Horst Drechsler, "demanded that the Herero cede not only the land directly required for the construction of the railway, but also a 20-kilometer- [over twelve-miles-] wide strip on either side of the track plus all water rights within this area"[10] Germans also desecrated the burial ground of Herero chiefs by turning it to agricultural uses.[11]

Another cause of the uprising was resentment at the German judicial system, which worked hand in glove with settlers to plunder and humiliate the Herero. German law deemed that the Herero had inferior status in court. Seven African witnesses were required to balance off one white witness, and it was difficult for Africans to take their complaints—even serious ones like rape and lynching—to court.[12] "Our people were being robbed and deceived right and left by German traders," a Herero underchief testified later:

> Their cattle were taken by force; they were flogged and ill-treated and got no redress. In fact the German police assisted the traders instead of protecting us. . . . Very often one man's cattle were taken to pay other people's debts. If we objected and tried to resist the police we would be sent for, and what with the floggings and the threats of shooting, it was useless for our poor people to resist. . . . They fixed their own prices for the goods, but would never let us place our own valuation on the cattle. . . . For a bag of meal they took eight cows.[13]

The racist premises that had led the settlers to take African land in the first place also made them believe they had a right to rape Herero women. The same underchief, Daniel Kariko, told how a settler tried to rape a woman from "a great old Herero family from which many big chiefs had come." She resisted, so he shot her.[14] After he was tried for murder but acquitted, he joined the German troops and "shot down [Herero] men, women, and children in the rebellion." Major Theodor

Leutwein, head of the German colony, believed that this murder "contributed its share towards the unrest among the Hereros which resulted half a year later in the outbreak of the rebellion."[15] Whereas Herero convicted of killing always received the death penalty, in the four cases of murder by white men that made it into court, the most stringent penalty was three years' imprisonment.[16]

War started in January 1904 when the Herero attacked German settlements. The revolt turned the Herero genocide into what criminologists might call a victim-precipitated genocide—using that term not to blame the victims but to indicate the dynamics of the situation and the victims' agency.[17] The Herero knew that rebellion would bring the end of their tribal life and that they would probably die. "There is no other way," counseled Chief Samuel Maherero. "Let us die fighting rather than die as a result of maltreatment, imprisonment, or some other calamity." The son of another Herero leader, Chief Zacharias, later testified that his father, "knew that if we rose in revolt we would be wiped out in battle because our men were almost unarmed and without ammunition. The cruelty and injustice of the Germans had driven us to despair, and our leaders and the people felt that death had lost much of its horror in the light of the conditions under which we lived."[18]

Although the Herero had few rifles and little ammunition, they were victorious in their first, surprise attack on the settlers. Leutwein, the civilian governor, tried to negotiate a peace, less out of sympathy with the Herero than because he believed that the colony needed an underclass of African laborers.[19] However, German officials in Europe were humiliated by the Africans' victory; if the revolt were not crushed, they thought, Germany would lose its standing as a great power.[20] Moreover, the settlers demanded that Germany back up their plans to completely appropriate Herero territory and, if necessary, exterminate the tribe. According to one historian, "The settlers in GSWA [German Southwest Africa] were not onlookers or bystanders but direct participants. They provided a major impetus for the genocide, because they complained vociferously to Germany and to the Kaiser about the lenient policy towards Africans, the Herero in particular. They wanted the Herero land and wanted it for free and did not care by what means they were to get it. When the conflict occurred, Germany clearly accepted the settlers' assessment and demands and decided that it was time to deal with the

Figure 3.1. Military portrait of Lothar von Trotha, the German officer who in 1904 ordered extermination of the Herero of Southwest Africa. Courtesy of Colonial Picture Archive, University of Frankfurt/Main.

matter once and for all."[21] The kaiser, putting the colony under military rule, replaced Leutwein with Lieutenant General Lothar von Trotha, a warrior who had already brutally suppressed rebellious blacks in East Africa. (Summarizing his approach to "race war" with Africans, von Trotha declared that "no war may be conducted humanely against non-humans.")[22] Von Trotha was this genocide's Hitler.

By late June 1904, reinforcements had brought the German force to nearly 20,000 men. Von Trotha planned to encircle and destroy the Africans at Waterberg, a site on the desert's edge to which the Herero had retreated. Many Herero fled into the desert, denying von Trotha a dramatic victory; but most died there of thirst, starvation, and, some said, poison that Germans had poured into the watering holes. Strangely, it was only *after* the Germans had clearly defeated the Herero that von Trotha issued his infamous order for complete annihilation:

> The Hereros are no longer German subjects.
>
> They have murdered and stolen, have cut off the ears and noses and other body parts from wounded soldiers, and in cowardice no longer want to fight. . . . The Herero people must leave the country. If the people does not do that, then I will force it to with the Groot Rohr [big cannon].
>
> Within the German border every Herero, armed or not, with cattle or without, will be shot, I will not take up any more women or children, will drive them back to their people or let them be shot at.[23]

The proclamation, writes the historian Isabel Hull, "provided the *ex post facto* justification for the genocide that had already occurred."[24]

Over the next year, German patrols hunted down unarmed Herero, shooting them as they foraged in the bush or bringing them back to headquarters for questioning and hanging. No distinction was made between prisoners of war and other Herero; thousands of men, women, and children were slaughtered without reason—other than to exterminate the group.[25] To explain von Trotha's "delirious cruelty," the sociologist George Steinmetz argues that the aristocratic general was "locked in a polarizing battle with a middle-class rival"—the previous head of the colony, Leutwein, who "represented for him the forces deposing the nobility from its ancient domination in Germany."[26] Class animosity may have reinforced von Trotha's resolve to exterminate, but he had been slaughtering Africans for years before he replaced Leutwein; he was both cruel and imperiously racist. On his orders, soldiers casually shot or incinerated blacks, who to them (as to the general himself) seemed more like "baboons" than human beings.[27]

Von Trotha's extermination order raised political protests in Germany, however, and colonial officials persuaded the kaiser to rescind it. Surviving Herero were herded into concentration camps, a method of social control that Germans had not used before. Death rates approached 50 percent before the camps were shut three years after their opening. "I was sent down with others to an island far in the south," reported a survivor. "There on that island were thousands of Herero . . .

Figure 3.2. Germans hanging 312 Herero in Southwest Africa, probably 1904. After Lieutenant General von Trotha's proclamation of extermination, the German army stationed in Southwest Africa killed Herero by every means possible—hanging, shooting, starvation, beating, even burning. Courtesy of Martin Plaut.

prisoners. . . . Men, women and children were all huddled together. We had no proper clothing, no blankets, and the night air on the sea was bitterly cold. The wet sea fogs drenched us. . . . The people died there like flies that had been poisoned."[28] Decrees declaring all the land to be German property further disenfranchised the survivors, who were now required to carry an identity badge. So ended what the historian Jürgen Zimmerer deems "one of the most brutal colonial wars ever fought."[29] More than three-quarters of the Herero population died; they killed about 125 Germans.[30]

From the Germans' perspective, the end of the Herero genocide was less a termination than a pause. Its effects continued, rippling outward. The influence of the slaughter, far from dying with its victims, actually grew stronger over time, feeding into the Armenian genocide of 1915 and the Nazi genocide that began thirty years later. During the Armenian genocide, German advisers to the Turks helped with military decisions and encouraged expulsion of the Armenians.[31] In Germany, the African

Figure 3.3. Captured Herero in chains. Some Herero survived the struggles with von Trotha's army only to be captured and humiliated. Among the initial survivors, some were sent to concentration camps, where large proportions of them died. Those who survived the camps were forced into servitude to white settlers. Courtesy of National Archives of Namibia.

genocide offered an example for the future, providing "ideas, methods, and a lexicon that Nazi leaders borrowed and expanded."[32]

The Herero genocide was the source not only of the German concentration camp but also of German studies in eugenics, the "science" of racial improvement. In 1908, Eugen Fischer, who became the Third Reich's chief authority on eugenics and a strong influence on Hitler's opinions about racial purity, traveled to Southwest Africa to conduct research on the "hybrid" offspring of whites and blacks. (In many cases, mixed-race children were born to African women who had been raped or otherwise coerced into sex by German settlers and soldiers.)[33] Further, the Herero genocide offered an early example of racial cleansing of a territory, although cleansing itself was the primary goal, irrespective of race; and it habituated Germans to the idea that it was legitimate to exterminate people who stood in the way of their national aspirations.[34] While the Herero genocide did not *cause* the subsequent Nazi genocide, it created a precedent and fostered a German national belief in racial purity and superiority.

Causes of the Herero Genocide

What caused the Herero genocide? What macro factors set the stage on which it occurred and put the Herero at risk? At the head of the list are German greed, presumption, and racism; bellicosity on both sides; and von Trotha's self-righteous cruelty. Aside from the Herero's willingness to fight, these factors can be grouped under the heading of colonialism, a macro factor also responsible to some degree in other genocides in my sample.

Colonialism involves a more powerful group's takeover of land popu-lated by an indigenous people and subjugation of the indigenous group for profit. In my sample, the colonization of Southwest Africa by the Germans is the clearest example of colonization leading directly to genocide, but in Guatemala, colonization of the Maya also played a role, even though that country's genocide occurred hundreds of years later. In Rwanda, too, colonization played a role, in that Belgian colonists had constructed the Tutsi as superior, racially, to the Hutu, and set the two groups in competition. One of Hitler's motives for starting World War II (which provided cover for the genocide of Germany's mentally and physically disabled) was to colonize Poland and other lands to the east. Moreover, a history of colonialism was a risk factor in the late twen-tieth- and early twenty-first-century genocidal wars in Central Africa. Colonialism can be considered a macro factor in its own right or as an ideology—a system of beliefs that structures economic and political policy and, more broadly, people's ways of interpreting the world.

Historians of the Herero genocide argue that destruction of the Afri-cans' culture did not depend on von Trotha's hate-filled intervention; de-struction would have happened in any case, albeit more slowly and with fewer deaths. The genocide scholar Dominik Schaller writes, "Leutwein and the colonial authorities in Berlin represented genocidal administra-tion, at least in intention. Cooperation with indigenous chiefs was only a temporary expedient. . . . Leutwein knew that the complete political dis-solution of the indigenous societies was a necessary precondition for un-disputed German supremacy. And he therefore tried to limit the power of the indigenous chiefs gradually and to abolish the political institution of chiefdoms."[35] Similarly, Zimmerer argues that von Trotha was not crucial to this genocide: "Leutwein's colonial aims would have also led to the destruction of African culture and tradition. Africans would have been transformed into a 'black' working class, devoid of any memory of their cultural origins or the Herero . . . identity. . . . In many respects the war just sped things up. The cultural destruction at which Leutwein aimed could also [i.e., like the destruction inflicted by von Trotha] be termed genocide, as cultural genocide is increasingly understood as a form of genocide."[36] Colonialism per se—quite apart from von Trotha's ruthlessness—was thus crucial to destabilization in Southwest Africa during the lead-up to the genocide.

Before I turn to other macro factors, let me say a bit more about colonialism, since it was a major influence on many twentieth-century genocides. According to two authorities on this subject, indigenous people all over the world have always been "prime targets for genocide" by colonists.[37] Because these exterminations have been scattered geographically, have covered hundreds of years, and have been less studied than genocides involving Europeans, there is no clear record for formulating generalizations about these events or gauging how greatly they differed from other, better-understood genocides.[38] If we knew more about colonial genocides, our understanding of the nature of genocide in general might change radically. For example, we would have to incorporate serial genocides, like those committed in Australia, Canada, and the United States against indigenous people, even though they do not easily fit the UN's definition of genocide, which is geared to big and fairly static events.

But the social anthropologist Dominik Schaller cautions against "generalizing conclusions" about colonial genocides. He points out that "seven European nations participated in the 'scramble for Africa' in the 1880s. Their motives . . . and colonial cultures differed considerably, as did their modes of governance and administration." The degree of violence against the indigenous population depended mainly on the identity of the administrator: when the chief administrator was a military man (as in the case of von Trotha), violence and even genocide were more likely.[39]

Schaller also cautions against using "colonial genocide" as a distinct category. Genocides against indigenous groups in North America, Australia, and Africa, he argues, vary too widely to be forced in a single conceptual framework. But even while heeding Schaller's cautions, one can state unequivocally that colonialism the world over helped prepare the ground for twentieth-century genocides and is partly responsible for the great number of such atrocities during the last century.

Racism, too, was a powerful factor in the Herero case. Self-serving Social Darwinist doctrines had taught the Germans that, as members of a "fitter" white race, they had a right to take over the lands of "unfit" black and brown peoples and to destroy them and their cultures with impunity. However, racism is difficult to separate from colonialism. The best approach might be to say that racism indirectly contributed to the Herero genocide by working through colonialism. What the Germans primarily wanted was the land, not to kill black people.

In the case of the macro factors of war and state failure, too, it is difficult to separate one factor from another. The war in Southwest Africa, as we have seen, was started by the Herero and brought Herero tribal governance to an end. But it would hardly be fair to say that the tribe's decision to go to war *caused* the failure of their "state" or the genocide itself. Drawing on the term introduced earlier, one might say that theirs was a "victim-precipitated genocide," meaning that the victim group took the first step toward its own destruction because it had no other choice.[40]

Aside from colonialism, another factor in the Herero genocide that can be treated as an independent force, in and of itself, is impunity: confidence that one can commit a crime without punishment. Whether one views the Herero genocide as a direct result of von Trotha's extermination order or as a more diffuse result of German colonialism, impunity was never in question. There was no power on earth that could have punished the Germans, individually or collectively, for their millions of injustices in Southwest Africa and their destruction of the Herero.

Macro Factors in Genocide More Generally

War and Other Major Upheavals

All eight genocides in my sample occurred during a period of upheaval or outright war. Thus, my study confirms the work of the many scholars who have argued that wars and major social struggles set the stage for genocide.[41] One of these is the political scientist Matthew Krain, whose large-scale study of the onset and severity of genocides found that involvement in war predicts these atrocities—and that civil war, in particular, is the best predictor. "Civil wars have more than twice the effect on genocide or politicide onset" as other kinds of wars, Krain writes.[42] Similarly, Hollie Nyseth Brehm's quantitative study of influences on the occurrence of genocide between 1955 and 2005 found that of all factors, civil wars have the most profound effect on the onset of genocide. The state, she points out, "is already inwardly violent toward a segment of its own population and the government is [already] threatened."[43]

My study also confirms the theory of the political scientist Robert Melson that state-sponsored mass murder becomes more likely when war is "intimately related to revolution."[44] We see such circumstances—and results—in the Armenian genocide. The Turks were fighting in World War I, on the losing side. They were also fighting against Russia, again losing. It was at this point that they initiated genocide on an unarmed population group in their midst: the Armenians. "The genocide of the Armenians," Melson writes, should be understood "as a stage in the Turkish revolution, which as a reaction to the continuing disintegration of the [Ottoman] empire settled on a narrow nationalism and excluded Armenians from the moral universe of the state."[45] This example, like others in my sample, alerts us to the fact that war, civil war, and revolution—intense violence and abrupt ideological change in close association—can sow devastation.

A particularly thoughtful discussion of war and genocide appears in the work of the British sociologist Martin Shaw, first in his book *War and Genocide: Organised Killing in Modern Society* (2003) and more recently in *What Is Genocide?* (2007). In the latter work, Shaw argues that *genocide is not only a form of social conflict, but also a form of war. . . . The difference lies in the construction of civilian groups as enemies . . . to be destroyed.*[46] The core of traditional warfare is a conflict between armed enemies, whereas in genocide the target is unarmed civilians. "For all the degeneracy of war, we can still grasp its core rationality of state against state, army against army." But "genocide removes the last vestiges of rationality and legitimacy that cling to more conventional war."[47] Shaw uses "genocidal war" to describe situations in which armed conflicts combine war and genocide.[48]

"Genocidal war" is an excellent description of the conflict between the Herero and the Germany army. "Genocidal war" also describes four other genocides in my sample: the conflict between the Indonesian army and the country's communists; Pol Pot's determination to exterminate Cambodians whom he decided were "enemies of the people"; the Guatemalan army's conflict with the Maya; and the violence by Rwandan Hutu extremists against Tutsi and moderate Hutu. Even the extermination of disabled people in Nazi Germany might be called a "genocidal war" because, although the aggressors in this case were not soldiers but medical men, they thought of their work as a mortal struggle against bad heredity.

Thus, war is often inextricably bound up with genocide. It may co-occur with genocide, as in the Armenian and Katyn cases, or precede genocide, as with the long-standing civil war that in Guatemala preceded genocide of the Maya. Moreover, war is closely related to another macro factor in genocide: state failure.

State Failure

Nations are described as "failed states" when they are so riven by internal violence—revolts; struggles among warring groups—that they can no longer provide security to their populations and thus, in the words of Robert Rotberg in the book *When States Fail*, lose legitimacy "in the hearts and minds of . . . citizens."[49] Whereas "war" refers to a type of struggle, "state failure" refers to a problem in governance. The two phenomena differ, but they also overlap, especially when state failure is caused by or results in civil war.[50] The failed-state phenomenon seems to have become more common in recent decades. The rate of emergence of new, relatively weak states has quadrupled since the year 2000 due to decolonization and the end of the Cold War. This has left a greater number than ever before of struggling, inexperienced nations vulnerable to takeovers by opposition groups.[51] The State Failure Task Force, an independent group that studied 114 state failures from 1955 to 1998, defines state failure in terms of four types of events: revolutionary wars, ethnic wars, adverse regime changes (such as state collapse and periods of severe instability), and genocides and politicides.[52]

Using matched case-control comparisons, the State Failure Task Force found that "*genocides and politicides almost never occur in an otherwise stable environment; instead they usually follow other kinds of state fail-*

ures, such as revolutions, authoritarian coups, or ethnic wars."[53] In five of my eight cases, the state was either failing or had recently failed, and in two others (Indonesia and Guatemala), the state was precarious.

- In the Herero case, colonization destroyed the tribe's "state"—the tribal confederation through which it governed itself.
- In the Armenian case, the Ottoman Empire was collapsing—spectacularly so—and its replacement, the Young Turk government, was self-destructing.
- The Katyn genocide occurred in the context of a "secret" state failure: Russia and Germany had recently signed the Ribbentrop-Molotov or Nazi-Soviet Pact of nonaggression, which included a clause dividing Poland and other eastern European countries into Nazi and Soviet "spheres of influence." This pact enabled Stalin to move into Poland, capture soldiers, and annex land without threat of Nazi interference. In other words, Poland was a failing state at the time the prisoners were captured, although they died innocent of that knowledge.
- The government of Cambodia, after a five-year civil war with Khmer Rouge forces, failed when it lost the war; Pol Pot's Khmer Rouge entered a country that had close to a blank slate in terms of governance.
- The Rwandan government collapsed when President Habyarimana's plane was shot down; but even before that, his government had been unable or unwilling to fall into line with the 1993 Arusha Accords, designed by outside countries to avert Hutu-Tutsi violence.[54]
- As a state, Indonesia was close to failing at the time of the attempted coup; Suharto's takeover and clampdown on communists achieved a quick recovery from state failure.
- Guatemala's government, too, was close to failure at the time of its genocide; it was trying to cope with a protracted insurgency and survived only because the military assumed dictatorial powers.

Thus, in seven of my eight cases, genocide was associated, usually closely, with outright or threatened state failure.

It is not hard to think of explanations for this. State failure, like war, results in social disorganization and breakdown—the very opposite of the circumstances that foster law-abiding behavior and social stability.[55] Moreover, when social dissention and chaos are contained by a corrupt force like the Guatemalan military, the result is not improved social solidarity but what one might call "antisocial efficacy": improved ability for an amoral, self-interested faction to commit enormous crimes, including genocide.[56] War and state failure create opportunities for the worst sorts of antisocial behavior.

My eighth case, that of the Nazi genocide of the disabled, took place in Germany, a nation that earlier had been close to state failure but had recovered when the Nazis came to power. As a now-stable state, it became an exception to the State Failure Task Force's finding that genocides and politicides rarely occur in stable environments. Even in conditions of stability, however, Hitler had to keep his "euthanasia" project secret and hide it under the blanket of war. Germany was not so stable, nor so closely controlled, that the T4 group could openly murder the disabled.

Ethnic and Racial Polarization

Genocide scholars of the 1970s and 1980s—a period when ethnic and racial prejudice was high on the Western world's social agenda—stressed discrimination and other social antagonisms as risk factors for genocide.[57] These themes continue to run strong today. Eric Weitz, in *A Century of Genocide*, emphasizes ideologies of race and nation in the causation of four cataclysmic twentieth-century genocides.[58] Moreover, the State Failure Task Force reports, "Discriminatory treatment of minorities and exclusion of some communal groups from the political elite are major factors in the genesis of geno/politicide,"[59] and Nyseth Brehm finds that the likelihood of genocide increases when the ethnicity of those in power is a recurring source of conflict in the society.[60]

In addition, one of the most influential of recent genocide studies, Michael Mann's *The Dark Side of Democracy: Explaining Ethnic Cleansing*, emphasizes ethnicity as a risk factor in mass murder. Specifically, Mann argues that "murderous ethnic cleansing" represents a perversion of modern democratic ideals. Democracy, Mann continues, means rule by the people (*demos*); but when *demos* devolves into *ethnos*, with a particular ethnic group dominating the others, its exclusionary practices can lead to genocide and lesser forms of murderous ethnic cleansing. This is the "dark side of democracy." Mann perpetuates and refines the argument of the 1970s–1980s that ethnic hatreds are primary risk factors in "the crime of crimes."[61]

But others disagree, and their voices grow increasingly loud. Krain, Shaw, and others point to a host of nonethnic genocides, including the Holocaust, in which, although Jews and so-called Gypsies were exterminated on the grounds of ethnicity, other victims were selected by religion, sexual orientation, or disability.[62] Krain's study found that ethnicity was only a "marginal" risk factor for genocide.[63] Perhaps, as I suggested in chapter 2, race and ethnicity are simply motives in a reservoir of reasons on which genocidists draw to justify violence.[64]

In my sample, ethnic or racial polarization was influential in four of the eight genocides (Herero, Armenian, Guatemalan, and Rwandan), while it played a marginal role in two others (Katyn and Cambodia). In the remaining two cases (the Nazi extermination of the disabled and the Indonesian genocide), ethnic or racial polarization was not relevant.[65] As appendix A suggests, racial or ethnic tension continues to be a factor in genocides around the world. However, further study may confirm the argument of Krain and Shaw that the impact of this factor is small or diminishing.[66] In any case, in my sample, this macro factor had less impact than war, state failure, or—a factor I discuss in a moment—prior offenses and expectations of impunity.

Ideology

Ideology figured large in earlier analyses of the causes of genocide, no doubt due to the influence of the Holocaust. Calling ideological genocides "perhaps a unique twentieth-century innovation," Helen Fein defined them as "cases in which the state redefines society by eliminating people in order to correspond to its political formula, its representation of itself, and to legitimate the state."[67] She found that ideological genocides were committed less frequently as the twentieth century went on: "most cases of contemporary genocide since World War II were committed by authoritarian, not totalitarian, states and are not ascribable to ideology."[68] Fein was, however, writing in 1993—a year before the Rwandan genocide reminded the world of the power of ideologies of ethnicity. Nyseth Brehm's work shows that exclusionary ethnic ideologies were a significant risk factor for genocide right to the end of the century.[69]

As noted earlier, colonialism can be considered an ideology; the same is true of ethnic and racial beliefs when these structure people's worldviews, as was the case with the Hutu Power philosophy that drove the Rwandan genocide. Thus, we are dealing here with an unavoidable overlap among macro factors. But if we include colonialism and ethnic or racial beliefs in the category of ideology, the conclusion to be drawn from my sample is that ideology powerfully influenced genocide throughout the twentieth century. Of my eight cases, only one—the Katyn Forest Massacre—was nonideological. (Stalin's decision to liquidate the Poles was largely strategic.) Moreover, of the various ideologies that shaped these genocides—nationalism, eugenics, and so on—the most common was communism and anticommunism, which affected three of the eight cases (Indonesia, Guatemala, and Cambodia). This pattern offers hope that, with the passing of the Cold War and its communism-anticommunism polarization, ideology may become a less potent risk factor in genocide.[70]

Prior Offenses and Impunity

The probability that states, like individuals, will commit a crime can be predicted by their prior behavior. Legally, earlier crimes may not be relevant, but criminologically, they shine a bright light on patterns of offending.

Criminologists have found that prior offenses are one of the best predictors of future criminal behavior. People who relapse into crime once are likely to do so again.[71] If they are convicted of three or more offenses, they may be labeled habitual offenders or career criminals—unless an extensive period of time goes by without further relapses, in which case old offense records have little predictive value.[72]

Genocidal states echo these behavior patterns. Some accumulate histories comparable to a prior record, and in these cases, prior offenses predict reoffending, just as they do for individuals.[73]

The influence of a prior record has evidently not been addressed directly in genocide studies.[74] The State Failure Task Force, the independent US study group, addressed it indirectly when it found that countries with a *history* of violent upheaval and state failure were much more likely to commit genocide than were those with relatively little

recent upheaval.[75] However, "violent upheaval" is not the same as genocide. How can we define recidivism when we are talking about genocide?

The best unit of measurement is "genocidal massacre," a term introduced by the genocide scholar Leo Kuper in 1981 and elaborated by
others since then.[76] Genocidal massacres are incidents aimed at exterminating a group, but they are smaller in scale and shorter in duration
than full-scale genocides. They can be committed by groups smaller
than a state (such as a tribe or militia), and they do not necessarily lead
to full-blown genocide, although a series of genocidal massacres such as
those committed against various North American indigenous peoples
can add up to genocide. Thus, "recidivism" in the case of genocide can
be defined as a history of genocidal massacres against the group that
eventually becomes the victim of genocide itself.

Three cases in my sample provide clear-cut examples of genocidal
recidivism. The Armenian genocide that began in 1915 was the culmination of a series of Ottoman massacres against the Armenians that
had begun in the nineteenth century. The Guatemalan genocide of
1981–1983 consisted of a series of genocidal massacres that cumulatively
constituted genocide. And the Rwandan genocide of 1994 came at the
end of a series of increasingly violent massacres of Tutsi by Hutu that
started almost as soon as the Hutu came to power in the early 1960s.
To this list, we need to add Indonesia's 1975 invasion of East Timor (a
separate country but part of the Indonesian archipelago) and brutality there for the next twenty-four years. Some people call Indonesia's
murders in East Timor—perhaps 100,000 killings out of a population
of 800,000—genocide; in any case, the Indonesian army attacked East
Timor viciously and with impunity just twenty years after its unarguable
genocide in its homeland.

The Genocide Prevention Task Force of the US Institute of Peace lists
a prior history of genocide or mass violence as one of the warning signs
for atrocity crimes.[77] Clearly, genocide can occur without such a prior
record, and a record of genocide does not necessarily lead to more genocide. However, when a group starts to collect the equivalent of a prior record of genocidal massacres, it is indeed at risk for committing genocide.

Closely related to the concept of a prior record for genocidal massacres is that of impunity. This macro factor is often absent from discussions of genocide prevention, which are more likely to focus on the

kindred idea of deterrence—crime prevention through threat of consequences. However, the two are conceptually different. Impunity refers to the expectation that one can get away with not only murder but genocide. In fact, historically it has been easier to escape punishment for genocide than for ordinary murder.

In every case in my sample, those who led the genocide and their followers expected impunity; in most cases, they were right. The Germans suffered no consequences for obliterating the Herero; the Turks dispossessed and killed Armenians with impunity; and so on through the century until we get to the Nuremberg "doctors" trials, in which twenty physicians were tried for "euthanasia" and medical experiments on humans during World War II. Some were acquitted, but the majority was convicted and seven were executed.

Thereafter, there was a gap in efforts to curb impunity, although there was no pause in *expectations* of impunity as states continued to commit genocide. However, efforts to curb impunity resumed in the 1990s with international trials for the genocides in Rwanda and the former Yugoslavia. These efforts continued into the early twenty-first century with trials of a few elderly men for the Cambodian genocide and of Efraín Ríos Montt for his 1980s genocide of the Maya.[78] They offer hope that impunity for genocide is ending.[79]

* * *

Let me propose another criminological analogy: the macro factors I have been discussing—colonialism, war, state instability and failure, ethnic and racial polarization, ideology, and prior genocidal massacres together with expectations of impunity—can be combined to create the construct of a "genocidal propensity" or "genocidal predisposition." To identify children at risk for becoming serious offenders, criminologists refer to a constellation of factors that constitute a criminal propensity.[80] Their lists include an early start in crime, antisocial parents, low-income backgrounds, and behavioral problems such as attention deficit disorder. They then try to find ways to treat children who are said to have this criminal propensity or predisposition so that remedial steps can be taken before the child grows up into a violent offender.[81] Following this criminological example, we might compile a constellation of the factors that put *groups* at risk for committing genocide by using the macro factors that in fact do predict it. We could call this a "genocidal propensity" or "genocidal predisposition."

One of these factors would be colonization or decolonization. Another would be the presence of war (especially civil war) in the group's current situation; state failure would be a third. Racial and ethnic polarization could be factored in, if relevant, as could the presence of a governing ideology and a prior history of genocide or genocidal massacres, especially if they had been committed with impunity. Together, these factors would constitute a genocidal propensity. Of course, not every one of these macro factors would predict genocide in every case, and there are perhaps other macro-level risk factors that should be included. My point is that with states as with delinquents, we can compile a kind of predictive instrument for criminal behavior.

The goal of creating such a predictive instrument would be the same for genocide as it is for delinquency: to prevent trouble before it occurs. If the United Nations or other international group were to pinpoint factors that put a state at risk for genocide, it could move into a troublesome situation ahead of time to head off disaster. This is indeed the logic behind *The Responsibility to Protect*, a 2001 report inspired by then-recent genocides in the former Yugoslavia and Rwanda. *The Responsibility to Protect* argues that when catastrophes are looming and the country in question is unable to protect its own citizens, other states have a responsibility to remedy the situation before humanitarian crises occur. By its authors' own admission, "To date, early warning about deadly conflict has been essentially ad hoc and unstructured."[82] International agencies involved in conflict prevention could benefit from an instrument such as the one I have just proposed to assess states' genocidal propensity.

* * *

Before leaving this discussion, I want to comment on two macro factors—regime type and poverty—that other scholars consider predictors for genocide.

With regard to regime type, the question is whether the type of government constitutes a risk factor for genocide. Are dictatorships more likely to commit genocide than democracies are? The State Failure Task Force, the independent study group with a large sample, holds that "policies of genocide are more likely to be implemented by autocratic regimes."[83] Similarly, the political scientist Rudolf Rummel has argued that democracies are less likely than dictatorships to commit violence against other nations.[84] But there are good reasons for reading such statements cautiously.

First, it is simply not true that decisions for genocide are always made by a single state or regime, working in isolation. This was true in the Herero case, but other genocides are likely to involve several states as perpetrators. For example, the United States played an indirect role in several Cold War genocides: during the Indonesian genocide, the US supported Suharto, just as during the Guatemalan genocide, it supported Ríos Montt. While genocide tends to occur within a single state, that does not mean that other states exert no influence on the leaders' decision-making processes.[85]

Second, the issue is less the *type of regime* than the regime's *stability*: stable democracies are less likely than democratizing or authoritarian regimes to commit murderous cleansing.[86] In other words, the type-of-regime risk factor is spurious, for it acts through stability.[87] In a definitive article titled "The State and Genocide," Anton Weiss-Wendt dismisses the regime-type debate by declaring, "The discussion of an 'ideal type of state' . . . is as fruitless as the construction of an 'ideal type of genocide.' Neither the state nor any of its constituencies possess certain innate characteristics that would make it prone to violence."[88] Thus, we can put aside regime type per se as a risk factor in genocide.

Is impoverishment a macro risk factor for genocide? Poverty did not contribute directly to genocide in any of my cases. Moreover, the political scientist Matthew Krain, in his large-scale study of the onset and severity of genocides and politicides, found that economic marginalization had no effect.[89] This is probably what we would predict, knowing that the world has for centuries had poor countries with no genocide. The supposed connection between poverty and genocide is another spurious relationship; if poverty plays any role, it is by working through other factors such as state failure.

From Macro to Micro and Back

Although this chapter is subtitled "The Macro Dynamics of Genocide," I have not said much about dynamics aside from mentioning that macro factors can interact with one another. In fact, by "dynamics," I mean not only these interactions but also the way influences flow from the macro level into the lives of ordinary people and, conversely, the way in which the lives of ordinary people help construct the macro factors of genocide. In what follows, I apply the specific macro factor of state instability and failure to the Herero genocide, first tracing flows of insta- bility from the individual to the group level and up to the state or macro level. (Indeed, one can go further, to a supramacro or international level, for even the struggles of an obscure tribe like the Herero had interna- tional repercussions.) Then I reverse the process, tracing cascades of instability from state to group to individual. The aim of this discussion is twofold. First, I want to get away from the abstractions of "macro fac- tors" by putting some meat on their bones—showing what they mean in actual situations. Second, I want to show the dynamics of macro factors in action.

To begin with the example of the nameless Herero woman who was raped and then shot, according to the narrator of this story—an under- chief who survived the genocide and later gave testimony to the British— she came from "a great old Herero family" that included chiefs, and she had just given birth. The situation was unstable from the start, for she found herself alone with a white settler. He tried to rape her, she resisted, and he killed her.[90] Concern would immediately have risen from the individual to the group level, first to that of her highly respected family, later to that of her tribe. The rapist was tried but acquitted—more cause for Herero resentment at injustice. Leutwein, the colony's governor, be- lieved that this shooting was a cause of the later uprising. Instability flowed outward from the individual to destabilize the state—meaning, in this case, the tribal collectivity.

How might the situation have looked to the settler? The woman's re- fusal to have sex must have struck him as outrageous. Settlers shared a racist version of Social Darwinist ideology according to which blacks were lower on the evolutionary scale than whites; thus, he would have felt superior and entitled. The colony's whites expected black services as a matter of course, just as they felt they had a right to Herero land. The ideology imported by the Germans had destabilized the situation with the woman even before their encounter, and he felt he had a right not only to rape but to murder her.

When the settler was put on trial for this murder, he would have been enraged. His anger would have spread through talk with settler friends to the group level. After he was acquitted, he joined the troops (a still larger group, representing the German state) who were now warring with the Herero and, according to the narrator, "shot down our men, women, and children." Instability flowed outward from him to genocide. It even had international repercussions, for according to Schaller, "the civilian government in Berlin finally managed to convince the Emperor and general staff that Lothar von Trotha's ravage would badly damage Germany's reputation as a *Kulternation*."[91] With Germany's international image at stake, von Trotha was forced to stand down, and the shooting phase of the genocide ended. Instability had flowed outward from the violent, nameless settler to the state's appointment of von Trotha. (Then, with von Trotha's resignation, stability flowed back in from the level of the state, forcing the settler to hang up his rifle and stop shooting Herero.)

For a third example of the influence of the micro on the macro level, one can turn to the Herero decision to start the war—specifically to October 1903, when the governor, Leutwein, went south to deal with a disturbance. While he was gone, settlers tried to goad the Herero into a misstep that would get them into trouble.[92] Chief Samuel Maherero described the results in a letter to Leutwein. First, white people lied to Samuel (as he was known), telling him that Leutwein had died. Then, they began brutalizing individual Herero: "They went so far as to kill two men of Chief Tjetjo's tribe. Even Lieutenant N began to kill my people in jail. Ten died and it was said they died of sickness, but they died at the hands of the labor overseer and by the lash. Eventually Lieutenant N began to treat me so badly and to look for a reason for killing me. . . . [He] called me to question me, . . . I saw his intentions and so I fled. Because of these things I became angry and said 'Now I must kill the white people even if I die.'"[93] Samuel and the other chiefs began meeting to plan for war. Instability at the micro level led to macro-level trouble. Then it flowed back from the "state" level to individuals who were sent to war.

While we can only guess at the emotional states of individual Herero, we can confidently speculate that with the failure of their traditional forms of governance, the group in general suffered from the condition that criminologists call "anomie." The term was coined in the 1890s by the French sociologist Emile Durkheim to describe reactions to situations in which one's sense of right and wrong, and one's expectations for the future, break down.[94] For instance, historical changes may make it impossible for people to continue to abide by what their culture has traditionally expected of them. Durkheim was not making judgments about what is right and wrong but rather saying that society—any society—plays the part of a moral legislator because its members invest it with moral authority. We look to our society for guidance on what to do. When the social rules break down, people experience the highly uncomfortable state of normlessness or anomie. Indeed, they become miserable, as no doubt the Herero did.

Here one can draw on another contribution to anomie theory, that of Robert K. Merton, who in a famous 1938 article explained rates of deviance and crime in terms of social structure.[95] Groups and societies, Merton argued, will have higher rates of deviance and crime when a disjunction develops between the goals set by the culture and the means available for meeting those goals. Merton used "anomie" to name this disjunction, which refers to a breakdown in a social group's ability to regulate itself. Anomie in this structural sense, as well as Durkheim's more psychological sense, certainly characterized Herero society—and characterizes most societies in which genocide occurs.

Colonialism and state breakdown made it impossible for the Herero to continue following their society's rules for right and wrong, for social relationships, for achievement, and so on, and thus the Herero, as a group and as individuals, could not help but enter a state of anomie or near normlessness. The concept of anomie helps us see how tightly linked macro and micro factors can be—so tight as to be inextricable.

When Chief Samuel Maherero realized that the Herero had run out of options (a kind of state failure), he was experiencing extreme anomie, a sense of alienation and social breakdown that left him no good choices, and so he embarked on a suicidal war. Other chiefs joined him because the entire group had become anomic. They were not *entirely* normless because they still had moral standards for warfare. According to underchief Daniel Kariko, "We decided that we should wage war in a humane manner and would kill only the German men who were soldiers, or who would become soldiers. We met at secret councils and there our chiefs decided that we should spare the lives of all German women and children. The missionaries, too, were to be spared, and . . . protected by our people from all harm. We also decided to protect all British and Dutch farmers and settlers . . . as they had always been good to us."[96] But henceforth Herero warriors would do their best to kill German soldiers and force them off their land. As their society and culture had begun to crumble, their original, pacific norms had broken down.

These scenarios show how one macro factor—state instability and failure—works in specific situations to help precipitate genocidal war. They also illustrate how state failure can be inextricably linked to other two other macro variables, racial polarization and war, and how it can interact with meso- and micro-level factors. Finally, these scenarios show how state instability and failure lead to anomie, the emotional condition that breaks down traditional barriers to committing crime—or to precipitating crime against oneself, as in the case of victim-precipitated genocide.[97]

This discussion of macro factors in genocide—showing how structural and group-level influences, particularly in the Herero case, dynamically interacted with one another—leads directly to chapter 4, a discussion of group-level factors that contribute to genocide.

4

The Emotional Dynamics of Genocide: Meso-Level Analyses

The Indonesian Genocide, 1965–1966

Genocides generate an extraordinary range of intense and devastating emotions. All those who participate—perpetrators, victims, collaborators, resisters, survivors, bystanders—experience emotions specific to their role, although within a single group, emotions can shift radically from minute to minute. Genocide induces revulsion not only in victims but also in outsiders and, sometimes, even in perpetrators.[1] Inevitably the most overwhelming event in the emotional lives of those who are directly involved, genocide traumatizes and scars most of them forever.

This chapter focuses on the emotions of groups of genocide perpetrators—passions and prejudices that are crucially important to the course of genocide because they drive what the group does *as a group*. The emotional dynamics of perpetrator groups interact complexly with those of individual perpetrators. Groups attract individuals who bring along emotions that take on a life of their own within the group. Groups create situations that then emotionally affect individuals by providing cover, inspiration, and enthusiasm or by cowing individual members into conformity and thus enabling people to commit atrocities they might otherwise condemn.[2] In *Ordinary Men*, a study of German soldiers during World War II, Christopher Browning found that even men who initially were horrified by their assignment to exterminate entire Jewish villages went on to shoot anyway, out of loyalty to comrades and reluctance to appear disloyal.[3]

Moreover, groups provide rationales for group behavior as well as the momentum that pushes individuals into violence.[4] Leaders of a genocidal group may provide a vocabulary of euphemisms—"baboons" instead of "Herero," "cockroaches" instead of "Tutsi," "vermin" instead of "Jews," "decontamination" or "liquidation" instead of "slaughter"—that enables individuals to evade emotional responsibility for what they do.[5] Group dynamics can persuade even opponents of a genocidal regime to become complicit and bask in the sense that mass murder is a communal good.[6] There is even an emotional division of labor in genocidal groups, with leaders experiencing emotions that differ from those of followers, and midlevel organizers experiencing frustrations and alarms different from those of the killers they direct.[7]

Among meso-level analyses of genocide, the one I undertake here is unusual in several ways. Whereas many meso-level studies concentrate on social and political groups such as specific towns or precincts, this one focuses on perpetrator groups. Moreover, whereas most previous meso analyses have looked at economic, organizational, or political factors, this one examines *emotional* factors that shape group behavior. This chapter tackles a type of midlevel analysis that, to my knowledge, has not been attempted before. As two genocide scholars write in a review of the literature, "Compared to macro- and micro-level research, meso-level analysis is the least developed among the three prongs of genocide research, and the field of genocide studies would benefit from greater attention to this level of analysis."[8] I hope to indicate a new way of doing meso research on genocide.[9]

One of the first steps in genocide is the reframing of identities, a group process that triggers a chain of emotions. Reframing is accomplished by embedding new perspectives on the identities of groups in new narratives. Usually perpetrators start the process by reframing the identities of those who are to become victims; in doing so, they also recast their own identities, thus changing the emotional dynamics of both groups.[10] However, reframing is not always initiated by perpetrators: in the Herero case, a major step in reframing was taken by the Southwest African chiefs in the meeting in which they decided to embark on a suicidal war. In this meeting, they definitively rejected the Germans, with whom some had been friends, recasting them as enemies and their own group as both victims of the Germans and as warriors.

Framing was first analyzed by the sociologist Erving Goffman, who described a frame as *a definition of a situation that is part of the organization of experience*, a kind of interpretative structure that helps us make sense of the world.[11] A frame is a conceptual understanding that individuals and groups impose on a situation. Building on Goff-

man's work, psychologists, social psychologists, and other sociologists have applied the concept of framing to genocide; many of them
originally focused on the social construction of victims, particularly
through processes of dehumanization.[12] More recently, framing studies have analyzed processes through which genocides and other violent
confrontations begin.[13] Stereotyping the enemy group as inhumane or
nonhuman or in some other way different, and representing one's own
group as righteous and aggrieved, are reframings that can set groups on
the road to genocide.

To be sure, no group is emotionally monolithic. Some people refuse
to be caught up in the stereotyping of neighbors. Resisters may hide
potential victims from genocidists and even loudly object to a turn toward killing. Individuals who work with genocidists at one moment may
protect victims at the next.[14] Yet to tell the story of a genocide and to
analyze its emotional dynamics, one must focus on the stories of the
groups involved.

I begin this chapter with the story of the Indonesian genocide of
1965–1966, emphasizing ways in which group identities were framed and
reframed over the course of this convulsive event. Next I discuss framing, identity, and the emotional dynamics of genocide more generally.
The final section of the chapter, on genocide "hot" and "cold," analyzes
the emotional temperature of the genocides in my sample and shows
how, in "hot" genocides, emotional momentum builds to a turning point
at which the genocide begins.

Framing and Identity in the Indonesian Genocide of 1965–1966

Geographically, culturally, and historically, Indonesia presents unusual
difficulties in governance. Geographically, this Southeast Asian archipelago consists of 6,000 inhabited islands covering over 3,000 miles
from east to west. Culturally it is "profoundly multiethnic," as the sociologist Michael Mann puts it,[15] with more than 300 ethnic groups and
over 250 spoken languages. Most Indonesians identify themselves as
Muslims; but five other religions are also recognized by the government,
and several more are practiced as well. Colonized by the Dutch, Indonesia did not gain independence until 1949, and the process established
the military as the key power in the new nation.

After independence and a short period of democracy, then-president Sukarno dissolved parliament in favor of a system he called Guided Democracy, under which he tried to balance the country's three main factions: the army, Islamic groups, and communists.[16] The country became increasingly polarized between the army and the PKI (Partai Komunis Indonesia, or Indonesian Communist Party), the largest communist group in the world outside the Soviet Union and China. In the opposite corner stood the PNI (Partai Nasionalis Indonesia), the faction of the army and political Right. The communist party also had tense relations with Islamists. These, then, were the chief political groups and their dynamics on the threshold of the Indonesian genocide.

In the period leading up to the genocide, the three factions collided over the best ways of addressing Indonesia's severe social problems. Social class divisions had grown, especially on the island of Bali, where the communists aggressively pursued land reform.[17] At the same time, famine spread, and people began to starve to death. "The grave economic conditions of the early 1960s," writes the historian Geoffrey Robinson, "were compounded by a succession of rat and mouse plagues, insect infestations, and crop failures . . . , and by the eruption of Gunung Agung [a volcano on Bali] in early 1963," which killed over a thousand people and ruined a huge amount of farm land.[18] People began to dread some new cataclysm.

Corruption was endemic in the military and government, but in retrospect, an even greater problem seems to have been the blurring of lines between army and government, an overlap that fused the two into a powerful conservative block.

The Coup and Takeover

Tensions erupted on September 30, 1965, with an attempted coup by midlevel army officers against top generals. Although the circumstances were murky,[19] the result was clear: six generals and an adjutant had been killed and dropped down a well. Within twenty-four hours, Major General Suharto took control and blamed the attempted coup on communists. Some people say that Suharto may have had advance notice of the coup,[20] which, if so, gave him time to plot his countercoup. In any case, even if the secret coup attempt had been instigated by communists,

Figure 4.1. The immense Pancasila Monument was erected by General Suharto to depict his own narrative of the Indonesian genocide of 1965–1966. The seven figures near the top are life-size portraits of the men whose murder started the genocide. Below them is a bas-relief relating Suharto's version of the events and exonerating him from responsibility for the genocide. Photograph by Vannessa Hearman, Department of Indonesian Studies, University of Sydney. Used with permission.

as he claimed, few of them could have been involved—certainly not every communist in the entire nation. Calling for a national cleansing of communists, Suharto unleashed a bloodbath that, when the violence finally died down in February 1966, left up to 500,000 alleged communists and their associates dead and tens of thousands more people jailed as political criminals. This was a political genocide.

Ethnicity was not an outstanding factor in the Indonesian genocide, nor, paradoxically, was ideology, even though Suharto targeted communists. "Ideological motives were there in the Indonesian case, of course," writes the historian Robert Cribb, "along with fear, revenge, adventure and so on but for the most part the perceived need to kill arose out of a sense of self-interest and self-defence, and was in no way dictated by a formal ideological world view."[21] Similarly, the historian Christian Gerlach insists that "the events of 1965–66 should not be reduced to 'political' violence even in a broad sense."[22] The term "communist," previously a political frame, became a catch-all into which all sorts of hatreds were thrown. Used loosely and expansively, the term "communist" allowed long-simmering antagonisms, many of which had nothing to do with politics, to explode.

Rage against communist women was a key aspect of the conservatives' reframing of the communist party as a mortal threat to the country. At the time, Indonesian women's roles were changing; to the conservatives who led the genocide, these changes symbolized growth in social disorder.[23] Communist women had organized the Indonesian Women's Movement, or Gerwani, a group that included about 20 percent of the country's women.[24] Suharto and his allies became obsessed with the sexuality of Gerwani women, claiming, at the time of the attempted coup, that the generals had been tortured and their genitals

Figure 4.2. This part of the bas-relief on the Pancasila Monument purports to show that the genocide was precipitated by seductive Gerwani women and communist men who killed the generals and shoved them down a well. Again, this was Suharto's version of events. Photograph by Annie Pohlman, School of Languages and Comparative Cultural Studies, University of Queensland. Used with permission.

mutilated by Gerwani members who danced naked at the scene of the crime. Even though the official post mortem on the generals' bodies proved that they had not been tortured,[25] and even though there was no other evidence for the charge, Suharto repeated the claim time and again, creating a new frame for understanding Gerwani women. This propaganda gave other Indonesians a motive for sexual violence against women, both during the genocide and afterward, when thousands of women were detained as political prisoners and many of them raped by nationalist-party officials.[26]

The mythology of the sexually dangerous political woman served to repress women generally until the end of Suharto's rule, three decades later—and even thereafter. The historian Annie Pohlman, a specialist on sexual violence during this genocide, writes that as a result of the violence, "women's organsing was depoliticized and women's organisations were brought under government control. Conservative gender values and ideas of femininity became ideological underpinnings for the New Order [Suharto's regime], with any deviation from these provoking anxiety and accusations of perversity and possible 'Communist' subversion. The legacies of this demonization of Communist ideology, and its association with sexual immorality and ideas of deviant political involvement by women continue to this day in Indonesia."[27] A Balinese historian writes that "rape of women accused of being members of Gerwani occurred everywhere, the example being set by local party leaders."[28] An anonymous source tells of a communist woman who, before being killed, "was ordered to take all her clothes off. Her body and her honour . . . were then subjected to fire. She was then tied up, taken to the village of Sentong in Lawang, where a noose was put around her neck and she was hacked to death."[29]

This same anonymous document describes how "Japik, a leading figure in the local branch of Gerwani, . . . was killed along with her husband. . . . They had been married only thirty-five days. She was raped many times and her body was then slit open from her breasts to her vulva."[30] Such extreme violence against communist women discouraged all women from playing a role in public life. Political activity became exclusively male terrain. Suharto used this genocide to reframe the role of gender in national life and block a very large group—women—from political participation.[31]

The Suharto Narrative

The Suharto regime devised a narrative line that blamed Indonesia's communist party for the coup and its bloody aftermath and that named itself as the country's savior. It created a new frame for understanding the country's recent history and new identities for the major participants. "Under Suharto anticommunism became the state religion, complete with sacred sites, rituals, and dates," writes the historian John Roosa in *Pretext for Mass Murder*.[32] As part of this reframing process, the government erected an immense public monument in South Jakarta, glorifying the murdered army officials as heroes and identifying the communist party as their killers. The monument's bas-relief depicts naked communist women prancing around the generals and shoving their bodies into a well.

As Suharto's regime consolidated control of the country, "it elaborated the events of 1965 into something of a mythic charter for the state," writes a team of cultural anthropologists, "justifying its rigid rule as a

Figure 4.3. This section of the Pancasila Monument shows Suharto restoring peace to Indonesia. The background depicts the genocide, while the foreground depicts women restored to their proper domestic roles. Photograph by Vannessa Hearman, Department of Indonesian Studies, University of Sydney. Used with permission.

protection against an ever present threat of subversion and its repressive policies as insurance of national security and unity."[33] From the army issued a steady stream of misinformation and fabrications about the perfidy of communist men and women.[34] At the same time, the army shut down communist media, making it impossible for those whom they defamed to counter this negative framing.

In the Suharto narrative, then, the genocide was self-defense, a necessary step to root out communists who threatened the state. This narrative, promulgated as it was during the Cold War, appealed to the United States and some of its allies who were also intent on fighting communism.[35] The US recognized the lies in Suharto's narrative and yet supported him. Only Robert Kennedy, the brother of the dead US president, objected.[36] Suharto, enjoying impunity, stayed in power until 1998. But by that point, the Cold War—itself a kind of megaframework for constructing international relations—had ended and, with it, US support of the regime. Faced with economic and political unrest at home and failing support abroad, the aging genocidist resigned.

An Extremely Violent Genocide

The Indonesian genocide provides as good an illustration as we are likely to find of Christian Gerlach's concept of genocide as an extremely violent event. The brutality that followed Suharto's countercoup was driven by a multiplicity of motives and committed by a wide range of groups through means both ordinary and gruesome. Set off by the emotional explosion that followed Suharto's grant of impunity to kill communists, the violence raced through the country, leaving behind emotional devastation and, among the perpetrators, the pleasure of belonging to the group that had successfully framed itself as the nation's redeemer. "The campaign," writes Robinson, "was accelerated by a well-coordinated nationwide propaganda blitz, depicting PKI members as traitors, barbarians, and atheists, and explicitly inciting acts of violence against them."[37] In some places, the killings were marked by ritualistic practices such as the piling up of corpses on rafts and nailing of penises to shop doors.[38] An anonymous source relates how in one area, "members and sympathizers of the PKI who were to be murdered had their hands tied. Then an Ansor [Muslim] gang, accompanied and protected by an army unit, . . . took them to the killing places. . . . Holes had already been prepared in these places. The victims were taken one by one up to the holes; nooses were put around their necks and then tightened until the victims collapsed. Then they were beaten with iron rods and other hard implements. After the victims had died, their heads were cut off."[39]

The killings were primarily organized by the army, which participated both directly, as when it shot groups en masse, or indirectly, as when it formed and provisioned militias to kill on its behalf. The savagery—which was worst where it was organized by the army—was concentrated in Central and East Java, Bali, and North Sumatra.[40] In North Sumatra, 2,000 to 3,000 communists were regularly—almost by scenario—killed: the army loaded them on trucks, the trucks were stopped by excited crowds, and the army handed over the prisoners to be killed.[41] The island of Bali, which lost 7 to 8 percent of its population, or 100,000 people, in less than six months, suffered most.[42] There, Gerlach writes, the "paramilitary wing of the Marhaenis Youth [a conservative youth organization] . . . started with stoning houses and attacking individuals, then turned to systematic nightly raids during which they captured leftists according to lists or denunciations, and decapitated them or slit their throats."[43] Six thousand Balinese were shot in three days. Along with alleged communists, children and other family members were murdered to forestall later revenge. Sometimes the military forced villagers to execute neighbors.[44]

These were strangely over-the-top reactions to what, after all, had been a failed coup attempt. Sukarno, the country's leader until Suharto took over, spoke of "burning down the house to kill a rat."[45] But what Suharto wanted was not to avenge the attempted coup but to rule the country and cleanse it of communists.

Opportunistic violence piggybacked on the army's killings. Little detailed information is available about this aspect of the genocide, and that may continue to be the case, given that Suharto forced people to remain silent about what had happened and that many of them have since died. However, it is clear that many victims were not communists. In the general chaos, perpetrator and victim groups overlapped, with killers sometimes later being killed. Cribb explains that the "ferocity" of the genocide "seems to have been a product of local factors."[46] Underscoring this view, the team of cultural anthropologists writes regarding Bali,

"Much of the bloodshed was in fact, we have found, motivated by social conflicts that were local, diverse, and shifting, conflicts that crosscut and shaped formal political allegiances and that were then manipulated by the state to give particular forms to the violence. These conflicts erupted over issues of caste, over access to and ownership of land, over economic inequalities, and over status and inheritance within extended families."[47]

In a country where violence was relatively acceptable, people took advantage of the upheavals to settle scores—sometimes inventively. "The ways in which people were killed," Gerlach observes, "indicate a high degree of popular participation, and extreme hatred. It seems that only a minority were shot. . . . Most were beheaded, stabbed, or had their throats slit with knives or swords. . . . Others were hacked to death, strangled, slain with clubs or rocks, drowned, or burned or buried alive."[48] To speak of such opportunistic violence in terms of popular participation is not to exonerate the military, for clearly the army was the prime mover behind this genocide. But neither can the violence be reduced to Suharto's simple, self-serving narrative. He had reframed a political group—communists—so expansively that it came to include everyday enemies, irrespective of political affiliation.

Crimes such as rape, gang rape, and sexual torture were practiced against both men and women, with women also suffering forced prostitution, sexual slavery, and forced abortion. Sexual violence, Pohlman writes, was crucial to the social construction of victim and victor.[49] While in some cases sexual violence against women during and after the genocide was merely expedient—a matter, for example, of one or more guards ganging up on a prisoner whom they deemed attractive—in other cases it was revenge for perceived sexual excesses by Gerwani women. Sexual violence was also a way for state security forces to demonstrate their dominance over communist men through sexual violation of communist women. Indeed, Pohlman concludes, it was a deliberate strategy to destroy the Left.[50]

Aftermath: The "Clean Environment" Policy—and Perpetual Impunity

Like an Old Testament patriarch, Suharto punished the relatives and descendants of dead communists for generations to come. He issued a Clean Environment policy declaring that parents, siblings, spouses, children, and even grandchildren of communists should be barred from holding government jobs, teaching, or belonging to a political party. The ostensible rationale was that such people might contaminate others with their political filth; in fact, the goal was to prevent retaliation by relatives of those who had been killed. Entire families were thus consigned to marginality for generations.

As for perpetrators' emotions, those of one group—a gang of thugs—are recorded in the acclaimed documentary film *The Act of Killing* (2012). The stars are the killers themselves, fifty years older but still delighted to be recognized as participants in a genocide, which they reenact with glee. Never punished for their murders, they have not the slightest fear of being punished this time around either, for they live in a society in which corruption is the rule and in which gangsters like themselves interpenetrate with the military and government. They killed in the first place for fame, money, and power; and they now reenact their most heinous crimes on film for the same motives, fully confident that responsibility will never brush them with its wing. "We were allowed to do it," one killer points out, "and never punished." Given the chance, they would happily torment and murder again.

On several occasions during the film, the gangsters do appear to repent—slightly—of the crimes they committed in their youth. One, named Anwar, has nightmares about a man whose eyes remained open even after decapitation. A second wants to apologize to relatives of all who died. A third observes that, although they said the communists were cruel, in reality, they themselves were the cruel ones. But one member of this gangster fraternity points out that atrocities are defined by the winners. Did the Americans not kill the Indians? They trade tips on how not to feel guilty, and they stage a scene—with who can imagine what motives—in which garroted actor-prisoners, lifting the wire from their necks, give Anwar a medal for executing them and sending them to heaven. Anwar wonders if his actual victims felt as much fear and terror as he did when playing the victim in this scene. Offscreen, the director, Joshua Oppenheimer, assures him that they felt more.[51]

Framing, Identity, and the Emotional Dynamics of Other Genocides

Framing and reframing drive the emotional dynamics of groups during genocide's early stages by reshaping identities. In this section, I suggest ways in which these processes operated in other genocides in my sample while also introducing related concepts and issues: the influence of stereotyping, ideology, and mass media on framing processes; us-versus-them thinking; and genocide and national identity. All these processes of framing and reframing are what the genocide scholar Daniel Feierstein calls "genocidal social practices." "Because a social practice is composed of shared beliefs and understandings as well as shared actions," he writes, "a genocidal social practice may be one that *contributes* to genocide or attempted genocide, including symbolic representations and discourses promoting or justifying genocide."[52]

Stereotypes and ideologies provide people with what the sociologist C. Wright Mills called "vocabularies of motive," meaning ways of speaking about others ("lice," "bourgeois," "atheist," and so on).[53] People use such vocabularies to frame or reframe the group that is being stereotyped or declared ideologically impure; in the process, they reinforce the frames through which they view themselves. Vocabularies of motive are woven into narratives of harm and safety, victimization and salvation, which people use to construct themselves as victims of another group—or as potential redeemers of a nation.

Before the Armenian genocide, for example, the negative stereotypes that Turks applied to Armenians were strong enough to encourage enormous massacres. But it was not until the winter of 1914–1915, when the Turks lost the battle of Sarakamish to the Russians, that Turkish hatred of the Armenians became ideological. The Turks decided that they had lost because Armenians had helped the Russians—as indeed they had, in small numbers; but in truth the accusation was an excuse for the Turks' foolish battle plan. At the same time, burgeoning Turkish nationalism—the new ideology of Turkey for the Turks—encouraged the feeling that there was no longer room in their country for the treacherous Armenian minority. Armenians were reframed as traitors, enemies of the newly emerging Turkish nation.

A second example can be found in the genocide of disabled people in Germany. Although they were no doubt negatively stereotyped in earlier years, they were murdered by the Nazis for ideological reasons—to protect the genetic purity of the Aryan nation. In this case, the vocabularies of motive included such terms as "unworthy of life," "degenerates," and "useless eaters."

Rwanda, where a radio station and weekly magazine controlled by the extremist Hutu elite disseminated hate information throughout the country, illustrates the crucial role media can play in reframing processes. The hardliners who fomented the genocide funded the radio station, Radio Télévision Libre des Mille Collines (RTLM), and the newspaper, *Kangura*, the main sources of news and entertainment for many Rwandans. For a year before the killing began, these media devoted themselves to spreading fear of Tutsi. "Songs containing anti-Tutsi sentiments were composed and broadcast on RTLM," writes the anthropologist Debra Komar, "as well as at large public gatherings held in athletic stadiums throughout Rwanda and from vehicle-mounted public address systems."[54] *Kangura* (Wake Up!) published the "Ten Commandments of the Hutu":

1. Every Hutu should know that a Tutsi woman, whoever she is, works for the interest of her Tutsi ethnic group. As a result, we shall consider a traitor any Hutu who
   - marries a Tutsi woman
   - befriends a Tutsi woman
   - employs a Tutsi woman as a secretary or a concubine.
2. Every Hutu should know that our Hutu daughters are more suitable and conscientious in their role as woman, wife and mother of the family. Are they not beautiful, good secretaries and more honest?
3. Hutu women, be vigilant and try to bring your husbands, brothers and sons back to reason.
4. Every Hutu should know that every Tutsi is dishonest in business. His only aim is the supremacy of his ethnic group. As a result, any Hutu who does the following is a traitor:
   - makes a partnership with Tutsi in business
   - invests his money or the government's money in a Tutsi enterprise

- lends or borrows money from a Tutsi
- gives favours to Tutsi in business (obtaining import licenses, bank loans, construction sites, public markets, etc.).

5. All strategic positions, political, administrative, economic, military and security should be entrusted only to Hutu.

6. The education sector (school pupils, students, teachers) must be majority Hutu.

7. The Rwandan Armed Forces should be exclusively Hutu. The experience of the October 1990 war has taught us a lesson. No member of the military shall marry a Tutsi.

8. The Hutu should stop having mercy on the Tutsi.

9. The Hutu, wherever they are, must have unity and solidarity and be concerned with the fate of their Hutu brothers.

   - The Hutu inside and outside Rwanda must constantly look for friends and allies for the Hutu cause, starting with their Hutu brothers.
   - They must constantly counteract Tutsi propaganda.
   - The Hutu must be firm and vigilant against their common Tutsi enemy.

10. The Social Revolution of 1959, the Referendum of 1961, and the Hutu Ideology, must be taught to every Hutu at every level. Every Hutu must spread this ideology widely. Any Hutu who persecutes his brother Hutu for having read, spread, and taught this ideology is a traitor.[55]

Thus did Hutu Power use the newspaper to frame Tutsi—and themselves. Similarly, the radio station RTLM broadcast daily discussions about the virtues of the Hutu and perfidy of the Tutsi. Even when defeat was at hand from the invading army, RTLM tried to reinforce the differences between "us" and "them": "As you know, life is shared between bad and good news. The good news is that only yesterday we [here the radio station identifies openly with the Hutu army] have killed more than 50 cockroaches [Tutsi] on all fronts. Let's hope that this good news is going to cheer up the 61st Battalion."[56]

Even monuments can play a role in reframing. After the Indonesian genocide, Suharto's forces built the elaborate memorial mentioned earlier, its bas-reliefs depicting (among other scenes) Gerwani women dancing lewdly and dropping the slain army officials down a well. This prominent piece of art demonized communists and glorified Suharto's bloody crackdown as a form of national protection.

"Violent political actors," writes the criminologist Vincenzo Ruggiero, "are embedded in popular narratives that they [the actors] may just re-iterate or, at times, dramatize. Such narratives . . . are based on . . . the division between *us* and *them*."[57] Us-versus-them thinking is evidently universal and seems to be hardwired into the human brain; without it, we would be unable to differentiate "our" group from other groups—a distinction that would have been crucial in the early days of human evo-lution.[58] Us-versus-them thinking pits anticommunists against com-munists, Tutsi against Hutu, and Guatemalans against Maya, hardening boundaries between in-groups and out-groups. When this is done at the national level, a nation itself undergoes reframing. In a much-quoted phrase, the sociologist Helen Fein describes this process as delineation of a "universe of obligation" that includes some people (those we are obliged to help) and excludes others, the outsiders.[59]

In Indonesia, the universe of obligation came to include anticom-munists and to exclude those who were defined as "communists." The psychoanalyst Erik Erikson described this generally as a process of "pseudospeciation," in which we divide up the world into a true spe-cies (our own kind) and the other (the pseudospecies).[60] Indonesian communists—and alleged communists—found themselves pushed out of the national nest to become prey to conservatives. They had to deal with the confounding emotion of being rejected by their own nation.

Genocides are centrally concerned with *identity*, here meaning the self-concept of the perpetrator group and its members. This becomes clear when we look at genocide from the perpetrator's angle. For many genocidists, the key dimension of identity is national; closely related is the dimension of race or ethnicity, because in the twentieth century, a "nation" was often defined in terms of its racial or ethnic homogeneity. At the time of the Katyn Forest Massacre, the image of Soviet citizens "persecuted by Polish 'lords' was widespread in the USSR" (write histo-rians of the killings), and "the notion of 'liberation' from the bourgeois 'Polish yoke' was popular. This stereotypical view was strengthened by the vilification of Poles in a propaganda campaign . . . justifying the

Soviet attack on Poland."[61] Not only political identities but also class, national, and religious identities separated Poland, a republic, from the Soviet Union in 1940. When Stalin signed the Poles' death warrant, he was influenced by these differences in identity. His main purpose was strategic, but he was also constructing a "universe of obligation" that excluded patriotic Polish soldiers.

Human groups often seem to need to compare themselves with other groups to achieve a sense of identity and self-satisfaction for their members. "Identity construction," write the sociologists David Snow and Doug McAdam, "can be accounted for largely by framing processes, by engagement in collective action itself, or by a combination of both. Framing processes that occur within the context of social movements constitute perhaps the most important mechanism facilitating identity construction processes, largely because *identity constructions are an inherent feature of framing activities*."[62] Snow and McAdam are analyzing nonviolent social movements, but their words apply equally well to genocidal movements and even to genocides that, like Katyn, involve no social movement at all but nonetheless end in ethnic or political cleansing. When identity is at stake, when leaders have framed the situation as a struggle for survival, when they have also framed the out-group as inferior, extermination becomes all the easier.

This brings us to dehumanization, the degradation process that often accompanies mass murder and that, many scholars believe, is a precondition for genocide. One of those who see it as a precondition is the social psychologist Herbert Kelman, author of the 1973 article "Violence without Moral Restraint: Reflections on the Dehumanization of Victims and Victimizers." In this rich and complex article, Kelman writes that "hostility toward the target, both historically rooted and situationally induced, contributes heavily to the violence, but it does so largely by dehumanizing the victims."[63] In "sanctioned massacres," as Kelman terms systematic mass violence, "the killing is not in response to the target's threats or provocations. It is not what he has done that marks him for death, but what he is—the category to which he happens to belong."[64]

Only extreme dehumanization can frame someone as belonging to the not-us category, according to Kelman. The only way perpetrators can "extract some degree of meaning out of the absurd events in which they find themselves participating is by coming to believe that the victims are subhuman and deserve to be rooted out."[65] Moreover, by dehumanizing their victims, they make themselves feel stronger and more confident. Franz Stangl, commandant of the Nazi extermination camp at Treblinka, made this point in an interview. "Why," the interviewer asked Stangl, "if they were going to kill them anyway, what was the point of all the humiliation, why the cruelty?" Stangl answered, "To condition those who actually had to carry out the policies. . . . To make it possible for them to do what they did."[66]

"But there may be dehumanization without massacre," observes the sociologist Leo Kuper, "and presumably massacre without dehumanization."[67] Helen Fein agrees: exclusion of the victim from the universe of obligation need not involve dehumanization.[68] In some cases, perpetrators need to be pushed into killing by the state. This was true in Indonesia and Rwanda, where many people resisted participating in genocide until soldiers threatened them with death or won them over with bribes. Dehumanization of the victim group alone had not done the trick for these reluctant killers.

More obviously, the Katyn victims were not dehumanized before execution. Thus, there are exceptions to Kelman's rule that dehumanization is a precondition for genocide. The Nazis' sometimes elaborate methods of dehumanization, coupled with the massive amount of research that has been done on that phenomenon, may blind us to the milder and sometimes ineffective dehumanization of other genocides—or make us forget that in some genocides, dehumanization simply does not take place.[69]

Genocide Hot and Cold

In *Violence*, the well-known study of the emotional dynamics of violence among perpetrators, the sociologist Randall Collins analyzes the social dynamics of violence in a host of individual and group situations—but not genocide.[70] In what follows, I show how Collins's concept of "a turning point," in which potentially violent situations spill over into actual violence, can be applied to some (though not all) genocides. Then I apply Collins's analysis of "hot" and "cold" violence to genocidal situations, showing how it, too, can help us understand the emotional dynamics of a group engaged in mass murder.

Turning Points

In violent confrontations between individuals, groups, or even armies, Collins writes, whether fighting actually breaks out depends on "a series of conditions or turning-points that shape the tension and fear in particular directions, reorganizing the emotions as an interactional process involving everyone present: the antagonists, audience, and even ostensibly disengaged bystanders."[71] These turning points mark a rupture with the emotions of the past and serve as catalysts for subsequent (though still contingent) actions.

A marked turning point or event that sets off the genocidal process characterizes most cases in my sample. Usually the timing and nature of the turning point was strongly affected by macro-level factors that altered the framework in which the groups were functioning.

In the Herero case, the turning point came when General von Trotha signed the extermination order; in the Armenian genocide, it came on the night of April 24, 1915, when the Turks began their attacks. For extermination of Germany's disabled population, the turning point came with the onset of World War II; for the Katyn massacres, it arrived when Stalin signed the Polish prisoners' death warrant. The turning point in the Indonesian case was the attempted army coup of 1965; in Cambodia, it came with the fall of Phnom Penh to the Khmer Rouge on April 17, 1975; and in the Rwandan genocide, it occurred when the president's plane was shot down. Only one of my examples lacked a marked turning point: Guatemala. The other seven cases were characterized by a moment that, to return to Collins's words, "reorganize[d] the emotions as an interactional process involving everyone present."[72] Victims were decisively reframed as enemies, the perpetrators as righteous avengers. Groups took on new identities. It seems likely that most genocides are characterized by sequences of small-scale turning points in addition to the cataclysmic turning point that sets many of them into motion.

At such turning points, the situation can tip away from, as well as toward, violence. Sometimes opponents back off. "Only where a strong emotional momentum is achieved . . . do we see a shift towards mass violence," writes the sociologist Stefan Klusemann.[73] Like Collins, Klusemann holds that one way to deal with tension and fear is to attack a weak enemy who can be physically and emotionally dominated.[74] In all of my cases, the victim group was not only weaker than the perpetrator group; it was unsuspecting or at least unarmed and unprepared—and in some cases, incapable of preparation.

In other words, genocidists are bullies. They mob near-helpless prey, and the victims' extreme fear makes them seem even more hateful. In genocide, one rarely sees an antagonistic confrontation of groups that are equals, and in my sample there is only one case (the Herero) in which the victim group was markedly antagonistic toward the genocidists. However, even the Herero, with their few ancient guns, were grievously underprepared to fight the German army. This helplessness of genocide's victims tempts some scholars to describe them as scapegoats—sacrificial creatures who are destroyed because symbolically they carry the sins of the killers.[75]

Collins elaborates his turning-point theory with the concept of "forward panic." A forward panic, he writes,

> starts with tension and fear in a conflict situation. . . . The tension is prolonged and built up; it has a dramatic shape of increasing tension, striving toward a climax. . . . There is a shift from relatively passive—waiting, holding back until one is in a position to bring the conflict to a head—to be fully active. When the opportunity finally arrives, the tension/fear comes out in an emotional rush. . . . The fighters . . . are in an overpowering emotional rhythm, carrying them on to actions that they would normally not approve of in calm, reflective moments.[76]

One might substitute "forward movement" or "forward rush" for Collins's "forward panic," but otherwise his term provides a model for many genocidal groups. In Indonesia, although the killings started at different times in different places, the first occurred a month or less after the attempted coup;[77] the time between turning point and forward rush was brief. It was even briefer in Rwanda, where genocidal forces had been in training even before the president's plane crashed.

The forward-rush concept even fits Guatemala's incremental genocide: although the genocide itself had no clear-cut starting point, the various genocidal massacres that constituted it did. On the day appointed for a massacre, paramilitaries would arrive before dawn and surround the village while the Maya were still asleep. After the victims had been captured and tied up, the violence began, often accompanied by carousing and rape.[78] The stalking of the village, which generated extreme tension and fear of discovery, ended with a forward rush of violence. "A forward panic," Collins remarks, "is a total victory, at least locally and on the physical and emotional level, and calls for celebration."[79]

Hot Genocides

Collins describes forward panic as "a hot emotion, a situation of being highly aroused, steamed up. It comes on in a rush, explosively; and it takes time to calm down."[80] These "hot" emotions are typical of most turning points into violence. Most of the genocides in my sample that had turning points were also "hot."[81]

To describe a genocidal massacre as work ending in carousing and celebration may seem to suggest sadism. Most genocidists are not sadists, however; they are "ordinary men," to use Browning's phrase, and most seem to dislike their work.[82] But we should not blink at the possibility of occasional enjoyment when we consider the emotional dynamics of genocidal groups. Take this scene from the extermination of the Herero, as reported by an African eyewitness, a guide for German soldiers:

> Some distance beyond Hamakari, we camped at a waterhole. While there, a German soldier found a little Herero baby boy about nine months old lying in the bush. The child was crying. He brought it into the camp where I was.
>
> The soldiers formed a ring and started throwing the child to one another and catching it as if it were a ball. The child was terrified and hurt and was crying very much.
>
> After a time, they got tired of this and one of the soldiers fixed his bayonet on his rifle and said he would catch the baby. The child was tossed into the air towards him and as it fell, he caught it and transfixed the body with the bayonet.
>
> The child died in a few minutes and the incident was greeted with roars of laughter by the Germans, who seemed to think it was a great joke.[83]

The soldiers had framed the baby as a not-human plaything. They had disengaged from moral values—and probably had done so long before this incident, for they had been executing Herero in equally unfeeling (if perhaps less playful) circumstances for weeks.

The merrymaking Guatemalan paramilitaries provide another example of enjoyment during genocide, as does a game played by Chechen tribesmen working for the Turks during the Armenian genocide: the Chechens planted two rows of swords in the sand, blade up, and forced captured Armenian girls to stand at the head of the rows; one by one, the Chechens would gallop down the rows, lifting the girls high in the air and flinging them down on the sword points. "It was a game—a contest!" a survivor remarked.[84] Genocide can be fun.

The "heat" of a forward rush also helps explain the camaraderie of a Rwandan group whose stories are told in Jean Hatzfeld's book *Machete Season*. During the genocide, "suddenly Hutus of every kind were patriotic brothers without any partisan discord," Ignace Rukiramacumu reports of the joyous weeks when he and his friends conducted a daily Tutsi hunt. "We were no longer in our each-to-his-own mood. We were doing a job to order. We were lining up behind everyone's enthusiasm. We gathered into teams on the soccer field and went out hunting as kindred spirits."[85] The heat may also explain why those who participate in extermination so often lack remorse. A member of Ignace Rukiramacumu's killing group explains, "I left every morning free and easy, in a hurry to get going. . . . I want to make clear that from the first gentleman I killed to the last, I was not sorry about a single one."[86]

Collins helps us understand such joy in cruelty. During a forward panic, "all the components that come out during the hot rush of a successful, unopposed attack are cycling back upon themselves: anger, release from tension/ fear, elation, hysterical laughter, sheer noisiness as itself a form of aggression—all of these are generating a social atmosphere in which persons keep on doing what they are doing, over and over, though it may make no sense even as aggression."[87]

The sociologist Jack Katz's *Seductions of Crime: Moral and Sensual Attractions in Doing Evil* further explains such seemingly incomprehensible cruelty.[88] Katz deals with street crime, not genocide, but he focuses on "the moral emotions": "humiliation, righteousness, arrogance, ridicule, cynicism, defilement, and vengeance. In each, the attraction that proves to be most fundamentally compelling is that of overcoming a personal challenge to moral—not to material—existence."[89] Shoplifting can be enticing; whipping an enemy can be delightful. Violating the law—the moral as well as the written law—can lead to a sense of elation, even pride. This can be seen in street crime, and it can be found in genocide as well.

Cold Genocides

Genocide does not always involve "hot" emotions, however, and two cases in my sample—the Nazis' extermination of disabled persons and the Katyn Forest Massacre—were chilly indeed. To manage the killings of the disabled, Hitler assembled a secret network of doctors; they began with the murder of babies and handicapped children. In hospitals and asylums, doctors and nurses killed helpless patients by injecting poisons, starvation, gassing, and allowing them to freeze. Doctors tended to prefer slow methods of death that were most easily concealed from the public. The program could not have been more coldly calculated or cruelly administered.

A disapproving witness described a tour of one of the institutions for killing children, led by the institution's director, Hermann Pfannmüller, who

> explicated his opinions in particular detail. . . . "For me . . . , these [disabled] creatures . . . represent only a burden for our healthy national body. . . . We do not kill . . . with poison, injections, etc., because that would only provide new slanderous campaign material for the foreign press and certain gentlemen in Switzerland [the Red Cross]." . . . As he spoke these words, [Pfannmüller] and a nurse from the ward pulled a child from its crib. Displaying the child like a dead rabbit, he pontificated with the air of a connoisseur and a cynical smirk something like this: "With this one, for example, it will still take two to three days [to starve to death]." I can still clearly visualize the spectacle of this fat and smirking man with the whimpering skeleton in his fleshy hand, surrounded by other starving children. Furthermore, the murderer then pointed out that they did not suddenly withdraw food, but instead slowly reduced rations.[90]

Clearly, the witness was repelled by Pfannmüller's unfeeling, dilatory murder of defenseless children.[91]

The group of physicians who ran the T4 program assembled a large bureaucracy to shield killers like Pfannmüller from criticism—another soulless aspect of the killing program. Parents who tried to retrieve children who had in fact been murdered were led on a wild-goose chase by paperwork that concealed the circumstances under which the child had died. However, the historian Götz Aly argues that most family members were as drained of feeling as those who ran the program. "The policy of secrecy . . . was not a matter of careful concealment but an opportunity for the [German] population to agree tacitly to government measures. . . . This 'secret Reich matter,' which was in fact public, essentially was an offer to the population to seek individual ways of avoiding responsibility [for handicapped family members]—an unconfessed complicity that eased the conscience."[92] In Aly's view, relatives of the handicapped group were as coldhearted as were members of the bureaucracy that ran the program.

Similarly, the Katyn Forest Massacre proceeded with cold calculation, from the planting of spies among the prisoners to the signing of the death warrant to the NKVD assembly-line shootings. No one showed a trace of anger or excitement; rather, those responsible proceeded with frigid intentionality. However, the executioners required large quantities of vodka to subdue their emotions.[93]

* * *

Hot and cold genocides are abstract types; in reality, genocides may alternate hot with cold emotions over time. In Indonesia, the army's initial organization of militias to fight communists, and its transportation of the militias from one island to another, was a phase of cool, rational planning, but when the killing began, the emotional temperature shot up. The cultural anthropologist Leslie Dwyer describes an emotional flare-up during the Indonesian genocide in which a "fifteen-year-old . . . who 'talked too much' for some people's liking was corralled in a wicker cage used to transport pigs and then thrown into the river to drown."[94] Genocides committed out in the open, for the world to see, run hot. In Rwanda, one of the most heated of recent mass murders, groups of genocidists swung their machetes in full view of running cameras.[95]

A ghastly example of a hot moment during a cold genocide occurred during the extermination of the handicapped when personnel at the "euthanasia" center in Hadamar, Germany, paused to celebrate the murder of their ten thousandth victim. After they had partied for a while, "the naked corpse was decorated with fresh flowers arranged attractively around flags bearing the Nazi swastika. . . . The body was then thrust into a furnace, at which point the staff burst into wild applause. Several staff members performed a mock eulogy of the victim while the others danced to the sound of a local polka band."[96] Then they went back to gassing people.

Framing, Power, and Social Identities

The concepts of framing and reframing help answer crucial questions about genocide and groups: What makes genocide possible? How do genocides get started? What were the precursors, and what led to the buildup of tensions until a turning point was reached and the killing started? The answers help us identify the push factors that put the emotional dynamics in play and led to a shift in social identities, with perpetrators reframing the victims as a problem so great that only their eradication would solve it.

A key issue, then, is which group defines the frame and whose frame "wins" in perceptions of good and bad, worthy and unworthy, acceptable and rejectable. This issue leads directly to the macro level and matters of political power. Before the genocide in Indonesia, that country experienced a mounting conflict between frames with contesting visions of national identity. The communists had one vision for solving the country's severe problems; conservatives had another. Tensions grew until the attempted coup triggered the genocide. The conservatives' framing of the situation won because Suharto had the power to impose it on the country—the power and political will to kill half a million Indonesians to solidify and preserve his view of what the country should be. He had that power because for most of the country's postcolonial history, Indonesia had been ruled by a military strongman.

Suharto's frame determined the emotional lives of Indonesians for decades to come, emotions connected to women's subordination and male domination, to deaths that could not be memorialized or even mentioned, to employment opportunities blocked and conferred, to an educational system that distorted history, and to a political system that refused moral responsibility for its own past. His frame was solidified partly by news media within Indonesia: newspapers were not allowed to report on the genocide, and Suharto tried to keep foreign journalists out of the country during it.[97] Even though some foreign journalists did get in and reported accurately on what was happening, the international media almost totally ignored the genocide. "Not least disturbing," one journalist wrote, "is the outside world's lack of concern for the greatest mass murder since the Nazi genocide in Europe. . . . The world knew little . . . [and] seemed to care even less, perhaps because the victims were only Communists and Communist sympathizers."[98] Suharto's frame had the power to dominate opinion worldwide.

But no frame lasts forever, even if it was established by a ruthless autocrat like Suharto. While he had considerable popular support at the start of his regime, it crumbled over time due to people's distaste for government corruption and Suharto's authoritarianism. Moreover, the end of the Cold War lessened US interest in supporting his regime, and in 1998, after an economic crisis further eroded his power, Suharto resigned. Declining health helped him dodge corruption charges for his accumulation of something like $15 billion; he died in 2008. After he was forced from office, his framing of the genocide gradually unraveled as Indonesians gained the confidence to speak truthfully about the past.[99]

* * *

But the emotional dynamics of genocide on the group level—even combined with macro factors identified in chapter 3—are still not sufficient to explain how people can commit genocide. For a full explanation, we need to look at micro-level factors that enable genocidists to ignore the humanity of their victims. These micro-level factors are investigated in chapter 5.

5

Extermination Up Close and Personal: Genocide on the Micro Level

The Cambodian Genocide, 1975–1979

The first question people ask about genocide is "How could they do it? How were the aggressors psychologically capable of such inhumanity?" That is also the main question I address in this chapter.

In chapter 3, I identified macro-level factors such as war and state failure that create the context for genocide, and in chapter 4, working on the meso level, I examined some of the emotions that drive what perpetrator groups do *as groups*. This chapter looks at micro-level factors that enable individuals to exterminate others, often with appalling cruelty. When we come down to it, it is *individuals* who open the canister of poison gas, deliver the neck shot, and smash infants against walls. Even after a group reaches a tipping point into violence, the individuals within it are still the ones who execute their enemies, usually in face-to-face situations. And yet in many cases these are people who do not resort to violence at other times in their lives. What in their personal situation enables them to kill during genocide?

In the first section of this chapter, as in the previous chapter, I take an unusual approach to its topic. Most scholars who study micro-level factors in genocide look to perpetrators' motives such as opportunities for looting, obedience to authority, desire to settle scores, and fear. I do this as well, toward the chapter's end. But I also want to get "behind" such motives to piece together a theory of not *why* but *how* individuals can kill during genocide, regardless of their specific motives. To be sure, there are drawbacks to this approach. There is no reason to assume that all genocide perpetrators undergo the same psychosocial process. Then, too, such a theory must be able to apply to all violent behavior, not just genocide—unless we assume that genocidists are somehow different from other humans, an assumption for which there is no evidence.

Despite these drawbacks, I am tantalized by the fact that scientists in a range of fields are producing research that can shed light on violent behavior. I want to try to put together a unified theory to explain violent actions during genocide. In fact, I do *not* expect this theory to apply in all cases, and I recognize that it is largely speculative. However, the theory does seem to apply in many cases, and it offers a new approach to understanding micro-level factors that affect genocide.[1]

The problem that confronts us in answering the "How could they do it?" question is to a large degree a "silo" problem. The literature on the social psychology of violence suffers because research generated in one area of specialization sometimes stays in its silo rather than being read by other specialists working on almost the same issue. Thus, findings are repetitive rather than cumulative; talent, time, and energy are wasted on duplications. To break down the walls of these silos, I pull together research from a range of fields, including criminology, neuroscience, primatology, social and clinical psychology, and sociology.

My answer to the "How could they do it?" question lies in a process I call *splitting*. It combines theory on moral disengagement in the fields of criminology and social psychology, investigations of empathy in clinical psychology and primatology, and the notion of "code-switching" in sociology. It is further bolstered by sociological investigations of ways in which frames, scripts, and cognitive landscapes shape behavior. The concept of splitting fuses discoveries from these various silos to form a micro-level explanation about the social psychology of genocide perpetrators. This is an explanatory model, an ideal type that will not fit every case. However, it explains the behavior of many genocide perpetrators across twentieth-century genocides.[2]

I have looked for a new way to answer the central question because others were not sufficient. The sociologist Randall Collins's theory about the rush forward into frenzied action does not fully explain genocidal killing because many soldiers and militia members will kill only if they are coerced or bribed with a promise of spoils.[3] Dehumanization, which has long been considered a universal predecessor or even cause of genocide, is also not a fully adequate, micro-level explanation because there are genocides in which little or no dehumanization takes place.[4] Nor is hatred a necessary precondition for genocide. Often people assume that genocides are a magnified version of individual hate crimes, where hatred by definition drives the crime. But genocide is seldom committed out of simple hatred. Rather, it is committed because the perpetrators are able to disengage morally from the victims, switch off their feelings of empathy, and objectify the victims as creatures whose humanity can be ignored.

The splitting theory comes close to the social psychologist James Waller's argument that "it is ordinary people, like you and me, who commit genocide and mass killing."[5] We *all* have the capacity to do evil, Waller argues; atrocities are committed not by sadists or madmen but by ordinary people who construct the victims of genocide as "objects"— mere things, not fellow creatures—through the processes of us-them thinking, moral disengagement, and victim blaming. In the language of chapter 4, genocidists *reframe* the victims as less-than-human objects. Waller and I both view cruelty as social in origin and consider committing atrocities to be the outcome of a *process* that changes the perpetrators' psychology—their world outlook.[6] We construct our theories from similar building blocks, such as the concepts of moral disengagement and us-them thinking. However, we use different building blocks as well, and we arrange those building blocks in a different order. Moreover, my explanation incorporates new material from the "silos" mentioned earlier.

The notion of "splitting" comes from psychology; also known as "all-or-nothing" or "black-and-white" thinking, it refers to an inability to see a person or group as partly good and partly bad. Splitting is a tendency to identify some people as completely virtuous and others as completely vicious, with no middle ground. Psychologists consider splitting to be a personality disorder with overtones of narcissism—splitters almost invariably locate themselves in the virtuous group, a narcissistic type of identification. During genocides, one side frames the enemy as wicked or impure and itself as virtuous—utterly in the right and therefore entitled to kill. Splitting denies the possibility that "we" and "they" might have something in common, including the capacity to be both good and evil. I have chosen the term "splitting" partly because it has overtones of pathological narcissism and partly because it reflects the relational dynamic of genocide, in which perpetrators feel they must split themselves off from the target group and destroy it.

My answer to the "How could they do it?" question runs as follows: psychological mechanisms involved in moral disengagement lead to a temporary and selective shutdown in empathy and identification with others; and that shutdown leads to the objectification that enables individuals to commit genocide. This is the *splitting process*. First comes moral disengagement, then neutralization of empathy, and finally the objectification that makes victims seem like objects, things we can get rid of rather than individuals like ourselves. Moreover, for genocide to occur, this sequence must be embedded in social situations that predispose the aggressors to behave inhumanely, such as the growth of Turkish nationalism before the Armenian genocide or the Nazis' acceptance of eugenics before their extermination of disabled people. Stars need to be aligned at the macro, meso, and micro levels for genocide to occur.

In what follows, I first lay out my argument for a three-stage splitting process as a genocide enabler or psychologically necessary precursor for perpetrators. I then summarize the Cambodian genocide of 1975–1979, an event that provides fertile ground for exploring the roles played by moral disengagement, empathy shutdown, and objectification in an actual genocide. In the final section, I return to the issue of micro-level factors but look at specific motives and cover all the genocides in my sample.

The Splitting Process

Although the splitting process passes through stages, it can happen very quickly. Moral disengagement, empathy shutdown, and objectification can surge through the individual like electricity through a wire. The stages may at times overlap, and if the process is frequently repeated, it may become chronic, brutalizing the perpetrator.

Moral Disengagement

Albert Bandura, a giant among contemporary psychologists, has identified eight "mechanisms" through which people morally disengage from humane behavior.[7] In his theory of the moral self, Bandura argues that individuals avoid violating their moral standards because to do so leads to self-condemnation. But if they can disengage from self-condemnation, they are free to commit harmful actions. (Bandura speaks generally of harmful actions, not specifically of genocide.) I will briefly discuss his mechanisms of moral disengagement, which fall into three sets, and exemplify them by reference to the Cambodian genocide, an event described more fully later in this chapter.[8]

Bandura's first three mechanisms of moral disengagement—moral justification, euphemistic labeling, and advantageous comparison—are the most crucial, in his view, for the cognitive restructuring that neutralizes self-condemnation. When these mechanisms are activated simultaneously, Bandura writes, killers are ready to massacre.[9]

The first of these three mechanisms, "moral justification," refers to individuals' invocation of ideologies and "nationalistic imperatives" to justify killing others.[10] In twentieth-century genocide, ideologies of race and nation often constituted a macro or background factor.[11] In the Cambodian genocide of the 1970s, for instance, Pol Pot's communist regime slaughtered or starved up to two million people on the ground that they were "enemies of the people"—foes of his highly ideological, nationalistic dictatorship. A second mechanism is "euphemistic labeling," "the language of non-responsibility," as Bandura calls it,[12] behind which genocidists hide their atrocities from themselves and others. Genocide produces a rich vocabulary of euphemisms; in the Cambodian case, "enemy of the people" was itself a euphemism for someone who should be killed, and killing was "reeducation." Third on Bandura's list is "advantageous comparison," through which those who are intent on harm frame themselves as heroes or martyrs and their foes as vermin or infidels who should be eradicated. It is Bandura's equivalent of us-them thinking. All three of these mechanisms involve the kind of redefinition of the victims discussed in chapter 4.

In Bandura's second set of mechanisms of moral disengagement, the mechanisms work together to minimize a perpetrator's sense of doing harm. They include "displacement of responsibility," as, for example, when one pleads obedience to authority: "I just did what I was ordered to do."[13] In the Cambodian case, an order to kill issued by party members was said to come from not only human authority but also Angkor, the mystical, national power that invested the regime with authority.

This second set of exculpatory mechanisms further includes "diffusion of responsibility," the psychological trick of spreading responsibility through a group and dividing up the dirty work so that each person does (or thinks of having done) just a small part. Nhem En, the teenager who photographed prisoners as they were brought into the main Cambodian torture center, S-21, speaks on film thirty years later as though he had little responsibility for the killings: he never went upstairs, he explains, to watch the torture.[14] Bandura further identifies "disregard or distortion of consequences," a mechanism available to those who can distance themselves from actual killings, making it easier to shut their eyes or discredit what is going on. Nhem En, when asked if he shared responsibility for the thousands of people tortured and killed at S-21, answers, "The world should thank me for my work. If I hadn't taken those photographs, . . . no one would know or care about Cambodia."[15]

Bandura's last set of disengagement practices concerns those who are being harmed. One such practice is "dehumanization," the act of draining the targets of qualities that might make torturers and killers identify with them. Importantly, this mechanism is not at the top of Bandura's list, where earlier genocide scholars might have put it, but close to the bottom; nor is it one of the mechanisms that, in Bandura's layout, contributes to the original cognitive restructuring that closes off self-condemnation. Rather, dehumanization in Bandura's schema is a facilitator that makes killing easier for the perpetrators, especially when combined with diffusion of responsibility.[16] In the killing fields of Cambodia, groups of party members would execute victims at night, when bonfires made those to be killed look grotesque and the group nature of the enterprise diffused responsibility. Bandura's eighth and last mechanism, "attribution of blame," comes into play when perpetrators shift guilt to the victims while claiming that circumstances compelled them to do harm.

Bandura emphasizes that these mechanisms work together and progressively, so that perpetrators increasingly disengage from self-blame over time: "Disengagement practices will not instantly transform considerate people into cruel ones." But over time, "the level of ruthlessness increases, until eventually acts originally regarded as abhorrent can be performed with little anguish or self-censure."[17] Violence feeds on violence, perpetuating and escalating itself.

Techniques of Neutralization

Three decades before Bandura began writing about mechanisms of moral disengagement, Gresham Sykes and David Matza identified similar mechanisms in one of criminology's classic articles, "Techniques of Neutralization: A Theory of Delinquency." (Here is a prime example of the silo problem; Bandura was evidently unaware of the earlier work on the same issue.)[18] Sykes and Matza's famous article helps answer the "How could they do it?" question by asking, "Why do people violate laws in which they believe?" They answer that people do so by learning "techniques of neutralization." These include

- denial of responsibility;
- denial of injury;
- denial of the victim;
- condemnation of the condemners; and
- appeal to higher loyalties.[19]

While Sykes and Matza's techniques of neutralization overlap considerably with Bandura's mechanisms of moral disengagement,[20] the fit is not perfect—Sykes and Matza were trying to explain delinquency, while Bandura reached further, trying to explain all inhumane behavior. But like Bandura, Sykes and Matza insist that cognitive restructuring must occur *before* negative behavior can take place. The techniques of neutralization are what make delinquency possible.[21]

It makes sense that cognitive restructuring must take place *before* we can harm others. Most stable societies are held together by prohibitions against violence. Children are taught antiviolence norms, and these are the norms that need to be neutralized if delinquency or violence is to take place. Sykes and Matza had this insight decades ago; other criminologists have not applied it to genocide until recently.[22] Regardless of which term we use—"mechanisms of moral disengagement" or "techniques of neutralization"—we are talking about the initial step into inhumanity, the first stage in the splitting process.

Empathy Shutdown

The psychologist Simon Baron-Cohen opens *The Science of Evil: On Empathy and the Origins of Cruelty* with a query similar to my central question: "How do humans come to switch off their natural feelings of sympathy for another human being who is suffering?"[23] (He illustrates the question with a photograph of two uniformed Nazis submerging an inmate of the Dachau concentration camp in freezing water, to study the effects.) Baron-Cohen defines empathy as "our ability to identify what someone else is thinking or feeling and to respond to their thoughts and feelings with an appropriate emotion."[24] His main argument is that to be cruel, we need either to be low in our innate biological capacity for empathy or to "switch off" empathy in a specific situation. In his view, everyone lies somewhere from high to low on an "empathy spectrum." Those who test at Level 0 are morally deadened psychopaths.

Baron-Cohen shows how various factors can damage the empathy "circuit" in the human brain, weakening its functions. Harmful factors include neurological and genetic problems as well as threats, corrosive emotions, and ideological beliefs.[25] (One ideological belief might be the idea that the victim group is the source of unfairness suffered by the genocidists; a sense of injustice among Cambodians helped fuel their genocide, for example.) Although Baron-Cohen explains that "in reality, empathy is more like a dimmer switch than an all-or-none switch,"[26] he typically speaks of a "switch" that turns empathy off and on. Switching off leads to objectification.[27]

The metaphor of an empathy switch helped solve a conundrum that had bothered me since a trip to the Nazi concentration camp at Mauthausen, in Austria. After I had toured the camp, my guide drove me a mile or two through rolling green hills to an idyllic scene: a village of picture-book, gabled cottages near a stream. And who had lived there? The top brass of the camp's command. I tried to imagine these SS officers returning home after directing tortures and pushing prisoners off the infamous "parachute" cliff above the camp's stone quarry. Did their return to their families—living that almost storybook existence—involve something like a change in personality? How did they manage the transition? When I encountered the concept of empathy switching, I felt I understood. Those Nazi officials switched their empathy back on. The transition was easy.[28]

Support for Baron-Cohen's picture of empathy as a variable capacity, even within one person, comes from sociology, neuroscience, and primatology. In *Code of the Street: Decency, Violence, and the Moral Life of the Inner City*, the sociologist Elijah Anderson develops a concept similar to that of an empathy switch: "code-switching," which he defines as radically changing one's behavior to conform to different sets of rules, depending on the situation.[29] Male, inner-city teenagers, he writes, may be polite and deferential in middle-class situations of the conventional world but need to switch to tough, masculine behaviors when they enter the street, with its different codes. These youths can switch from "decent" to "bad"—and back—almost instantly. "With some number of campaigns to his credit, the winner [of a campaign for street dominance] may feel self-confident enough to challenge someone who has already established himself. . . . But he is likely to roll on decent youths first. In self-defense, otherwise decent youths will sometimes mimic those who are more committed to the street. On the streets and in the halls at school, they sometimes adopt the 'street look,' wearing the street uniform, but also swaggering, using foul language, and generally trying to 'go for bad,' all in the interest of acquiring respect."[30]

Of course, it is a far cry from the inner-city culture analyzed by Anderson to the genocidal culture of mass murder, but the psychological mechanisms form parallels: both involve a kind of code-switching. Code-switching can be difficult, Anderson finds, but the young men he studied had little choice but to do it. Growing up in impoverished, inner-city neighborhoods, they had to survive when they left home and entered the street. Although Anderson does not define code-switching in terms of empathy, he implies that inner-city kids need to leave empathy inside when they exit home. And, because he demonstrates that people can flick moral codes off and on, his work supports Baron-Cohen's notion of an empathy switch.

An example of code- or empathy switching appears in the biography of Vann Nath, an artist who survived Cambodia's S-21 prison by painting pictures that pleased the prison's director, Deuch. Deuch asked Vann Nath to draw a portrait of Pol Pot; while it was in progress, Vann Nath dared to ask for colored paints, to make the portrait even better. Deuch

told Peng, "a brutal guard, the most feared of all," to bring in art supplies; but Peng, whose "daily work was to kill people," warned, "If you
cannot do the work, just wait and see." "I started to paint in color," Vann
Nath writes, "and three days later produced a beautiful color painting. I
had tried my best, knowing my fate was tied to the picture." But he was
frightened, knowing that there would not be a second chance "because
Peng, the chief butcher, had already said so."

> A while later I heard footsteps and saw Deuch enter, accompanied by
> Peng and another man. Standing next to the wall, I waited for their reac-
> tion, feeling shaky and chaotic.
>   Deuch stood silently in front of the painting for several minutes and
> then burst into a loud laugh. "Good. . . . Good," he said. "It's all right."
>   These few words meant the difference between life and death for me.[31]

Deuch had code-switched from ordering death—his default position—to sparing a prisoner.

The empathy-switch concept is further supported by sociological
work on framing and cognition, notably recent sociological work that
deals with framing on the individual level. Without denying that frames
are collectively constructed and also adopted on the group level, sociologists talk about the multiple frames to which individuals are exposed
(by politicians, popular culture, family tradition, schools, and so on) and
that they incorporate into their mental "tool kits." Individuals draw on
these tool kits (of narratives, symbols, and worldviews) to solve problems and devise strategies for action.[32]

The multiple frames (acting as lenses) and scripts (providing tem-
plates for action) that we carry in our heads often compete with or contradict one another.[33] Thus, our behaviors can be contradictory, and we
may act in ways that violate our basic values. We may switch off empathy
with some people or groups. Moreover, our choice of scripts may be
shaped by "cognitive landscapes" that present us with ecologically structured standards for behavior.[34] By cognitively scanning a local "landscape" or social context, we discover behavioral guidelines that tell us
when to switch codes or when to reduce the volume on empathy. In *Why
Did They Kill? Cambodia in the Shadow of Genocide*, the anthropologist
Alexander Laban Hinton gives an example when he tells how, after the

Khmer Rouge takeover, rich and poor changed status, with the poor now taking "revenge upon their class enemies," the so-called new people, even to the point of turning them into war slaves. Hinton quotes one such captive: "We were hungry, too tired to wash or clean our clothes, and we lost all sense of hygiene. We didn't care what we ate as long as we could put something in our stomachs. We didn't mind where we had a shit, or who saw us. Disease spread through the village—cholera, malaria, dysentery, diarrhea, and skin infections." "Such conditions," Hinton observes, "often reduced a person to an animal-like state of being. Like water buffalo, 'new people' were sometimes required to pull a plow or cart and might be whipped if they failed to work hard enough. . . . Since 'new people' were less than fully human, there were fewer moral inhibitions in harming them. A 'new person' who did something wrong could be 'discarded' . . .—a euphemism for execution."[35] In this example, the peasants had scanned the social context, decided to adopt Khmer Rouge values, and brutalized the "new people" who were framed as their former oppressors. Even the city people adopted the new script, reframing themselves. Codes switched for everyone, and it became difficult to maintain any interpersonal empathy whatsoever.

How, exactly, does empathy work in terms of mental processes? Answers can be found in the work of Tania Singer, the director of social neuroscience research at the Max Plank Institute, in Germany. Through ingenious experiments, Singer and her colleagues have shown that "empathy is a highly flexible phenomenon."[36] Defining empathy as what happens when "the observer's emotions reflect affective sharing ('feeling with' the other person),"[37] Singer points out that it does not always carry us in positive directions. "For example, a torturer may use empathy in order to sense how to increase his victim's suffering; in competitive environments (from sports to business operations to warfare), successful tactics take into account the negative . . . effects that action will have on the opponent."[38]

While Singer does not talk about an empathy switch or code-switching, she does identify mental processes that affect degrees of empathy, including contextual appraisal (which may inform us that an empathic response is not appropriate in this situation), cognitive processes (through which we assess our competence to react to the mental states of others), and the relationship between the empathizer and the target. "The way we attend to the emotions of others substantially modulates our empathic responses to them."[39]

Gender, too, may affect empathy, as Singer discovered through a study that engaged volunteers in a game. Confederates of the researchers cheated and then allowed their cheating to be discovered. The volunteers were then hooked up to fMRI (functional magnetic resonance imaging) machines that measured their brain activity while they watched a cheater receiving pain. In the men, but not the women, empathy-related brain activity ceased. "At least in men," Singer concludes, "a desire for revenge won over empathic motivation when they were confronted with someone experiencing pain who they believed deserved to be punished."[40] Empathy can thus be canceled out by hostility, a discovery that shows how empathy shutdown works in some circumstances.[41]

The primatologist Frans de Waal sheds further light on the conditions under which empathy shutdown occurs. He begins with the evolution of humans' capacity for empathy. "Empathy engages brain areas that are more than a hundred million years old," he writes. "The capacity arose long ago with motor mimicry and emotional contagion, after which evolution added layer after layer, until our ancestors not only felt what others felt, but understood what others might want or need."[42]

But, de Waal points out, empathy needs some sort of filter so we do not collapse by feeling the suffering of everyone we meet. It needs "a turn-off switch." "Like every emotional reaction, [empathy] has a 'portal,' a situation that typically triggers it. . . . Empathy's chief portal is identification. We're ready to share the feelings of someone we identify with, which is why we do so easily with those who belong to our inner circle: For them the portal is always ajar. Outside this circle, things are optional."[43] The more physical and psychological distance we have from people or groups, the less we are likely to identify with them and thus feel empathy. "Empathy builds on proximity, similarity, and familiarity," de Waal writes.[44] We are more likely to shut down empathy toward strangers and enemies. Here de Waal directly ties lack of empathy to genocide.[45] When we lack it, we objectify and dehumanize people, and that can lead to mass killings.

Another variable affecting empathy, according to de Waal, is gender: "Cross-cultural studies confirm that women everywhere are considered more empathic than men."[46] This echoes Tania Singer's finding of gender differences in empathy and may help explain why the vast majority of genocidists are men, not women.[47] Such differences may well have evolutionary roots in maternity and child rearing.

Notwithstanding the evolutionary roots of empathy, it is socially activated. It is variable, complex, and contingent.[48] Although empathy is frequently associated with kindness, it can also be used to calculate cruelty and, indeed, may feed into genocide when it encourages identification with perpetrators. In the effort to understand genocide, the idea of an empathy switch is particularly useful because it helps explain empathy shutdown.

Objectification

When empathy shuts down, the result is objectification, the reduction of someone to the single, simplistic identity of an enemy (useless eater, communist, Tutsi). Aggressors can now treat victims as if they had no right to self-determination but rather are property, to be disposed of at will. Having completed the splitting process, aggressors are liberated to kill as much and as viciously as they want.

Have these aggressors become psychopaths, as some commentators (including Baron-Cohen) maintain?[49] Not in a criminological sense. Criminology, too, is concerned with people who seem to have no conscience and be incapable of remorse. But the psychopath studied by criminologists has many additional characteristics not necessarily shared with the genocidist, such as glibness, deceitfulness, impulsivity, and a craving for excitement.[50] In addition, criminal psychopaths act alone, not in groups. Most significantly, criminal psychopaths reveal these traits in early childhood, whereas genocidists' lack of conscience develops in response to a specific situation in adulthood and does not generalize beyond it. They may be brutalized by committing genocide, but there is no reason to think that they commit other crimes once the genocide is over.

How does the endpoint of the splitting process—objectification—differ from that of dehumanization? They overlap, but with Bandura, I suggest that dehumanization is a nonessential step in the splitting process—part of moral disengagement; and in my view, objectification is the process's endpoint. Dehumanization degrades victims, who are then easier to kill. Objectification turns people into things in the minds of the perpetrators, making them seem like impersonal objects that one is allowed or even obligated to destroy. Victims can be objectified without being dehumanized, and vice versa, although the two processes often work together. In my view, the splitting process does not *require* dehumanization, but it does require objectification, without which intentional killing cannot occur.

Detailed accounts of warfare make it clear that many soldiers do not complete the splitting process: they cannot disengage from the rules of moral behavior that they have been taught from childhood; they cannot shake off empathy with those whom they are supposed to kill; they cannot objectify the enemy. These are combatants for whom the question is not "How can I do it?" but rather "How can I avoid doing it?"

The findings about warfare hold true for genocide as well, to judge from Christopher Browning's *Ordinary Men*, a study of 500 members of a German police battalion who, during World War II, participated in the murder of at least 83,000 Jews. Browning finds that participation in atrocities fell on a spectrum of behavior. About a dozen members of the police battalion, when offered the opportunity to drop out at the start of the outfit's assignment, took it. During the battalion's murderous tour through Poland, some soldiers took pity on Jews like kitchen helpers who had acquired a kind of "personal identity" for them; in my terms, they could not completely shut off empathy with these victims. "Direct proximity to the horror of the killing significantly increased the number of men who would no longer comply," Browning continues; and in addition, some police officers evaded orders when they were not directly supervised.[51] Others simply followed orders, and "a nucleus of increasingly enthusiastic killers . . . volunteered for the firing squads and 'Jew hunts.'"[52] People's ability to split themselves off from humanity seems to differ by situation and, perhaps, individual capacity.

This conclusion is reinforced by the behavior of the "guards" in the psychologist Philip Zimbardo's Stanford Prison Experiment, in which college-age, male volunteers who had been screened for emotional stability were randomly assigned to act as either guards or prisoners in a simulated jail. The mental health of the "prisoners" deteriorated rapidly. A few guards showed sympathy with the prisoners, but most of them became abusive and power hungry; and three in particular became "aggressive and dehumanizing."[53] The experiment had to be terminated after six days out of concern for the mental health of the "prisoners." The escalating cruelty of the "guards," who had been selected for participation in the experiment due to their evident "normality," seems to demonstrate, again, that the ability to switch off empathy, objectify others, and complete the splitting process is situationally induced but also varies by individual.

Similar variations in people's capacity for cruelty showed up in Stanley Milgram's obedience experiments, in which volunteer "teachers" were told by the experimenter (dressed up as an authority figure in a white lab coat) to deliver shocks to a "learner," who was really in league with the experimenter and simply pretended to experience pain from the shocks. The degree to which teachers complied with the experimenter's instructions to deliver ever-greater shocks varied considerably according to the conditions of the experiments. For instance, teachers were more likely to deliver what they thought were extremely strong shocks when they could neither see the learners nor hear their pretended cries of pain; but when they could actually see and hear cries from a learner who was evidently receiving an electric shock through their actions, the degree of compliance with the experimenter's instructions fell. If the teacher had actually to *touch* the learner, compliance decreased even further. And as the experimenter physically distanced himself from the teacher, compliance fell again.[54] Although Milgram's experiments have recently been exposed as scientifically weak,[55] they may have yielded a core of truth. In them, too, splitting—or splitting-like behaviors—occurred on a continuum that depended on situational conditions and, apparently, also on individual willingness to harm another person.[56]

Having explained the splitting process, I now return to the "How could they do it?" question, examining it in light of Cambodia's genocide.

The Cambodian Genocide

The Cambodian genocide, 1975–1979, took place against a background of civil war, international conflict, and state failure—the type of macro setting, as we have seen, that foments genocide. About ten years before the communist Pol Pot came to power, an anticommunist, Lon Nol, had been elected prime minister of Cambodia; but Pol Pot's forces, fighting in the jungle, were already strong enough to challenge him. The two sides clashed until April 1975, when Pol Pot and his followers, the Khmer Rouge (Red Cambodians), won the struggle and renamed the country Democratic Kampuchea. They stayed in power until they were ousted by Vietnam in January 1979.

During the civil war, the United States—to support Lon Nol, damage the Khmer Rouge, and destroy what it suspected were secret Vietnamese supply lines—secretly bombed Cambodia, dropping 2.7 million tons of bombs.[57] The bombing drove Cambodians into the arms of Pol Pot's Khmer Rouge forces, with their fiercely anti-US ideology. Tens of thousands of Cambodians were killed during the bombings, which came, inexplicably, from a country—the United States—with which Cambodia was not at war.

On the threshold of the Khmer Rouge takeover, the country was in tatters from the civil war and bombings. Hundreds of thousands of Cambodians had been killed in the civil war between the forces of Lon Nol and Pol Pot. The country's rural economy had been almost destroyed; ties of family and village had been broken. But more destruction lay ahead as Khmer Rouge soldiers entered the capital city, Phnom Penh, and emptied it of inhabitants, driving them into the countryside. The elderly, hospital patients, women in labor—all were mercilessly torn from their homes and set on the road.

Pol Pot revolutionized the organization of Cambodia in line with communist ideology from the Soviet Union and, especially, China's Mao Zedong. During the first period of his regime, before collectivization, many Cambodians, especially people under thirty, seem to have been fairly satisfied with the Khmer Rouge.[58] But dissatisfaction grew as the regime created large collective farms that disrupted traditions of agricultural and also family life.

Hundreds of thousands of Cambodians were relocated to collective farms, some in previously uncultivated areas of the country. On the collective farms, everyone had to eat communally, separate from their relatives and among strangers. In some cases, men and women were forced to live apart, and parents were separated from children. During meals, supervising cadres, who themselves barely understood the party line, instructed weary farmers in communist ideology.

Schools closed; religious worship was forbidden; and the police and courts ceased to function, as did markets. Money was abolished, and no one could leave the farm to which they were assigned. People had to wear the peasant uniform—black pajamas—and labor in the rice paddies. "For most Cambodians," writes Alexander Laban Hinton, "life during Democratic Kampuchea . . . was like a giant prison camp."[59] In one subdistrict, where people were forbidden to use "old, happy words," young cadres eavesdropped to detect "morals offenders" and then executed the culprits.[60]

The changes not only destroyed older bases for morality in family and village life; they also created divisions among groups and individuals as the Party Center reframed the value of various groups. Former city dwellers were now despised, as were intellectuals. Both were subordinated to the so-called old people, meaning the peasants who had come to power with the Khmer Rouge and had traditionally worked the land. Young people—the blank slates on whom Pol Pot hoped to inscribe his ideology most deeply—were given authority to discipline "new" city people and even have them executed. In addition, Buddhist monks, carriers of the traditional religion, were ostracized and executed, partly because the communist line deemed religion an opiate of the people and partly because they lived off alms without contributing productive labor to the country.

The Pol Pot regime controlled its population more closely and ruthlessly than has any other state in history.[61] "Old" people and the party-affiliated cadres morally disengaged from "new" people, foreigners, the monks, and those who tried to cling to family life. All loyalties were now directed toward Angkor, the ancient spirit associated with Party Central and its prime minister, Pol Pot.

In under four years, over two million Cambodians died out of a total population of eight million—one-quarter of the people. Of those who died, perhaps one million were intentionally murdered, while the rest died of hunger and disease, although it is impossible to be sure. Democratic Kampuchea was sealed off from the outside, and Party Central rarely allowed outsiders to enter. Cambodians could neither send letters nor make telephone calls. Immobilized on their collective farms, Cambodians had little in their lives aside from hard labor, threats, and indoctrination sessions. Even if they had the energy to empathize with those who were hauled off to be killed, they could do nothing. Democratic Kampuchea was a terrorist state that sought total control over its workers.

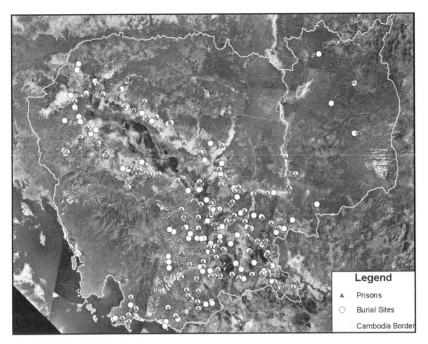

Figure 5.1. Prisons and mass graves in Cambodia, 1975–1979. This map of Cambodia (demarked by the outline) shows that there were dozens of prisons in Democratic Kampuchea in addition to the Tuol Sleng prison in the capital city of Phnom Penh. By no coincidence, many of the prisons were close to burial sites. Copyright Cambodian Genocide Program, Yale University. Used with permission.

"Three tons per hectare," or about seven and a half acres: this was the production goal that the Party Center set for rice production on the collective farms. But the goal was unachievable; previously, farmers had produced only one ton per hectare, and some of the land opened up by Pol Pot was unsuitable for agriculture. Cambodians spent twelve hours or more each day in the fields, cultivating rice and building dams to irrigate new areas for cultivation; but as it became clear that the production goal could not be met, they were fed less and less, until finally they received only a small portion of rice gruel each day. When they faltered in their work, exhausted and starving, young cadres—better fed and unsympathetic—would blame them for insufficient loyalty and might have them dragged off for "reeducation."

Pol Pot, born in 1925 and originally called Saloth Sar, was an exceedingly strange man, but it is difficult to explain his strangeness due to his personal remoteness and paranoid secrecy. Even after he came to power, many associates did not know who he was. Born to a family of relatively prosperous farmers when Cambodia was still a French colony, he studied electronics in Paris as a young man but kept failing his exams. He showed more aptitude for politics and was drawn to Marxism in a period when the idea of "power to the people" magnetized youths worldwide. Pol Pot became a communist and, after his return to Cambodia, rose through party ranks, ever more nationalistic in his views and ever more authoritarian. His warm and open face, with its disarming smile, belied his disregard for human life; his disinterest in pomp seemed testimony to his dedication to communism. Even before he won the war against Lon Nol, Pol Pot started purging people from the party, sending them off to be shot with no opportunity for self-defense, and in another ominous sign of what was to come, he built prisons in areas controlled by the Khmer Rouge. When the Lon Nol government collapsed, Pol Pot became prime minister of the new government of Democratic Kampuchea. He also adopted the name Pol Pot (the origin is obscure) and the moniker Brother Number One.

Vastly ambitious but also utterly deluded, Pol Pot revolutionized the country, but with policies that were poorly thought out and disastrous in their consequences. After the Vietnamese ousted his government in 1979, he lived for years on the border between Cambodia and Thailand, where he continued as head of the Khmer Rouge—a governmental entity without a country that, incredibly, the United Nations recognized for many more years, thanks to pressure from the United States and China. Surrounded by remnants of his Khmer Rouge forces, he continued to order brutal killings of former confederates, and even when confronted with figures on the number of deaths under his regime, he persisted in denying responsibility. But cancer, age, and a stroke slowed him down. Pol Pot died in 1998 under unexplained circumstances—perhaps due to old age, perhaps by suicide, perhaps through poison.[62]

Pol Pot saw his regime as a continuation of the Angkorean empire that, in the years 800 to 1400, had ruled northeastern Cambodia. He used the concept of Angkor to reshape international and internal relationships. As the Khmer Rouge began to preach "Cambodia for the Cambodians," the neighboring Vietnamese, who had helped put the Khmer Rouge in power, were reframed as enemies. Relationships between the individual and the state shifted radically as loyalty was re-defined as self-sacrifice—really, a willingness to be eradicated—for Angkor. Angkor in the sense of the country's communist party, Hinton remarks, was "the Khmer Rouge panopticon,"[63] its omnipresent prison of total surveillance. The party structure was said to have "the eyes of a pineapple."[64] Angkor—the Khmer Rouge reminded people—was constantly on watch for disobedient behavior.

The genocide began slowly and without systematic planning, more a result of Pol Pot's inability to govern and his paranoid fear of plots than a deliberate decision to exterminate. If former city dwellers now working in the rice fields complained of lack of food or faltered in their work, youthful cadres might hustle them into trucks that would drive them to burial pits, where they were killed with blows to the back of the head. The cadres were controlled by Party Central and district chiefs, but otherwise they were a law unto themselves; serving simultaneously as police, judges, and executioners, they jeered at "new" people, assuring them, "To keep you is no profit, to destroy you is no loss."[65] Often they killed not only the person who had somehow offended but also his or her entire family. According to Hinton, this excess was motivated by traditional Cambodian acceptance of the notion of disproportionate revenge ("a head for an eye," he calls it).[66] "The Khmer Rouge used this ideology to inflame the feeling of resentment . . . [and] make its follow-ers 'burn with rage'" as they sought to punish enemies of the people.[67]

Who were the Khmer Rouge's victims? Most were ordinary Cambodi-ans, but the regime also killed disproportionately large numbers of Bud-dhist monks, Muslim Chams, Vietnamese, and Chinese. Of the 250,000 Chinese in the country in 1975, over half were dead by 1979, "the worst human disaster ever to befall the large ethnic Chinese community of Southeast Asia," writes Kiernan.[68] Of the approximately 250,000 Muslim Chams in Cambodia when the Khmer Rouge took over, about 100,000 were dead by 1979. Over 100,000 Vietnamese were expelled from the country and another 10,000 murdered.[69] (Because these religious, ethnic, and national groups were targeted for eradication, the Cambodian kill-ings fit the UN's definition of genocide.) Cambodians who went to their deaths also included former Lon Nol supporters, party officials whom Pol Pot came to distrust, and intellectuals. A journalist coined the term "killing fields" for the sites of mass murder where prisoners were forced

Figure 5.2. Tuol Sleng, also known as S-21, was the prison in Phnom Penh where thousands of Cambodians were tortured and murdered. Formerly, it was a high school; today it is the Tuol Sleng Genocide Museum. Photograph by Ben Kiernan (1980), Yale University, and used with his permission.

to dig their own graves and then killed not with bullets, which were too valuable to waste on them, but with sharpened bamboo poles and the edges of spades. Babies were smashed against trees; and in an extreme economy measure, many prisoners were reportedly buried alive. According to Yale University's Cambodian Genocide Program, the atrocity left behind 309 mass grave sites, 19,000 grave pits, and 1,386,734 bodies.[70]

In the most grisly manifestation of the Khmer Rouge's disregard for human life, it took over a former high school, Tuol Sleng, renaming it Security-21 and turning it into a central prison. At S-21, prisoners were tortured to force them to name others who were spies for the CIA, the Russian KGB, or the Vietnamese. Most prisoners knew nothing about the CIA or KBG and had no traitorous intent, but the naming of enemies was crucial to the feeding of Pol Pot's paranoia. About 12,000 people died in S-21 or at the nearby killing field of Choeung Ek.[71] Almost no one who entered the prison survived.

In S-21, prisoners lived on floors, chained together in rows, growing filthy and lice ridden, and dreading the summons to the torture rooms. As the victims delivered their "confessions" and named others who, like themselves, were traitors to the revolution, guards wrote down what they said for delivery to Pol Pot, whose suspicions were thus confirmed.

About 100 staff members ran the death machine that was S-21. They were mainly young men from rural backgrounds, as were the prisoners themselves. While the guards were undeniably cruel, one should recognize that they performed their gruesome tasks under threat of death and that some met the same end they had meted out to their wards. According to David Chandler, the author of a book on S-21, the guards were as terrified as their victims.[72]

Toward the end of Pol Pot's regime, he went on a killing frenzy. He decided to invade Vietnam from eastern Cambodia and so, to first get rid of potential enemies in his own country, started purging party members, soldiers, soldiers' families, and even civilians in that area, murdering up to 100,000 in a veritable orgy of murder.[73] Cambodians began fleeing into Vietnam, and the Vietnamese finally put an end to Pol Pot's agitation on their borders by invading Cambodia. The Khmer Rouge machine collapsed in early 1979, having lasted less than four years. Pol Pot fled to his jungle refuge on the Thai border.

Motives as Micro Factors

The first part of this chapter looked at micro-level factors—those involved in the splitting process—that enable individuals to exterminate others. This section uses the genocides in my sample to examine another sort of micro-level factor: motives—the inducements or goals that cause people to commit genocide. These are the factors that scholars most commonly have in mind when they speak of genocide at the micro level.[74] For genocides in my sample considered collectively, the six most frequent motives were

- to deliver just deserts ("the victims had it coming to them");
- to act on an ideological conviction (for example, that the victims were ethnically contemptible);
- to obey authority ("my superiors told me to kill");
- to gain economically ("we wanted the victims' land, rugs, women");
- to avoid harm ("others would have killed me if I hadn't participated"); and
- to enjoy oneself ("killing them was fun").

In most genocides in my sample, *just deserts*, or the conviction that the victims deserved to be killed, was a key motive. Germans who killed the Herero felt the Africans deserved to die because they had started the rebellion; the Soviet officials who planned the Katyn Forest Massacre considered their prisoners to be counterrevolutionaries and anticommunists. The only two genocides in which the idea of just deserts did not play a significant role were the Nazi extermination of the disabled—the doctors did not argue that their victims were to blame for their disabilities[75]—and the Guatemalan genocide, in which the goal was mainly strategic.

The motive of *ideology* (including racism) was used to justify the majority of genocides in my sample. "The idea of racial superiority," writes the historian Jon Bridgman of German brutality against the Herero, "the contempt for native life styles and life, were part of a belief in the civilizing mission of the white man."[76] In Indonesia, anticommunist ideology, including the belief that communists were likely to be atheists, motivated many of the killings. The relationship between ideology (a set of ideas that together form a worldview) and motives for genocide is somewhat abstract, but it becomes clearer if one thinks of ideology as a resource or pool of beliefs on which people draw when they are deciding on personal courses of action. For example, Pol Pot's ideology included the conviction that survival of the Khmer Rouge revolution justified mass killings. Party officials spread this ideology through indoctrination sessions, and eventually some who listened adopted the ideology to justify their own genocidal behavior. They did not *have* to—they were not the blank slates that Pol Pot hoped for; but many actively decided to behave in line with Pol Pot's ideology.[77]

Obedience to authority was a strong motive in five genocides in my sample. Among the German soldiers, some objected to brutality against the Herero; but I have identified only one who actually defied von Trotha's extermination decree in order to help the Africans.[78] Others complied for a range of reasons, from a sense of racial superiority and belief that the Herero deserved to be punished to simply following orders. At Katyn, the NKVD executioners may have had little sense of whom they were shooting or why; but their job was to be expert executioners, which involved obedience to instructions. Obedience to authority did not play a major role in the Armenian genocide, where those who massacred the Christians were richly rewarded freelancers; nor was it a motive in the Nazi effort to wipe out the disabled, where again the killers—at least those at the higher levels of the organization—were well-rewarded volunteers. Similarly, during the Indonesian genocide, although some participants were forced to kill, others did so willingly and indeed enthusiastically. Elsewhere, however, obedience to authority was a strong motivator.

Economic motives played a key role in five of the eight genocides, sometimes at the group level and at others for individuals. In the Herero case, Germans wanted the land; in the Katyn case, the Soviets wanted eastern Poland. Members of the Special Organization who were mobilized to kill Armenians turned genocide into a pot of gold that include precious rugs, jewelry, and girls who could be sold into sex slavery; meanwhile, on the state level, authorities appropriated Armenian homes and other property to resettle refugees and help build a Turkish middle class. The staff of the killing centers for the disabled in Nazi Germany received extra pay for productivity,[79] while at their headquarters, officials received bonuses and budget credit based on the amount of gold they extracted from victims' bodies.[80] In Rwanda, in many cases Hutu joined the genocide in the hope of stealing something from the farm of the person they killed or even slipping into ownership.[81] "A lot of people were killed because the killers wanted to take their things," one Rwandan reported.[82]

Fear, too, motived genocidists. Staff at the Nazis' killing centers had no choice but to participate in the extermination program. Christian Wirth, the supervisor of the Hartheim Castle killing center in Austria, explained to his staff, "We must build a crematorium here, in order to burn mental patients. . . . Mental patients are a burden upon Germany and we only want healthy people. . . . Certain men will be chosen to work in the crematorium. Above all else, the motto is silence or the death penalty. Whoever fails to observe this silence will end up in a concentration camp or be shot."[83] The staff were literally prisoners, unable to leave Hartheim Castle and forced to perform their unpleasant tasks under threat of death. Fear motivated some Indonesian genocidists as well, as when they murdered the survivors of already-executed communists out of fear of retaliation at a later point. In Cambodia and Rwanda, genocidists often faced the choice of killing or being killed.

Fun or pleasure sometimes motivated genocidists in my sample. Members of the Special Organization who killed Armenians had great (and sometimes sadistic) fun terrorizing, raping, and killing their victims.[84] Similarly, during the Guatemalan genocide, the civil patrols that destroyed Mayan villages enjoyed the killings, raping, and drunken partying in the aftermaths. That some Hutu took pleasure in killing Tutsi has been documented by a number of scholars.[85]

These micro factors—revenge or just deserts; ideology; economic gain; fear; fun and pleasure—were mentioned most frequently in the accounts I read of the eight genocides. Others appeared less frequently, such as scientific pride in the work in the case of the Nazi physicians, strategic considerations (especially important in Guatemala and Katyn), and a tradition of disproportionate revenge in Cambodia.[86] Nor was it unusual for a single genocidist to act out of multiple motives, as some Hutu did when they killed out of fear, greed, and belief in the Hutu Power ideology.

The micro factors discussed here are relatively rational and conscious motives for participating in genocide. Less rational are the micro factors involved in the splitting process, which depends largely on processes and impulses of which genocidists may be unaware.

* * *

To return to the initial question, then, How could they do it? A better question may be, How could *we* do it, were we in the same circumstances? I begin with the assumption that anyone can participate in genocide under the "right" conditions; genocide can break out anywhere, if conditions are suitable, because what leads people to commit genocide is a combination of factors working on macro, intermediate, and personal levels. In this chapter, I have focused on personal factors, suggesting a two-part answer to the basic question. First, people can commit genocide (and other violent acts) only after going through the process of splitting—moral disengagement, empathy dimming, objectification—a process that can happen quicker than it takes to read this sentence. No one is immune to splitting, but some people seem to be more susceptible than others, perhaps due to innate factors related to gender and level of empathy. The second part of the answer lies in motives, which can best be understood in the context of the macro and meso factors in play. We have to get up close and personal and, at the same time, to see the full picture.

Whereas this chapter has concentrated on the social psychology and motives of individuals who commit genocide, chapter 6 radically shifts the scale of the inquiry, asking what states do to prepare themselves to commit genocide.

6

Mobilization for Destruction

The Armenian Genocide, 1915–1923; The Nazi Genocide of the Disabled, 1939–1945

How do states prepare to commit genocide?

One way, improbable as it may seem, is by making movies. The Nazis took this step to help accomplish the extermination of disabled children. One film begins by asking, "What causes more suffering in the world than the stupidity of the compassionate?" and answers with the story of an actress who marries a doctor with hereditary mental problems. Maria and Michael predictably produce a feeble-minded baby and, filled with the stupidity of the compassionate, try to rouse it from its insensate condition. After a year, Michael kills the child—which is what he should have done in the first place and what, perhaps, should have been done to him as an infant, since he was so clearly a bearer of degenerate heredity.[1]

Concocting this plot may seem an unlikely prelude to genocide, but the Nazis, foreseeing resistance to their "euthanasia" program, made propaganda films to soften acceptance of the killings. Preparation for genocide always includes seemingly trivial steps toward the final conflagration.

Genocide, in other words, is never spontaneous. The architects of disaster plan their grim strategies carefully, taking the measure of the enemy, mapping out plans, building support, and in many cases mobilizing specialized groups to do the dirty work of killing. In the latter regard, states intent on genocide act much like organized crime syndicates, creating and training gangs to commit their crimes. But they have the great advantage of being not syndicates but states, which can quietly change or twist the law so as to make the genocide seem legitimate.

This chapter begins with detailed accounts of two genocides, the Armenians killed by the Turks and the disabled people "euthanized" by Nazis, examples that provide two specific answers to the question, How do states prepare for genocide? Next comes a section on "genocidal organizations," a concept I have developed to analyze how genocides are executed. I define these organizations, give examples, and draw conclusions based on my sample. In the chapter's final section, I focus on Giorgio Agamben's concept of a "state of exception": the circumstance in which authorities create a legal void to assure impunity. States of exception, like genocidal organizations, are part of the calculated mobilization for destruction.

The Armenian Genocide, 1915–1923

The Armenians, who lived for over 2,000 years in what became eastern Anatolia—the land in northeast Turkey closest to Russia—were one of the first groups to adopt Christianity as their official religion. When they were incorporated into the Ottoman Empire—the vast state that at one point covered eastern Europe and parts of the Middle East as well as what is today called Turkey—the Armenians coexisted in general harmony with Ottomans, but they were regarded as infidels, denied the rights that Ottomans enjoyed, and had to acknowledge second-class status. Thus, they were vulnerable to mistreatment.

While traditional Muslim law required Christians to pay an extra tax and display subservience, reforms forced on the Ottomans by European powers guaranteed equality to Christian minorities. Thus, there was a double standard: Muslim customary law mandated inequality, while new treaties and the reformist Ottoman Constitution of 1876 assured equality.[2] A clash was inevitable. When the Armenians pushed for reforms that they had been promised, such as equal taxation and protection from Kurdish and Ottoman raids, the Ottomans retaliated with increasing brutality—and impunity, since there was no one to stop them. During the nineteenth century, victimization of Armenian communities steadily increased.

By the early twentieth century, the Ottoman Empire was in its death throes. "Between 1878 and 1918, the empire lost 85 percent of its territory and 75 percent of its population," explains the historian Taner Akçam.[3] Sultan Abdul Hamid II, faced with calls for Armenian equality, lamented, "By taking away Greece and Rumania, Europe has cut off the feet of the Turkish state. The loss of Bulgaria, Serbia and Egypt has deprived us of our hands, and now by means of this Armenian agitation, they want to get at our most vital places and tear out our very guts. This [Armenians' demands for equality] would be the beginning of totally annihilating us, and we must fight against it with all the strength we possess."[4] While the sultan continued to resist genuine reforms that would refashion his empire into a modern state, the Armenians, influenced by nationalist ideologies taking hold in Europe, demanded better protections and more autonomy. Radical Armenians went so far as to push for complete independence. They forged alliances with Western nations that supported their demands—alliances that insulted and infuriated the sultan, whose response was increasingly harsh.

Between 1894 and 1896, the Ottomans suppressed Armenian demands in massacres and atrocities that killed perhaps 200,000 people. These attacks, which went for the most part unpunished, further marginalized the Armenians and turned them into fair game.[5] The genocide scholar Vahakn Dadrian goes so far as to talk about an Ottoman "culture favouring the resort to massacre as an instrument of state policy."[6]

Massacres continued into the new century: in 1909, in southeastern Anatolia, Ottomans plundered and slaughtered 15,000–20,000 Armenians. But the twentieth-century massacres had a "very different character from earlier ones," explains Akçam, partly because the crumbling Ottoman Empire was now trying to turn itself into a kind superstate based on Islamist ideology.[7] The most immediate impediment to this drive for Muslim unity seemed to be the Armenians.

But the Armenians were more than an impediment; they appeared to be an active threat to the unity of the Turkish state. Due to pressure from western European nations, in 1914 the Ottoman government was forced to accept the Armenian Reform Agreement, giving international inspectors permission to enter Turkey to check up on Armenian conditions. To the Turks, this seemed a step toward a breakup of their land in Anatolia and establishment of an autonomous Armenian region.[8] "All parties participating in the negotiations of the reform agreement," writes Akçam, "knew that this was the beginning of an independent Armenian State"[9]—or would be if the Turks did not take drastic action.

The Ottomans—beguiled no less than the Armenians by the nationalist ideas flowing in from the West—had started to rethink their national identity.[10] Under the influence of German ideas defining nationality in terms of racial, ethnic, and cultural unity, Ziya Gökalp, the government's ideological leader, fantasized about a new Islamist empire based on language and culture that would stretch through Russia into China and India.[11] Turkish "supermen," in Gökalp's imagination, would unify the new Turkish state—and cleanse it of outsiders.[12]

Meanwhile, a liberal party, the Committee of Union and Progress (the "Unionists" or "Young Turks"), having wrested control of the government from the sultan, projected plans for modernizing the country and turning "Ottomans" into "Turks" with a single national and ethnic identity.[13] In the chaos of World War I (in which Turkey allied itself with the losing Central Powers), a conservative triumvirate ("the three pashas") of the Unionist party came to power with a nationalistic, Turkey-for-the-Turks agenda. Its goal of Turkification involved massive reorganization of Anatolia's population: forced removal of Greeks, Armenians, and other Christians; dispersal of non-Turkish Muslims (Kurds, Arabs) throughout the country; and incorporation of the hundreds of thousands of Muslim refugees flooding in from the Balkans. It seemed clear that the Armenians, regarded increasingly as a foreign blot that must be excised, should be pushed out to make room for the refugees.

The Unionists, as part of their involvement in World War I, decided to attack Russia, on their eastern flank. Most of the large concentrations of Armenian peasants in that area were apolitical,[14] but a minority of radical Armenians allied themselves with Russia in the hope that a Russian victory over Turkey would lead to an independent Armenian state. The Unionist war minister embarked on his Caucasus Campaign with dreams of becoming another Napoleon; instead, he suffered devastating losses at the battle of Sarakamish, losses he blamed on Armenian treachery. (In fact, Russia would have won the battle even without its relatively small contingent of Armenian allies.) It was probably at this point that the Unionist triumvirate began secret meetings to discuss cleansing Turkey of the Armenians.[15]

It would be difficult to overstate the chaos in Turkey in the spring of 1915, when the genocide started. Turkey had lost its Caucasus campaign at Sarakamish. It was fighting in World War I, and its European enemies had landed at Gallipoli, the country's most vulnerable point, strategically. The triumvirate, notwithstanding its visions of Turkish glory, had to face the reality that the Great Powers of the West might defeat them and carve up their country—and perhaps even make the Armenian lands autonomous. To them, this possibility was unacceptable. Desperate and enraged, they initiated expulsion and genocide of the Armenians. Part of the triumvirate's strategy was to empty Armenian homes for refugees from the Balkans and transfer Armenian wealth to the new Turkish middle class that they hoped to create.[16]

Turkey, just coming into being as a new nation, fit two conflicting models at once. It can be seen as an example of what the political scientist James C. Scott, in *Seeing like a State*, calls "authoritarian high modernism," in which a government actively tries to engineer a nation's population and other characteristics according to rational, scientific criteria.[17] Simultaneously, it fits Christian Gerlach's model of an extremely violent society.[18] At the time of the genocide, Turkey was simultaneously rational and chaotic.

The Unionists' first move in carrying out their plans against the Armenians was to round up Armenian leaders and intellectuals in Constantinople on the night of April 24, 1915—the date Armenians still commemorate as the start of the genocide. The Turks had already formed what they called (literally) a Special Organization, a semisecret, centralized structure with branches across Anatolia and ties to administrators in every province. Its branches, supervised by army officers, consisted of motley gangs of ex-convicts, gendarmes, Kurds, and refugees.[19] In April 1915, these local branches of the Special Organization received orders to march able-bodied Armenian men to the outskirts of their villages, force them to dig burial pits, and shoot them. After that, they dragged women, children, and the elderly from their homes and started them on a death march into distant deserts to the east.

On the deportation routes, Armenians were whipped along by men on horseback or abandoned by the roadside to starve or die of thirst; some were rowed into lakes and rivers and thrown overboard. Convicts who had been specially amnestied to join the Special Organization, along with Kurdish bandits and Turkish gendarmes, were encouraged to rape and pillage the deportees. Some Special Organization members sold young girls into sexual slavery; others permitted Turks to incorporate girls into their families or harems. While some Armenians who lived in Turkey's western cities escaped deportation, those who lived in the eastern provinces died horrible deaths in an ethnic cleansing that peaked during 1915 but lasted until 1923 and claimed over one million lives.

The Armenian genocide, due to the planful, systematic manner in which it was conducted, is often called the first "modern" genocide. That it achieved its goal so successfully, helping to create the new nation that the Unionists had dreamed of, is one reason why today Turkey persists in denying the genocide; its citizens are naturally reluctant to admit that their state was founded on atrocity.[20] Although Turkey itself, near the end of the slaughter, held trials and condemned the Unionist triumvirate to death (in absentia: the three pashas had fled), the genocide was committed, essentially, with impunity. In fact, it almost faded from memory, which is why Hitler encouraged his generals to invade Poland by asking, "Who, after all, speaks today of the annihilation of the Armenians?"[21]

The next section describes one of the genocides that Hitler unleashed three decades after the Armenian massacres: that of disabled people, the most vulnerable population in his domain. This "euthanasia" genocide, like the Armenian genocide, demonstrated high-modernist thinking at work in the way it sought to engineer the composition of a nation's

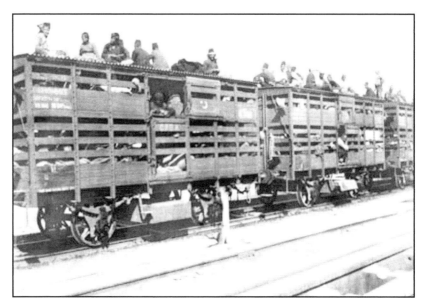

Figure 6.1. Ethnic cleansing during the Armenian genocide. The Turks forced many Armenians to traverse the deportation routes on foot, but they crowded other Armenians into cattle cars to make the journey eastward by rail.

Figure 6.2. Body of an Armenian woman. This Armenian woman was starved, raped, and decapitated on a deportation route near Bitlis, Turkey. Courtesy of Hasmik Grigorian, Library of the Armenian Genocide Museum-Institute.

population. And like the Armenian genocide, it involved creation of a genocidal organization to do the killings.

The Nazi Genocide of the Disabled, 1939–1945

Hitler's genocide of the disabled was an outcome of his belief in eugenics, the so-called science of improving good "stock"—and eliminating bad. He linked the vigor of Germany to Aryan purity and, by implication, to eugenic eradication of those whom he considered hereditarily impure. "The highest purpose of a folkish [people's] state," he wrote in *Mein Kampf*, "is concern for the preservation of those original racial elements which bestow culture and create the beauty and dignity of a higher mankind. We, as Aryans, can conceive of the state only as the living organism of a nationality which not only assures the preservation of this nationality, but by the development of its spiritual and ideal abilities leads it to the highest freedom."[22] Hitler began planning his "euthanasia" program as early as 1935[23] but cannily waited to implement it until 1939, when World War II had begun, calculating that complainers would have a harder time making themselves heard.[24]

The "euthanasia" program was kicked off with a "model" case of 1938 involving a severely deformed baby born to a family called Knauer; the father purportedly asked the clinic to kill the baby, but the clinic's director refused on the grounds that he did not have the authority. The father then appealed directly to Hitler; the Führer instructed various physicians, including his personal physician, Karl Brandt, to visit the child to pronounce a diagnosis. Brandt authorized "euthanasia," the baby was killed, and the killing of handicapped children began.[25]

Genocide of the disabled was anticipated by the sterilization law of 1933, mandating compulsory sterilization of people with mental and physical disorders. Then, in autumn of 1939, began the children's "euthanasia" program—a secret program run by the Reich Committee, a group of physicians including Karl Brandt who were invited to join and freely agreed to participate (although they used pseudonyms and other ploys to avoid identification).[26] The Reich Committee office distributed forms to hospitals, physicians, and midwives asking for the names of children under age three who suffered from deformities, mental illnesses, mental retardation, and other abnormalities. These children were transferred to asylums, if they were not there already, and killed with lethal injections or left to starve.

The "euthanasia" program owed its success not only to its ideological appeal but also to a variety of pragmatic and venal considerations. Disabled people filled hospital beds that, in the Nazis' opinion, were needed for wounded soldiers. There were also more insidious motives. Physicians who murdered handicapped children received bonuses when they reached their "quotas," were rewarded with research grants, and enjoyed considerable prestige in the Nazi hierarchy.[27] Their subordinates received generous liquor allowances to help them through their unpleasant work of killing helpless children, and sometimes they were allowed to keep the belongings of those they helped murder. Inspired by "career considerations and personal profit," the Reich Committee's physicians and psychiatrists, as the historian Henry Friedlander puts it, turned "mass murder into a profession."[28]

Rudolf Lonauer, the T-4 physician who headed the Hartheut Castle killing center near Linz, Austria, can serve as an example of those professionals. Born in 1907, Lonauer was in his early thirties at the time of his appointment and thus typical of the youthful cadre of physicians who became Nazi medical leaders.[29] He was already manager of an asylum for the mentally ill in Linz (it became a feeder institution for the Hartheim gas chamber) and head of the Department of Nervous Diseases at Linz Hospital. Lonauer's father was a founding member of the National Socialist Party in Linz, Hitler's hometown and a seedbed for Nazism, and Lonauer himself joined the party at an early age. He had a severely epileptic brother who by all rights should have been funneled to the gas chamber but, perhaps protected by Lonauer, died of natural causes during the war.[30] Lonauer and his wife, Maria Hoffer, another National Socialist, made a handsome couple, a local example of upwardly mobile Nazis as they strolled through Linz, she in furs and an elegant hat. Like other T-4 officials, Lonauer was paid by the head for those whom he consigned to "euthanasia." He enjoyed jaunts to the local concentration camp at Mauthausen, where he selected prisoners to be executed at Hartheim and partied with the institution's commanders.[31] In April 1945, just before the US Army arrived in Linz, Lonauer killed his wife and two small daughters, reportedly by injecting them with poison, and then committed suicide. Evidently he feared more than capture and a trial; it seems that his entire world had depended on National Socialist foundations and that once those gave way, he could not imagine a future for himself or anyone close to him.

By 1941, about 5,000 children had been murdered.[32] Faced by public opposition, Hitler ordered a stop to the adult euthanasia program, which included chronically ill adults, the blind, the deaf, and residents of old-age homes and almshouses; but thereafter the program actually expanded again to include criminals and other "asocials."[33] By then, the program was known as Aktion T4 after the street address of the Berlin villa that housed its offices.

As the T4 program grew, its medical directors looked for a more efficient means to kill. In the winter of 1939–1940, in a special chamber of a disused jail near Berlin, they conducted their first experiment with carbon monoxide gas. The method worked so well that six "euthanasia" killing centers were established throughout Germany and Austria; their mock "shower rooms," where victims were gassed, and crematoria became models for those later built at the infamous death camps. A number of officials who were trained in the killing centers subsequently ran the gas chambers at Auschwitz and other extermination centers.

Figure 6.3. Handicapped Jewish prisoners. The Nazi genocides included a program to exterminate the mentally and physically handicapped. Some of those who died were Jewish, but many were non-Jews from Germany, Austria, and Poland. Copyright United States Holocaust Memorial Museum. Courtesy of Robert A. Schmuhl.

The T4 program expanded yet again as the Nazis moved into Poland and western Russia, where patients in asylums were gunned down by the mobile killing units of another genocidal organization, the Einsatzgruppen. In April 1941, the pretense of killing the mentally and physically ill for eugenic reasons was dropped entirely, and a new operation, 14f13 (so named after a filing system), was initiated to get rid of concentration-camp inmates too debilitated to work. T4 physicians continued to participate by making the selections, however,[34] and the original "euthanasia centers" were now used to gas concentration-camp prisoners.

The fundamental motive for this genocide was specific and narrow. Whereas the Herero and Armenian genocides were partly concerned with territory, land was hardly at issue here. Rather, the disabled were considered foreign bodies within the "living organism" of the German nation, a biological problem that crossed national, ethnic, racial, religious, and even political boundaries. However, the Nazi genocide of the disabled did resemble the Armenian genocide in that it too was concerned with social cleansing and national identity.

The broad historical significance of the genocide of the disabled lies in its serving as a dry run for the Final Solution. The "euthanasia" killings, Friedlander writes, "were Nazi Germany's first organized mass murder, in which the killers developed their killing technique. They created the method for selecting the victims. They invented techniques to gas people and burn their bodies. They employed subterfuge to hide the killings, and they did not hesitate to pillage the corpses. . . . The killers who learned their trade in the euthanasia killing centers of Brandenburg, Grafeneck, Hartheim, Sonnenstein, Bernburg, and Hadamar [the six killing centers] also staffed the killing centers at [the extermination camps of] Belzec, Sobibor, and Treblinka."[35] For example, Franz Stangl, who later headed the Polish extermination camps of Sobibor and Treblinka, got his start at the Hartheim Castle "euthanasia" center in Linz, Austria.

The elaborate, highly rationalized, and bureaucratic killing machine created to carry out "euthanasia" of the disabled in its early stages forms the basis for one of the most original explanations of the Nazi slaughters: *Modernity and the Holocaust* (1989). In it, the sociologist Zygmunt Bauman argues that the Holocaust did not grow out of some dreadful social malfunction but grew out of the normal conditions of the modern world, including, notably, bureaucracy, the goals of rationality and efficiency, reliance on science (as in the "science" of eugenics), and disregard for traditional human values.[36]

Bauman's modernity thesis has been undercut by more recent studies exposing the ad hoc, irrational quality of the Nazis' planning and the fact that many of their killings took place not in "efficient" gas chambers but in savage and chaotic face-to-face encounters. But the modernity thesis does apply fairly well to the genocide of the disabled, which, in its early stages at least, was indeed meticulously planned, highly rationalized, and elaborately bureaucratic (including false paper trails to persuade families that their relatives had died natural deaths). Ironically, Bauman ignores the genocide of the disabled to focus on the Holocaust, but his modernity thesis—together with Scott's analysis of the "industrial-strength social engineering" of "authoritarian high modernism"[37]—fits better with the first stages of the "euthanasia" genocide than with most other aspects of Hitler's genocidal policies.

In all, at least 70,000 children were killed (or "disinfected," in the Nazis' euphemism) during the first phase of this genocide and 275,000 disabled adults murdered during its next phase. Perhaps another 20,000 people were killed during Operation 14f13, and thousands more were shot by Nazi officers in Polish and Russian hospitals and forests. The total murdered in this genocide of the mentally and physically disabled may have been as great as 750,000.[38] At the Nuremberg Doctors' Trials, after the war, twenty-three physicians were tried either for participating in the "euthanasia" program or for experimenting on concentration-camp prisoners. (Some did both.) Sixteen were convicted and seven hanged, but most personnel of this genocide went unpunished. Their victims, for the most part, remain unremarked even by specialists in Nazi history like Bauman, and for the most part they go unmemorialized. Today, however, some monuments are being erected in their memory, like the blue glass wall inaugurated in Berlin in 2014.

Genocidal Organizations

As shown by the examples of the Armenian genocide and of the disabled in Germany, genocidal states sometimes create specialized units to carry out their killings. In the Armenian case, the unit was the Special Organization—the officials who ran it and the network of gangs they mobilized to kill. In the case of the German disabled, the unit consisted of the group of physicians who planned the genocide—the Reich Committee (later T4)—and the medical personnel who actually committed the murders. In both cases, the genocidal organization was at least a semisecret unit—as it had to be, since its goal was to murder a large number of people without raising suspicions or objections. Other genocides in my sample also illustrate this tendency of genocidal states to establish a covert branch to carry out their work.

I considered the label "deviant organizations" to characterize these groups but rejected it due to the suggestion that the organization strayed from an originally legitimate objective, which is not the case with genocidal groups. I also considered the historian Charles Tilly's rather odd term "violent specialists"; but in his definition, the category consists of legitimate workers (military personnel, police, jailers, and so on),[39] and I wanted a name for illegitimate organizations. Nor did I like "criminal organizations": I wanted to explore ways in which genocidal organizations resemble organized crime, but neither "criminal organization" nor "organized crime" implies the exclusive focus on death work that is part of my meaning here. "Death squads" offered another possibility; but death squads are usually small (three or four members), and they kill relatively small numbers of people.[40] Insofar as genocidal organizations have been discussed in the scholarly literature, they have been called "paramilitary groups" or "state-sponsored militias."[41] But those terms do not cover all the types of murderous gangs that turned up in my sample.

I settled on the term "genocidal organizations," which I define as organizations dedicated to the mass killing of civilians or prisoners of war. Created expressly for this purpose, a genocidal organization is a group of people working together, following specific rules and performing specific functions, to do the work of genocide. A genocidal organization has "antisocial capital"—group resources mobilized for a destructive goal.[42] Borrowing a term from the work of the social psychologist Herbert C. Kelman, I define the work of genocidal organizations as "sanctioned massacres."[43] This is what genocidal organizations do: they use their antisocial capital to commit sanctioned massacres.

The criminologist Alex Alvarez was among the first to ask why genocidal states rely heavily on paramilitary militia groups when they have military and police forces readily available.[44] Alvarez identified the type of organization that I call genocidal organizations; he focused on fairly recent armed groups and events (Arkan's Tigers in the former Yugoslavia, the Interahamwe in Rwanda) and based his conclusions on these recent examples of paramilitary militias.

But Alvarez's observations apply as well to other kinds of genocidal organizations. He notes that paramilitary militias are "trained in violence, yet not bound by formal codes of conduct";[45] are looser and less formal in structure than regular military forces; and are created for the express purpose of engaging in collective violence. Their membership is fluid. Those who join are amateurs compared to trained soldiers, and many join for personal gain and profit. Regular militaries are formally connected to the state, but the relationship of paramilitary groups to the state is less clear:[46] states like to rely on them because their connection can be denied. Paramilitary groups often recruit young men (such as soccer fan clubs) who are drawn to violence. Such recruits are preorganized in the sense that they may already know one another, and if they live in a strife-torn area, they may be particularly vulnerable to indoctrination. For such recruits, "these organizations provide meaning, status, and a sense of belonging and identity."[47]

Writing at close to the same time as Alvarez, the criminologists Ruth Jamieson and Kieran McEvoy identified the same sort of phenomenon, which they called "state crime by proxy." States intent on violating international prohibitions against human rights violations and crimes against humanity, they write, use surrogates such as indigenous paramilitaries, mercenaries, and private contractors, thus making the task of prosecuting them more difficult.[48] My term "genocidal organizations" designates such state-crime proxies.

Examples of Genocidal Organizations

The Herero genocide. In the Herero case, the agent of destruction was the German army. Although not created for genocidal purposes, it *became* a genocidal organization after von Trotha issued his order of total destruction, at which point its goal became sanctioned massacres. While this army differs from other genocidal organizations in that it remained a formal organization, during the period of the massacres, its behavior was often ad hoc and unprofessional.[49] As a genocidal organization, it had two tiers, the supervising officers and the soldiers who did the killing.

The Armenian genocide. The Special Organization, created before the Unionists decided on a strategy of genocide but repurposed to that end, had two tiers. Its directors—the first tier—consisted of high-level Unionist officials who worked closely with the heads of local Unionist party organizations in each province and who gave orders to the second tier, which consisted of hundreds of armed gangs authorized to plunder and kill.[50] This two-tier Special Organization necessarily operated clandestinely because it was assigned to do illegal work that the government itself could not accomplish openly.[51]

The Nazi genocide of disabled people. In this case, too, the genocidal organization had two levels. The first consisted of the Reich Committee—

physicians who ran the secret program—while the second consisted of the institution-based physicians and other medical personnel who did the actual killing (or, in later stages, selected the prisoners to be gassed). This genocidal organization was unusually complicated, partly because it covered two entire countries (Germany and Austria) and included six killing centers and partly because of its bureaucratic complexity. The Reich Committee had to work with local health authorities and heads of institutions for the handicapped. It had to establish a Transport Office to bus children to their deaths and to supply lethal substances to physicians who preferred poisons to starvation. The killing centers required the services not only of physicians but also of SS overseers, secretaries, cooks, and crematorium workers. Other layers of bureaucracy were added when the T4 program expanded to include adults.

The Katyn Forest genocide. The genocidal organization in this case was part of the NKVD, Stalin's police force. The NKVD included the secret police and, under it, small groups of trained executioners. The secret police conducted the undercover interrogations of the Katyn prisoners and supervised the exile to Kazakhstan of the prisoners' families. It also closely monitored the executions through on-site supervisors who reported back to Moscow (sometimes twice daily) on the progress of the massacres.[52] Although these functionaries did not belong to an organization specially created to conduct the Katyn massacres, the two-tiered killing organization was roughly comparable to the genocidal organizations of the Armenian and Nazi atrocities.

The Indonesian genocide. The army was largely responsible for this genocide, although its work was aided by militias (which it subcontracted), by freelance vigilantes, and by civilian gangs. Although the army does not fit the definition of a genocidal organization—it was not created for this purpose and had other duties as well—the militias and civilian gangs that it mobilized, constituting a complex network of killing units, do fit the definition.[53]

The Cambodian genocide. In this case, the only group that might be described as a genocidal organization was the personnel of the S-21 prison. But S-21 bore little resemblance to the paramilitary groups analyzed by Alvarez. It was fluid in personnel, insofar as some of the guards were killed and then replaced, but it did not constitute a cohesive group whose members gained identity and status from working at the prison;

nor did the guards enter the work for personal gain or profit. Thus, I do not count it as a genocidal organization.

The Guatemalan genocide. In the Guatemalan case, too, there was no specific genocidal organization. The army directed the genocide, but it was not created for this purpose and had other responsibilities as well. The civil patrols that committed the Mayan massacres—small gangs that executed villagers and burned their houses—were temporary organizations that disbanded at the end of a massacre.

The Rwandan genocide. The Rwandan genocide involved a two-tiered genocidal organization consisting of a small, top tier of fanatics and a second, larger tier of militias and those who, out of fear or greed, latched on to them.[54] The top tier included leaders of the Hutu Power political party and other members of the *akazu*, the group that gathered around the wife of President Habyarimana. Disaffected with the president himself due to his apparent willingness to compromise with the Tutsi, these extremists published the incendiary Hutu Ten Commandments, funded the rabid Interahamwe militia, and supported the propagandist media station Radio Télévision Libre des Mille Collines. The Interahamwe began as a soccer fan club that provided food, drink, and companionship for purposeless, often homeless young men. The top-tier extremists gave these youths military training and indoctrinated them in the Hutu Power ideology, turning the Interahamwe into a hypermasculinized cult or pseudofamily.[55]

The Nature of Genocidal Organizations

Thus, six of my eight cases had a genocidal organization. Of these, four were two-tiered (five, if Katyn is included). In these two-tiered cases, members of the top tier managed and directed the genocide, while the second tier served as their instruments.

Irrespective of organizational complexity, these groups shared two characteristics: their gender composition and their confidence in impunity. They consisted almost entirely of men. There were two exceptions to this rule: the lower tier in the Nazi destruction of the disabled included nurses; and in Rwanda, the *akazu* included a few women. But the exceptions really prove the rule, for even these organizations were overwhelmingly male in composition. More important than the sex of the groups' members were their gender characteristics—the emphasis of most of them on fighting and masculinity and in some cases the permission they were granted to brutalize the enemy's women. As for impunity, even in genocides that lacked a special organization, perpetrators acted without fear of consequence. Individuals had various motives for committing genocide—the settling of scores, greed, fear, a desire to purify or defend their country, blind hatred, or (in the NKVD executioners' case) obedience to orders. But in every case, they believed they could get away with what they did. In most instances, they were right.

Genocidal organizations are similar in several respects to organized crime. Organized crime, like genocide, is criminal activity that occurs within a centralized enterprise run by criminals in order to break the law. Like genocidal organizations, organized crime usually has a dominant, formal structure that branches out into smaller gangs. In genocidal organizations and organized crime alike, the smaller units in the network are fluid in membership, and in both cases, one aim of participants at all levels in the hierarchy is financial profit or political gain. In both, the central group tries to protect the smaller units from prosecution. Thus, there are a number of resemblances that warrant calling genocidal organizations a form of organized crime.[56]

The main differences between the two types of organization lie in the nature of their work, the stability of the organization through time, and their relationship to the state. Genocidal organizations, while they often attract members through the promise of financial gain, have as their main goal the eradication of a population. When that goal is accomplished, they usually disband—unlike organized crime groups, which perpetuate themselves. While genocidal organizations are in operation, they are likely to work for the state—which is seldom the case with organized crime. Genocidal organizations are a form of state-organized crime.[57]

Criminologists have kept genocide at arm's length partly because it seems alien to their usual research. As this comparison shows, however, there are points of convergence. Genocide in fact bears many resemblances to other crimes insofar as it involves types of street-level offenses such as homicide, rape, and theft. It also involves the formation of genocidal organizations that are structured like organized crime. Moreover, some genocidal organizations, such as the Reich Committee and the NKVD, pursued their work in ways that resemble occupational and corporate crime, in which legitimate forms of work are perverted to criminal ends.[58] Genocide is not foreign to other types of crime but offers familiar territory for criminological exploration.

The Changing Nature of Genocidal Organizations

The nature of genocide has changed since World War II. In the first part of the twentieth century, genocide usually was committed by strong states, with little nonstate involvement (by, for example, freelance militias). But today genocide often occurs in weak states, under conditions of civil war or state failure. "In these cases," writes the political scientist Ariel Ahram, "the army and police have receded or collapsed, leaving violence in the hands of various competing insurgent factions and increasingly autonomous paramilitaries and extra-judicial groups."[59] Without denying that atrocities continue to be committed by strong states, Ahram holds that, increasingly, genocidal events are characterized by a state role that is "muted or indirect," while the role of militias becomes "far more prominent."[60]

In my terms, the nature of genocidal organizations is changing. Whereas in the first half of the twentieth century these organizations were usually mobilized and directed by a strong state and remained dependent on it, today genocidal organizations may be mobilized by independent rebel groups and other nonstate actors. Moreover, they are likely to be militias. This development, Ahram observes, has important implications for genocide prevention. Given the increasing role of militias in genocide, "preventing genocide means . . . peeling away militias from the coalition of violence. . . . International sanctions must be applied not only against states that sponsor non-state militias, but also against the militia leaders themselves."[61]

States of Exception and License for Impunity

As part of a genocidal regime's organization for destruction, it will formally or informally create a legal exception that makes the killings legal—or at least seem to be. This happened in all eight of my cases. The appearance of legitimacy gave the killers a kind of license for impunity.

In the book *State of Exception*, the Italian philosopher Giorgio Agamben draws attention to a peculiar phenomenon, a kind of legal "void" that makes violation of a state's laws seem legal. "The state of exception is neither external nor internal to the juridical [legal] order," Agamben writes, but is rather "a threshold, or a zone of indifference, where inside and outside . . . blur with each other."[62] Law is not abolished but suspended, "deactivated."[63] A state of exception need not be announced publicly and indeed usually is not; it can simply be created by the people in power to enable killers to do their work without hesitation.

A state of exception was introduced in various ways during the genocides in question. During the Herero genocide, it was simply assumed: the German authorities took for granted that international law did not apply to Africans, and the settlers did not believe that German national law applied to Africans.[64] The Herero, falling into one of Agamben's "juridical voids," had no legal protections against being slaughtered; moreover, those who slaughtered them had no fear of legal consequences, for as far as they were concerned, none existed. In the Armenian case, the Unionist triumvirate authorized the Special Organization to despoil, deport, and kill Armenians, an authorization that put the bands of killers beyond oversight of the parliament.[65]

The situation was different in Nazi Germany, where Hitler steadfastly refused to pass a law authorizing the "euthanasia" program, for such as law would make it public. Instead, he issued a secret authorization on his own letterhead ("as if mass murder was his 'private affair,'" quips Henry Friedlander),[66] stating that the leaders of the program "are charged with the responsibility of enlarging the competence of certain physicians . . . so that patients who . . . are considered incurable, can be granted mercy death after a discerning diagnosis."[67] "The letter," the historian Robert Proctor writes, "was not an order . . . but an empowerment . . . , granting physicians permission to act."[68] It guaranteed impunity. This letter was passed around among members of the Reich Committee and later among judges who, after getting wind of the program's existence, tried to investigate what had happened to wards of the court who had disappeared. The letter persuaded them, too, even though the killings were in fact against German law.[69]

Stalin simply issued an order for liquidation of his Polish prisoners. He and his close associates in the Politburo knew that the order vio-

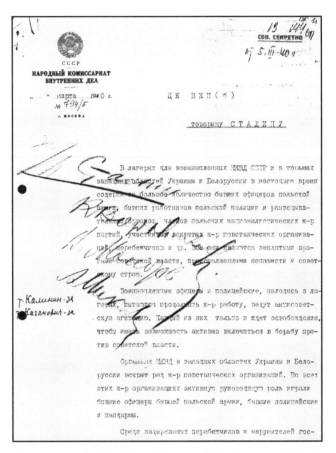

Figure 6.4. Document authorizing Katyn Massacre. This document of March 5, 1940, signed by Stalin and members of his Politburo, authorized extermination of the Polish prisoners held at Katyn and other Russian camps.

lated their own laws and the Geneva Conventions on treatment of war criminals, but in this case as in countless others, they felt free to act with impunity.[70] In Indonesia, Suharto ruled for thirty years on the basis of a law enabling the military to operate outside the law; thus, the army and its affiliates could arrest people on suspicion and kill them without trial.[71] In Cambodia, a state of exception was the rule of the land, for under Pol Pot, there were neither courts nor judges.[72] In Guatemala, Ríos Montt, brought to power by a military coup, suspended the constitution, dissolved the congress, and ruled by decree. He appointed himself president and commander in chief of the armed forces. When he so directed, civil patrols could kill Maya and others designated as state enemies without worrying about punishment.[73]

In Rwanda, as soon as the president's plane crashed, the order to kill Tutsi went out from the highest levels of government, delivered by the Hutu Power radio station. This led militia members to believe that killing Tutsi was not only lawful but patriotic: a way to demonstrate loyalty to the nation. Moreover, to disobey this order was to run the risk of being butchered oneself.[74] Thus, an informal state of exception encouraged the killers. Moreover, the government created what Human Rights Watch terms "a generalized environment of lawlessness" that "gave the militias full license to commit egregious human rights abuses, including rape and murder, with impunity."[75] This environment of lawlessness, too, signaled a state of exception. Empowered by law (an apparent government order) on the one hand and lawlessness on the other, Hutu were given every reason to commit genocide.

* * *

The creation of genocidal organizations, contrivance of a state of exception, and assurance of impunity: these are three of the pillars on which twentieth-century genocide was built. They are the main ways in which states mobilized for destruction. But even as states deliberately mobilized, taking calculated steps to destroy their enemies, their planners drew on ideas about gender—masculinity and femininity—of which they were not even conscious, on taken-for-granted notions about the nature of men and women that powerfully shaped their conscious calculations. Chapter 7 explores the role of gender in genocide.

7

Gender and Genocide

The Rwandan Genocide, 1994

The term "sex" is usually used to refer to the biological characteristics that differentiate women and men, while "gender" is usually used to speak of femininity and masculinity, meaning the various roles that societies assign to women and men. "Gender" refers to socially constructed relationships, experiences, and expectations that are *associated* with sexual characteristics but in fact differ from group to group, culture to culture, man to man, woman to woman, and across time.

Every culture has a sex-gender system spelling out who cares for the children, who does the farming, who drinks in the evening at the local pub or bar—and who goes to war. We can define "masculinity" and "femininity" as ideal types within a culture or across cultures, observing that across cultures masculinity is usually associated with soldiering and femininity with child care. However, even within a single culture, those ideal types will vary across households and individuals. There are multiple genders—even within a single culture.

Gender—even though it is a major structural factor in genocide—did not play a prominent role in the genocide literature until recently. Perhaps it was slighted because it seems less important than ethnicity, state failure, war, and other macro factors; and certainly—if one is not attuned to it—gender is easier to overlook. Gender is invisible even in some reports on Rwanda, where women played key roles in planning the genocide and where gender strongly shaped decisions about who would be killed and how. Gender also tends to be invisible in research on the aftermaths of genocide, again even in Rwanda, where after the killings, huge numbers of Hutu men either fled the country or were imprisoned, leaving Hutu as well as Tutsi women to assume important functions in government and the country's reconstruction. "Women" and "gender" are not the same, but once the social roles of women in genocide are recognized, gender follows close behind.

The same is true of men and their gendered roles in genocide. Usually, men's genders too are invisible, in peace and in war. We tend to *assume* that men are those who do the fighting, run the governments, commit the crimes, and get killed in battle or mass murder of civilians. But the political scientist Adam Jones has introduced the term "gendercide" to sensitize people to the gender-selective nature of mass killing. "Noncombatant men have been and continue to be the most frequent targets of mass killing and genocidal slaughter," he writes, "as well as a host of lesser atrocities and abuses."[1] The Katyn Forest Massacre provides an excellent example: all the victims (but one) were men because the Russians rounded up Poles who were active in the military and police or who were members of the intelligentsia—roles not available to women, although one tends to *assume* women's exclusion, rather than thinking of gendercide. Katyn was a highly gendered genocide, but the way it was shaped by gender is obscured by our of-course assumptions about gender roles.

Later in this chapter, I look at gender variations in behavior and victimization during genocide, but first, I want to establish a foundation of conclusions about gender and genocide on the basis of my sample. According to my data, during genocide, men tend to enact or "accomplish" extreme forms of masculinity through murders and rapes, while women, "doing" gender in traditional ways, by and large avoid violence or become victims. I draw the terms "accomplish" and "doing" from an influential article by Candace West and Don Zimmerman, "Doing Gender," which sees gender "as a routine accomplishment embedded in everyday interaction." "Doing gender," these authors argue, "involves a complex of socially guided perceptual, interactional, and micropolitical activities that cast particular pursuits as expressions of masculine and feminine 'natures.'"[2] My basic argument in this chapter is that gender is also accomplished during the—far-from-everyday—interactions of genocide. Those who "do" gender during genocides, like those who "do" it in everyday interactions, organize their activities to express gender, albeit often in extreme forms.

In this chapter, I address three fundamental questions about gender and genocide. First, in what ways is genocide a gendered event? How is it gendered for victims? For perpetrators? (Here I also discuss gender differences in empathy.) Second, what does it mean to say rape is genocidal? Increasingly, scholars talk about rape as an instrument of genocide. But when is rape genocidal, and what are the purposes and meanings of genocidal rape? Third, how does international law define and punish rape during genocide? Does it deal adequately with this phenomenon, or should international law be changed to deal more effectively with the gendered aspects of genocide?

I address the questions in this order, but before I start, I review the Rwanda genocide of 1994, a powerful example of how gender and genocide interact. With details of the Rwandan genocide at hand, one can more easily find answers to the three central questions.

The Rwandan Genocide, 1994

The 1994 Rwandan genocide shocked the world through its horrific, and highly public, violence. Whereas most mass murderers since von Trotha had tried to keep their genocidal intentions quiet, if not secret, the men and women who mobilized the Rwandan genocide literally broadcast their intentions: hate speech against Tutsi, transmitted by radio as well as newspapers, became a means of recruiting perpetrators. Once the genocide began, appalled observers around the globe followed the violence over television and radio in something close to real time. Further shocking was the refusal of the United Nations and United States, either of which might have been able to stop the genocide, to intervene. Their apparent indifference gave the perpetrators confidence in impunity and led to the deaths of over one million people in a mere three months.[3] Also distressing was the genocide's sexual violence—the Hutu use of rape and sexual mutilation to destroy Tutsi women. At least 250,000 women were raped, some by carriers of the AIDS virus who intentionally infected their victims.[4] Other rape victims included men and the onlookers—including family members—who were forced to witness the rapes.

In the background lay a failing state. President Juvénal Habyarimana's regime began to implode in the late 1980s. The economy of Rwanda—a small country, no larger than Vermont—was based on agriculture; but landholdings became fragmented as fathers subdivided lots for sons upon marriage. Rwanda had the highest population density in Africa, with 305 persons per square kilometer (less than half a square mile) just before the genocide,[5] and almost half of the population lived in extreme poverty.[6] Young people could not marry because sons could not get land to support themselves and a family.[7] "It was as if Rwanda was plunging free fall into a nightmare," writes the government professor Mahmood Mamdani.[8]

Also in the background lay the secondary status to which women were relegated in pregenocide Rwanda. *Shattered Lives*, a report issued by Human Rights Watch just two years after the atrocity, detailed ways in which the markedly patriarchal society created a context for violence against women. "Within Rwandan society, women have traditionally been regarded and treated as dependents of their male relatives. Throughout their lives, women are expected to be managed and protected by their fathers, their husbands and their male children. Traditionally, the role of a Rwandan woman in society has centered around her position as wife and mother."[9] Girls were prepared for lives as submissive wives and mothers. Wives were valued by the number of children they bore, and female children were valued less than boys. Women frequently experienced domestic abuse. "The Rwandan government," the *Shattered Lives* report continued, "estimates that one-fifth of Rwandan women are victims of domestic violence at the hands of their male partners. One Rwandan proverb states that a woman who is not yet battered is not a real woman."[10]

Relations between the two main ethnic groups, the Hutu and Tutsi, were deteriorating as Hutu leaders deliberately racialized their differences. Actually, "reracialized" might be a better word, for racial framings of these ethnic differences went back to the days of Belgian colonizers and may have originated with them.[11] The two groups are nearly identical in language, appearance, and culture, and they intermarry. One Rwandan recalled when he was a schoolboy: "They used to tell us to stand up, when they told Tutsi to stand up, I did it and when they told Hutu to stand up, I stood up also. My teacher . . . gave me a small letter that I had to take to my parents. There was written that they had to explain me clearly about my ethnic group."[12] Neither the schoolboy nor his teacher could tell which group he belonged to. Hutu treated the Tutsi, who constituted 10–15 percent of the population,[13] as second-class citizens. Power-sharing efforts by Hutu President Habyarimana—halfhearted though they were—frustrated the extremist Hutu Power group. This faction nursed grievances from decades earlier when Tutsi ruled Hutu. Moreover, although the two groups' physical differences were often indiscernible, Hutu extremists resented the attribution of more "European" characteristics (such as greater height and more delicate features) to the Tutsi. The journalist Philip Gourevitch tells a story about a Tutsi friend, a physician named Odette. When Hutu arrived at the hospital to arrest her, they made a mistake. "I had a colleague who had the same name," Odette told him. "She was Hutu and she denied that she was me, but she was much taller than I am and they said, 'There's only one Tutsi doctor named Odette.' So she was imprisoned and tortured, and in 1994 she was again mistaken for a Tutsi, and killed."[14] The extremists, moreover, had built up a mythology about the sexual superiority of Tutsi women, a folklore that heightened the vulnerability of these women to rape.

In the years preceding the genocide, Hutu periodically butchered groups of Tutsi in genocidal massacres that went unpunished, encouraging further impunity. In 1990, a Tutsi army, the Rwandan Patriotic Front[15] headed by Paul Kagame, appeared on Rwanda's northern border, threatening to invade and rescue Tutsi from these predations. Many Hutu were frightened by the prospect of invasion and loss of their governmental dominance. At first, Kagame's army did little, partly because the United Nations persuaded the two sides to sign a power-sharing peace agreement, the Arusha Accords. However, the accords drove the Hutu Power faction into a new frenzy of hatred. "Mobilization for the final extermination campaign," Gourevitch remarks, "swung into full gear only when Hutu Power was confronted by the threat of peace."[16]

Hutu Power financed formation of the Interahamwe militia and operation of several news outlets, including the radio station, Radio Télévision Libre des Mille Collines (RTLM), and the newspaper, *Kangura*, which spewed anti-Tutsi propaganda, encouraging moral disengagement and thus starting the splitting process that makes genocide psychologically possible. These media pushed open an ever-widening gulf between Hutu and Tutsi, stressing the notion of Hutu identity. Popular songs with anti-Tutsi lyrics were broadcast from RTLM and blasted through public-address systems during athletic events.[17] *Kangura*, deriding Tutsi as *inyenzi*, or "cockroaches," printed the "Hutu Ten Commandments" (quoted in chapter 4). These strongly gendered and racialized orders— they assumed a male audience that would be sexually attracted to Tutsi women—branded as "traitors" Hutu men who had contact with Tutsi women (even as secretaries) and demanded that every Tutsi public servant be replaced by a Hutu.[18] "*Kangura* . . . was the first and most virulent voice of hate," according to one report. "Although it had a relatively small circulation of approximately 10,000, *Kangura* was distributed to the local burgomasters and actively supported by powerful government and military patrons. . . . *Kangura* often warned the Hutu to be on guard against Tutsi women. According to *Kangura*, 'the *Inkotanyi*'" (meaning "fierce fighter" in Kinyarwanda and referring to the Rwandan Patriotic Front) "'will not hesitate to transform their sisters, wives and mothers into pistols' to conquer Rwanda."[19]

Leon Mugesera, a Hutu Power leader, told a 1,000-person meeting that the Tutsi "belong in Ethiopia": "We are going to find them a shortcut to get there by throwing them into the Nyabarongo River. I must insist on this point. We have to act. Wipe them all out!"[20] Mugesera offered a role model of someone who had completed the splitting process and was ready for genocide.

When on April 6, 1994, President Habyarimana's plane was shot down, killing everyone on board, the Hutu Power faction invited the army to take over the government; when moderate Hutu resisted, the extremists killed them and assumed power. At the same time, the Rwandan Patriotic Front resumed its invasion. Paul Kagame, the leader of the invading Tutsi army and, after the genocide, Rwanda's president, has since been accused of engineering the downing of Habyarimana's plane.[21] In any case, with the invasion, Rwanda was fighting a civil war in the midst of a genocide. (The civil war had begun in 1990, with the massacres of Tutsi and appearance of Kagame's army on Rwanda's northern border. This army, which did its share of killing and terrorization, gave Hutu a strong motive for fearing a Tutsi takeover of the government and killing Tutsi.)[22] Interahamwe militia members, using lists of names and addresses prepared by the extremists, began killing Tutsi and moderate Hutu in the capital city, Kigali. Soon they fanned out into the countryside, helping local officials compile lists of those who should be killed.

Knots of young men—militia members, soldiers, police officers, and ordinary citizens—gathered at crossroads to create roadblocks. People could not pass without showing an identity card defining them as Hutu or Tutsi. These cards, a relic of Belgian colonialism, proved to be a death sentence for Tutsi. Hutu would pull them aside and slaughter them or, if they were female, rape and then kill them. If there were too many people to murder all at once, the Hutu would slash their Achilles tendons so they could not run away but had to lie in the roadway, watching the massacre until their turn came. With the killers often inebriated, the atmosphere mixed hysteria with glee. Some victims paid bribes for a quick death.

In rural areas, militia members would organize a village's men, show them how to kill, and set them to work. "Many people did not know how to kill," a Hutu later explained to the French reporter Jean Hatzfeld,

> but that was not a disadvantage, because there were *interahamwe* to guide them in their first steps.
>
> At the beginning the *interahamwe* came in by bus from the neighboring hills to lend a hand.
>
> They were more skilled, more impassive. . . . They gave advice on . . . which blows to use, which techniques. . . . They used their spare time to initiate those who seemed uneasy with this work of killing.[23]

Hutu who did not want to participate—and they were numerous—were forced to do so with threats of fines or death and with promises of being able to loot the victims' property. Some who killed were terrified of a Tutsi takeover.[24] Even so, some Hutu helped Tutsi hide and successfully resisted participation.

Tutsi fled to churches for protection; Hutu would wait until a church was full, then surround it and go on a killing spree. Some victims were impaled; others were forced to have sex with close relatives and then kill them; pregnant women were eviscerated; men were emasculated; women had their breasts sliced off and sticks or machetes shoved into their vaginas. Some women were abducted and gang raped for days or weeks. Tutsi women who most resembled their stereotype (small noses, long fingers) had their noses and fingers chopped off.[25]

Estimates of the number of Tutsi killed vary widely, but the number slaughtered may have been about 750,000, or three-quarters of Rwanda's

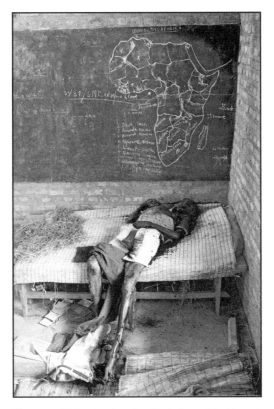

Figure 7.1. This schoolteacher lies below a blackboard
on which he had posted a map of Africa. He was one
of hundreds killed in the village of Karumbamba in
May 1994. Associated Press (photo Jean-Marc Bouju).
Reprinted with permission.

Tutsi population.[26] Perhaps 250,000 Hutu were also killed, because they
either were married to Tutsi, looked like Tutsi, tried to protect Tutsi, or
refused to participate in the genocide.

The genocide ended about three months after it began, when Kagame
and his invading Tutsi army reached Kigali and took over Rwanda's
government.[27] Almost immediately, the United Nations set up its International Criminal Tribunal for Rwanda (ICTR), on which over the
next decade it spent well over $1 billion,[28] trying seventy-five people
and creating an International Residual Mechanism to deal with final
appeals and fugitives' trials when it shut down in 2015. Because it was

impossible to prosecute everyone who had a hand in the genocide, the UN went after only the main offenders, meting out a number of life sentences. Rwanda itself tried and executed at least twenty-two people for genocide-related crimes, but it abolished its death penalty in 2007 to encourage other, non-death-penalty nations to extradite Rwandan fugitives for trial before the ICTR. Other offenders, too, were tried in Rwanda's court system, but even after it had sent 120,000 men to regular prisons, it still had a huge backlog of cases to deal with.

To handle the backlog of about two million cases,[29] Rwanda set up a supplementary system of *gacaca* (pronounced gah-CHA-cha) courts based on informal traditional justice, run by trained local people and aimed at a combination of retributive and restorative justice. The *gacaca* system, in operation from 2001 to 2012, could mete out sentences of life in prison but was less punitive when the accused confessed, and indeed, the majority of its cases were property crimes settled by fines.[30]

None of the three court processes was entirely satisfactory, but impunity had ended—at least for Hutu.[31] People who committed genocide were punished. The Tutsi invaders, however, also killed civilians—perhaps as many as 60,000[32]—and they were not brought to trial.

Genocide as a Gendered Event

In twentieth-century genocides, perpetrators were almost exclusively male, due to the traditional composition of armies, militias, and other fighting groups. As long as genocide is framed as a battle against an enemy—and how else could it be framed?—it will probably continue to be a predominantly masculine pursuit. Women do participate as perpetrators, but in small numbers and generally in conformity with their group's gender roles. Men and women are both victims of genocide, but because they are usually victimized in different ways and may die at different times, we need to redefine how we count the victims of genocide, as I explain in more detail in the following sections.

These generalizations about the gender identities of perpetrators and victims play out somewhat differently by genocide; each event is driven by its own assumptions about gender, and in each, men and women enact gender in different ways.[33] Generally, however, whereas gender stereotypes motivate some men to fight, they make women more vulnerable to victimization.

The Gendering of Genocide in Rwanda

The Perpetrators

Several scholars have studied gender among the perpetrators of the Rwandan genocide. Adam Jones, the scholar who introduced the concept of "gendercide" or gender-selective mass killing into genocide studies,[34] looks at the "gender crisis for younger Hutu men," who in the early 1990s were landless and unemployed and thus lacking prospects for a better future or marriage.[35] Militias and the work of genocide solved these men's problems, giving them a purpose in life, power, drinking buddies, and a sense of camaraderie. "You can get free beer," one recruiter said. "Come with us tomorrow [to kill Tutsi] and then you can join us at the bar."[36] Jones quotes another Rwanda scholar, Gérard Prunier, who observes that for marginal Hutu men, "the genocide was the best thing that could ever happen to them. . . . They could steal, they could kill with minimum justification, they could rape and they could get drunk for free. This was wonderful."[37] Jones and Prunier both maintain that the Hutu Power leaders who engineered the genocide (perhaps, it now appears, with the help of Kagame)[38] took full advantage of this crisis in masculinity.

Another author, Jean Hatzfeld, through interviews with men imprisoned for rape and murder of Tutsi, produced a graphic picture of masculinities in a soccer group that played and drank together before the genocide, swung their machetes together during the genocide, and went to prison together thereafter. "We no longer saw a human being when we turned up a Tutsi [hiding] in the swamps," one prisoner told Hatzfeld. "The hunt was savage, the hunters were savage, the prey was savage—savagery took over the mind. Not only had we become criminals, we had become a ferocious species in a barbarous world."[39] These killers assumed the masculine hunter role of their ancestors.

The women who participated in planning, promoting, and organizing the genocide included Agathe Habyarimana, the president's wife, around whom a group of Hutu Power politicians gathered; their group was sometimes called the *akazu* (little house) and sometimes the "zero net-work," since its goal was a Rwanda with zero Tutsi. Another activist was Pauline Nyiramasuhuko, minister for family welfare and the advance-ment of women under Habyarimana, who with her son trapped Tutsi in a stadium, where they were raped, tortured, and killed, some by being set on fire. Agathe Habyarimana managed to avoid prosecution, thanks to protection by officials in France, to which she fled at the genocide's start; but Nyiramasuhuko, the first woman convicted by the ICTR, was sentenced to life imprisonment—for genocide and incitement to rape— with eligibility to apply for parole after twenty-five years.

Local women, too, participated as perpetrators. Some looted the bodies and homes of dead Tutsi; some told militia members where Tutsi were hiding; some encouraged their sons and husbands to kill.[40] But in their case as in that of more prominent women, their roles as perpetrators were sharply curtailed by codes of gender in the highly patriarchal society of Rwanda. In all ways, women were treated as in-feriors; they were not even allowed to inherit land. (This rule created major problems after the genocide, when the wives of husbands who had been killed could not obtain title to the family land.) Their sec-ondary status helps explain why relatively few women participated as perpetrators and why, when they did participate, they played limited roles.

This secondary status also helps explain why many Hutu women took roles as bystanders to the genocide, watching as the violence ignited and burned through their villages. However, like bystanders to other geno-cides, they were not morally neutral. As Hollie Nyseth Brehm writes, "If women were feeding their husbands at night despite knowing that they were gone during the day killing Tutsi, what does that make them? Per-haps not perpetrators, but . . . not completely innocent either."[41]

Two sources of systematic data speak to women's participation in the genocide as perpetrators. The economist Philip Verwimp, in a sample of 1,838 Rwandans, found that less than 10 percent of adult perpetrators were women, but he gives no further breakdowns on their offenses.[42] More recently, a criminological team has drawn conclusions from con-victions in Rwanda's *gacaca* courts—a total of over 1,068,000 cases by the time these courts closed down.[43] Ninety-one percent of the cases had male defendants. Women constituted about 11 percent of the looting defendants but only 5.5 percent of the murder defendants—meaning that when women were involved, they committed relatively minor crimes. Women tended to receive more lenient sentences than men for crimes in the same categories—perhaps due to differences in offense severity. Thus, these researchers, like everyone else who has investigated the issue, conclude that the vast majority of those who committed crimes during the Rwandan genocide were men.[44]

The Victims

The Rwandan genocide's notoriety for mass rape can lead one to overlook the many other forms of sexual violence suffered by its victims, including, according to an analysis of victims' narratives, harassment, threats, having breasts or other body parts beaten, forced nudity, witnessing sexual violence against others, molestation, mutilation, and forced abortion. One victim was terrorized by merely hearing about sexual and other violence: "It was also another form of torture, they would come and say to me, We killed Aime, we stripped her naked and paraded her through the Round-About. . . . They said they took the pastor's wife naked from church and paraded her through the Round-About, your relative Masamaza, they said, has been crucified at the Round-About."[45] Another reported mutilation:

> They lay her down, took a spear, inserted it in her and stirred it in her. They first kneaded her body as if helping her to give birth. Because of fear the baby came out. We thought that they were helping her to give birth so as to separate her from the baby.
>
> When the baby was half way out, they sent a spear upwards and stirred until when the spear came out of the mother's mouth.[46]

A man reported a forced abortion: "And there was a woman who was pregnant. She was a very fine woman and good shaped and I wonder if there is any other woman in Rwanda like that woman. They laid her body down and operated on her stomach and removed the baby with a spear. For God's sake, I never forget the memory of that woman."[47]

Nor should one overlook male victims of sexual violence. It is impossible to gauge the number of the victims because Rwandan men, like their counterparts elsewhere, are extremely reluctant to report sexual victimization. Kristin Bell, from whose analysis of victims' narratives I have just quoted, was given access to a nonrandom sample of seventy-two Rwandan victims, of whom thirty-three were male. Some of these men reported being held in sexual slavery. While most reports of sexual slavery came from women, "the Rwandan sample also included a young man who had been in sexual slavery and raped by several women," Bell writes. "These women referred to him and another man as their husbands and said the men were there to 'fulfill their needs.'"[48] This victim recalled of his captors, "One of them got of a piece of cloth and another one tied me here and they started raping me. Then as days went on, they could drug me and then [I] started to enjoy it."[49]

Despite exceptions, it seems clear that rape was the most serious form of sexual violence during the Rwandan genocide and that Tutsi women were its most frequent victims. In retrospect, the mass rape of Tutsi women seems almost inevitable. One risk factor was the inferiority of women generally in pregenocide Rwanda: disempowerment made them vulnerable to sexual violence from the start.[50] Tutsi women were particularly vulnerable because they were objectified as sexually desirable, if remote and disdainful of Hutu men. Moreover, part of the planning for the Rwandan genocide involved circulation in the media of sexualized stereotypes of Tutsi women; one female government official was depicted (like the Gerwani women during the Indonesian genocide) having sex with multiple partners simultaneously.[51] "Tutsi women were made for sexuality and beauty, for royal courts," a journalist explained to a Human Rights Watch investigator. "That's how we were educated. People from the north, where there were few Tutsi, wanted to take Tutsi as mistresses because they were forbidden to have them. Tutsi women were seen as spies because they know how to present themselves to whites and to Hutu men, so they became an arm of the RPF [Kagame's army]. Hutu understood the propaganda. It was time for revenge."[52] These gender and ethnic stereotypes further diminished empathy with Tutsi women and increased their objectification. For Hutu men, it became easy to think of raping them.

Rape victims were picked for their beauty, age (many were young girls), and sometimes politics (as when during the genocide Hutu women were raped in punishment for protecting Tutsi); but the main reason was the intersection of gender with Tutsi ethnicity. According to the Human Rights Watch report on sexual violence during the Rwandan genocide, most of the women interviewed reported that their rapists used ethnic hate language:

> Rape survivors recounted comments such as: "We want to see how sweet Tutsi women are"; or "You Tutsi women think that you are too good for us"; or "We want to see if a Tutsi woman is like a Hutu woman"; or "If there were peace, you would never accept me." When asked why rape was so widespread, one Rwandan woman . . . said, "Hutu men wanted to know Tutsi women, to have sex with them. Tutsi women were supposed to be special sexually." Other women noted that their attackers said, "You Tutsi girls are too proud," apparently setting the stage for their degradation.[53]

As these snippets of language show, the rapes were motived more by revenge than desire.[54] They were also motivated by determination to establish power and dominance over the victims as both women and Tutsi. Rape has always been a tool for constructing masculinity as a gender of potency and control, with the right of subjugation.[55] In the Rwandan mass rapes, Hutu violators simultaneously asserted their right to destroy women and to reconfigure Rwanda as a country without Tutsi. And they hammered home the framing of Hutu men as masculine.

Intent to harm is further demonstrated by the nature of the rapes. Women were seldom, if ever, raped in private by a lone attacker but rather suffered mass rapes in highly public settings.[56] Some rapists used sticks, machetes, and boiling water to ruin the women's reproductive organs.[57] Some deliberately infected their victims with sexual diseases, including AIDS, and deliberately impregnated them. Many women were tortured as well as raped; some were kidnapped and held in houses where groups of men raped them until they died or were killed. The public nature of the rapes worked to torment not only Tutsi women but also Tutsi men, many of whom were forced to witness violence against family members that they were incapable of preventing. That these rapes were destructive in intent is further shown by the fact that most Hutu women were spared. Here we see a key difference between genocidal rape and "ordinary" rape: the former is explicitly designed to destroy the victim and her group. It is intended (as Daniel Feierstein argues about genocide in general) to reconfigure society.[58]

Male and female victims suffered similarly during the Rwandan genocide, but they also suffered differently. Both met deaths of great cruelty, but many of the women were also raped before death. Women who survived rape often had to cope with sexually transmitted diseases, and those who were impregnated—somewhere between 2,000 and 5,000 of them—had to cope with bearing "hate babies."[59] Stigmatized for giving birth to these infants, some women committed infanticide, while others abandoned the children; but most kept them, living with these constant reminders of what they had suffered.[60]

In genocides in which the men are killed and the women raped but allowed (in at least some cases) to survive, men experience the most violent crime of all—murder—while the women experience less lethal violence but suffer for a longer time. This is an important gender difference in genocide. It raises two issues: how do we count genocide victims, and how do we determine a genocide's endpoint?

Traditionally, the victim count in genocide was based on the number of people who died immediately or soon thereafter; in other words, in cases where the women were raped but allowed to live, the figure tended to be biased toward male victims. This traditional tallying method led to miscounts of the total number of victims and ignorance of the impact of gender on such atrocities. "Acts that do not result in death have not been taken seriously in estimating the toll of victims by students of genocide," writes the genocide scholar Helen Fein.[61] We need to find new ways to count genocide's victims, one that goes beyond "the hegemonic focus on killing"[62] to include both victims who outlive the immediate violence and those harmed by gender-based atrocities.

We also need to find a new way to date the termination of genocides. Do they end when genocidists call it quits? When the last victim dies? When, as in Rwanda, the last child born to a mother with AIDS dies? It is tempting to look for a figure that can be determined relatively simply; but it is fairer to count all those who die as a consequence of genocide, regardless of the time of death in relation to the event.

Gender in Other Genocides

I have been analyzing gender dimensions of the Rwanda genocide, focusing first on the perpetrators and then on the victims. But how did gender affect other genocides in my sample? I have less information on them—Rwanda, aside from the Nazi atrocities, is probably the most studied genocide in history—but enough information is available to assess, at least in outline, ways in which gender fed into the other genocides. They were quite different from Rwanda, and they varied greatly among themselves.

A sense of affronted masculinity colored the reactions of the German high command when it removed its Southwest African colony from civilian control and put it under Lieutenant General Lothar von Trotha. If the Herero revolt were not crushed, writes the historian Isabel Hull, Germany would not seem to be a true colonial power. In addition, a quick victory seemed necessary "to demonstrate absolute German military superiority, because the military . . . had become synonymous with monarchical stability, social discipline, and Germany's future as a prosperous Great Power."[63] This concern for military prowess and invincibility characterized German reactions throughout the genocide. Von Trotha issued the extermination order not for any military advantage—he had already defeated the Herero—but because he and his superiors in Berlin were worried about Germany's self-presentation as masculine: firm, tough, and unyielding. Declaring and executing genocide were gendered actions—a nation's way of "doing" gender.

In the case of the Armenian genocide, the tactics of the ruling Committee on Union and Progress reflected the complexity of late Ottoman attitudes toward gender. While the Unionists had Armenian men (the ones who might fight back) shot in their villages, they designed a different policy (deportation and death at the hands of the Special Organization's gangs) to get rid of Armenian women, children, and the elderly. In other words, patriarchal protectionism prevented the Unionists from having women shot with the men, but their hatred of Armenians enabled them to find another, backdoor approach to murdering the women and their dependents. Noteworthy too is the complexity of feelings about gender among Ottomans who took Armenian children into their homes to save them from deportation and death. Although protectionism played a role in this kind of assimilation, so too did predation, because adopted girls were often forced to join harems or marry their Ottoman saviors. Some ran away a year or two later, even abandoning babies to escape.[64] Young boys taken into Turkish families experienced sexual violence in the form of forced circumcision, which served to subjugate them in several ways: they were feminized by the very experience of sexual violence, and they were robbed of a sign of their Armenian identity.[65]

In signing the death order for the 22,000 Poles exterminated at Katyn, Stalin enacted a version of masculinity. His most explicit concerns were to increase the power of the Soviet Union and minimize resistance to his takeover of eastern Poland. Such military strategizing and willingness to kill characterize an ideal, warrior type of masculinity, as does war making more generally. However, Stalin showed none of the grandstanding authoritarianism of, say, von Trotha; his style of masculinity was more secretive and wily.

The Nazis' secret "euthanasia" program was organized by men and run by them, according to the gender division of work under the Nazis, who stressed domesticity for women and public roles for men.[66] One woman—Herta Oberheuser, the physician at the Ravensbrück concentration camp—was included in the Doctors' Trial, held at Nuremberg after World War II to try medical personal involved in the "eugenics" program and in medical experimentation on humans. (She received a twenty-year prison sentence, was released early for good behavior, and resumed medical practice but had her license revoked after she was recognized by a Ravensbrück survivor.) But during the Nazi extermination of the disabled, women mainly assisted doctors as they starved children to death or injected them with poisons. These were nurses who worked in institutions with pediatric "clinics"; like the physicians, nurses received extra pay for murdering disabled children.[67] Killing did not require a break with their usual, gender-dictated duties: feeding the ill (or, in this case, not feeding them), giving injections, taking orders from doctors. The historian Henry Friedlander quotes from a US intelligence report written just after the liberation of the Kaufbeuren "hospital" in Bavaria, where disabled children were killed: "The perpetrators or passive collaborators involved were in no way conscious of their crimes; they were *Germans* and not *Nazis*. Among them were Catholic sisters.

The chief nurse who had confessed without coercion, that she had murdered 'approximately' 210 children in the course of two years by intra-
muscular injection, asked simply, 'will anything happen to me?'"[68] She
had merely done as the doctors had instructed.

Shifting gender roles were both cause and effect in the Indonesian
genocide. That women—particularly members of the Gerwani or communist women's movement—were becoming more active in the public
sphere deeply alarmed conservative men, including the Muslims who
formed a predominant sector of the population. As chapter 4 showed,
the genocide included a violent backlash against these shifts, with Gerwani women and even women who had no links whatsoever with the
communist party being raped, sexually mutilated, and murdered.

The mythology of the deviant communist woman helped fuel the
genocide, as shown by the following account of one woman, Ibu D:
"After raping me, they herded me down the street completely naked,
walking towards the police office that was about five kilometres away.
All the time the blood was flowing out of (D points to her genitals).
Along the road, people shouted out, screaming at me. 'Communist
woman! Kill her! Cut up her body, just like she cut up the Generals!'"[69]
This myth survived until the end of Suharto's presidency, writes the
sociologist Saskia Wieringa: "Long after the Partai Kommunis Indonesia . . . was destroyed . . . , the spectre of communism—especially in
relation to women—was still called up to justify the harsh repression of
any democratic anti-government forces in the country. . . . The 'woman'
was no longer defined as a comrade in the revolutionary struggle; under
the New Order, she was a submissive wife and devoted mother. General
Suharto became the super-patriarch as father of the development family he wanted his New Order state to become."[70] Suharto's repression
of several generations of "communists" reshaped gender roles, driving
women back into the home and consolidating men's hold on public activities. Only with Suharto's resignation did the rigid gender roles of his
era begin to relax.

In Guatemala, the genocide was committed by soldiers or militia members enacting an extreme version of masculinity through a
scorched-earth policy. They used rape to destroy the Maya, morally,
physically, and culturally. Soldiers, after invading a village and raping
the women, would sometimes thereafter require the women to cook a

meal for them, thus further humiliating the victims. "By invading their homes, their bodies, and their work," the historian Virginia Garrard-Burnett observes, "the military was able to demonstrate that it fully dominated even the most intimate spheres of the women's worlds."[71] When survivors became pregnant through rape, they were ostracized; later, their children were rejected socially.[72] This unraveling of their community strengthened Ríos Montt's program of destroying Mayan independence. It contributed to the reconfiguration of Guatemalan society that Ríos Montt aimed at.

The situation was somewhat different in Cambodia, where the Khmer Rouge had declared that women would be equals. Women did participate as perpetrators in the genocide, but they tortured and killed less frequently than men did (for instance, there was apparently just one woman interrogator at the S-21 prison),[73] and they were not well integrated into the country's power structure. Until very recently, there was little evidence of rape during the genocide; but with the indictment of key perpetrators, starting in 2007, discussion of victimization has become more widespread in Cambodia, and more evidence of rape may come to light.[74]

In sum, genocidal groups enact extreme forms of masculinity in which they are all-powerful and invincible, and their organizations are strong, comradely, patriotic institutions.[75] In different ways, all of the genocidal groups examined here reinscribe through their behavior— albeit in diverse ways—the belief that women are inferior to men, and they sometimes reinforce that view through violence against women.[76] Genocidal action often—but certainly not always—reflects a sense of ownership of women, of females as objects with which (if one is male) one can do as one pleases.[77] The main perpetrators of genocide are men, with women playing small or nonexistent roles; when women do participate, their roles are closely related to gender definitions in their larger social field. Genocide, my data show, is *always* a gendered activity. Symbolically, genocidal rape feminizes the victim group (including men who are raped or otherwise sexually violated), demonstrating its powerlessness, while at the same time it masculinizes the victors.[78] The gendering of genocide accomplishes shifts in social power, helping to achieve the perpetrators' goals of reordering society.

Just as individuals create the meanings of gender through daily inter-actions, so too do nations. We are not used to thinking of nation-states as entities that "have" or "do" gender, but even this brief examination of eight genocides shows that the actions of nations, like those of individuals, construct gender attributes and roles. Through victimization, genocidists masculinize themselves and feminize the victims—regardless of the victims' sex or genders. Gender is indeed omnirelevant, as West and Zimmerman claimed in their famous article,[79] and in the case of genocide, the dominant gender is extreme masculinity—not surprisingly, since so often the nation during genocide is represented by its militias or army. However, even the nature of these extreme masculinities varies from nation to nation and genocide to genocide, as gender is constantly re-created by new interactions.

Gender and Empathy

To participate in genocide, as chapter 5 showed, one must switch off empathy, the ability to share the feelings of others. Do women and men differ in their capacity to empathize? If so, this might help explain men's greater participation as perpetrators in genocide.

Every study of this matter concludes that women do have a greater capacity to empathize than men do. The capacity seems to be neurological in nature and may well be evolutionary in origin,[80] although it varies greatly by context. Women score higher than men do on questionnaires measuring empathy, and girls and women respond more empathetically to the distress of others. By the age of three, girls are ahead of boys in their ability to infer what others are thinking—an important first step in empathy. Girls are more concerned with fairness, while boys are more competitive. Related is the fact that throughout the world and across eras, girls and women have had lower crime rates, especially for violent crime.[81]

The classic neuroscientific experiment in this area, described in detail in chapter 5, is that reported by Tania Singer and Claus Lamm in 2009. Both men and women responded empathetically when a player whom they liked (because he had previously played fairly) was in pain. However, men did not respond empathetically when they saw a player whom they disliked (because he had previously cheated) in pain; women did.[82] Singer and Lamm hesitate to state definitively that women have a greater capacity for empathy because the evidence is not yet all in; but their study suggests that this is the case.

Men and boys may have more reasons to rein in empathetic responses. We know that empathy depends on context; for instance, Singer and Lamm report that "being in a competitive gaming relationship results in counterempathetic responses."[83] That males sometimes find themselves in competitive or dangerous situations is illustrated by Elijah Anderson's study of violence and morality in a US inner city; this study, also described in depth in chapter 5, demonstrates that young men living in rough, impoverished ghettos learn "codes of the street" that provide security. "Imbued with the code of the street, they either don't know the rules for decent behavior or may see little value in displaying such knowledge."[84] This purely sociological study, like Singer and Lamm's neurological study, indicates factors that may mute males' empathy and make it possible to objectify and harm others. (It would be interesting to know whether military training has a similar effect.) Weak or nonexistent empathy may go part of the way toward explaining why men are more likely than women to be genocide perpetrators. Gendering in the broader society may help create genocidists who then reinforce the society's gender codes.

What Is Genocidal Rape?

The UN definition of genocide, listing only "national, ethnical, racial or religious groups," does not include women as one of the collectivities with whose destruction it is concerned. Yet recent atrocities have made it clear that genocidists *do* aim at destroying women as a group, not necessarily by killing them but by immobilizing them psychologically and reproductively, thus making reproduction of the larger group to which they belong physically and culturally impossible. To be sure, the UN Genocide Convention does recognize *acts* that can help in the prosecution of mass rape: "causing serious bodily or mental harm to members of the group; deliberately inflicting on the group conditions of life calculated to bring about its physical destruction in whole or in part; [and] imposing measures intended to prevent births within the group."[85] However, it does not protect women "as such."

The 1990s genocidal events in the former Yugoslavia and Rwanda demonstrated to the entire world that women "as such" can be destroyed by genocide and crimes against humanity.[86] The Serbs' rape camps (eventually deemed to have constituted crimes against humanity, not genocide) and the vast scale of rapes by the Hutu, together with horrific sexual mutilations by both groups, proved beyond question that rape was used to destroy targeted groups. Scholars began calling this kind of behavior "genocidal rape."

"Genocidal rape" is mass rape aimed at destruction of the victim group—not just the immediate victims but the larger group to which they belong. We might prefer the term "state rape," coined by the criminologists John Hagan and Jaimie Morse.[87] "State rape" is a better term in that it indicates the usual source of the violence; on the other hand, it is not necessarily linked to genocide, and not all genocidal rape is committed by states or in states. Another possibility is "wartime rape," the term preferred by the legal theorist Laura Sjoberg. Sjoberg sees "wartime rape" as an act that feminizes the victim and the victim's group, regardless of the biological sex of the perpetrator or victim. In her interpretation, through sexual violence, the raping group masculinizes itself, and the raped group is humiliated through feminization.[88] Although Sjoberg's reading of the symbolism of wartime rape is enlightening, not all genocides occur during war, and thus, I prefer the term "genocidal rape." Moreover, "genocidal rape" is clear about both the cause and effect of the violence.

In the traditional "spoils of war" or "biblical" model of genocide, the nature and purpose of mass rape are unclear, but in any case, they are irrelevant because the deaths of the men and the culture matter most. We still know little about the history of genocide, but it is becoming clear that the traditional model took a male viewpoint, in which what happened to the women was not paramount.

Using the data assembled for this book, one can construct a partial history of genocidal rape dating back to the early twentieth century. After the Herero had lost their war with Germany, remnants of the tribe, mostly women, were sent to a concentration camp on Shark Island, off the southwestern coast of Africa—wet and very cold in climate. The prisoners called it "Death Island" due to the high mortality rates from malnutrition (the Germans underfed the prisoners), exposure to the elements, and exhaustion from heavy labor. Female prisoners were frequently raped,[89] but these rapes were casual and opportunistic, not intended to destroy the group. Thus, they cannot be classified as genocidal rape. They were the *result* of a social reconfiguration, not the cause of it.

In the Armenian genocide, on the other hand, rapes of women on the deportation routes *were* genocidal, part of the overall plan for the Special Organization to rid Turkey of Armenians. Rape is not relevant to the genocides of disabled people by the Nazis or the Polish soldiers at Katyn, because there are no reported rapes for either.[90] During the Cambodian genocide, at least one female prisoner in the S-21 prison was raped, and "hundreds of thousands of victims" were forced to marry "in order to breed the new revolutionary progeny";[91] but as yet, there is no evidence of systematic rape of the ethnic and religious groups targeted by the Khmer Rouge.[92] In Indonesia, in contrast, rape was widespread during and after the genocide of 1965–1966; because the sexual violence aimed at destroying communists as a group, it was genocidal. Similarly, the rapes of Mayan women during Guatemala's genocide of 1981–1983 aimed at group destruction.

Thus, there were at least four twentieth-century genocides in which rape was used systematically to put the victim group out of existence— four instances of genocidal rape. The traditional spoils-of-war model applies only sporadically. Mass rape was no doubt genocidal in earlier times as well—and in other twentieth-century genocides not covered in this study.[93]

Firm conclusions about the causes of genocidal rape cannot be drawn from my small sample, but it is noteworthy that a key difference between the four genocides that included it (Armenia, Indonesia, Guatemala, and Rwanda) and the four that did not (Herero, Nazi extermination of the disabled, Katyn, and Cambodia) lies in state failure or extreme social instability. In the cases where rape was *not* used systematically to destroy the targeted groups, the state had not fully collapsed. In the cases where rape *was* used systematically to destroy the target group, state failure was at hand (Turkey/Armenia and Rwanda) or the state was experiencing the extreme social instability that usually precedes state failure (Indonesia and Guatemala).

In cases where rape *was* used systematically, moreover, it was constituted as a tool of nation building. Gendered violence was part of the project of forming a new, ethnically homogeneous nation. Sexual violence established dominance not only over the women of the targeted group but also over the men who were helpless to prevent it—and who, perhaps, had themselves been sexually victimized.

Genocidal Rape in International Law

Recognition of genocidal rape in international law took place against a background of over forty years of national and local campaigns for rape law reform that involved, first, making the distinction between sex and gender and, second, recognizing that law itself could be gendered.[94] The traditional law of rape was gendered in that it worked to protect perpetrators and discourage victims from pressing charges. It defined rape as unlawful carnal knowledge by a man of a woman by force and against her will, excluding husbands and requiring forcible penile penetration of the vagina. Rape was framed as essentially a crime of theft—of a man's property: his wife or daughter.[95]

Starting in the 1970s, rape law reformers sought to change nearly every element in this definition. They objected to the law's depiction of rape as a crime of theft from a man. They also objected to its requirement of consent ("against her will"), which forced victims to prove they had not consented to being victimized. Traditional rape laws essentially put victims on trial by allowing investigations of their past sexual history to show that they *might* have consented. These laws were blind to male victims, and they did not cover any kinds of sexual violence other than penile penetration of a vagina.[96] Reformers realized that the traditional law was less concerned with sex than with gender—that it contributed to the construction of men as owners of women and of women as likely false accusers. Rape law reformers and, gradually, legislators came to understand that rape law should be degendered—made sexually neutral and fair.

More recently, the crime of rape has again forced a rethinking of gender and criminal law, this time in the arena of international law against genocide. The new reform movement took place against the backdrop of earlier genocide litigation.[97] At the Nuremberg Military Tribunal (1945–1946), jurists relied heavily on documents rather than victim testimonies that might have brought women into court—or at least given them a say in the charges.[98] Moreover, the tribunal's charter made no mention of sexual violence. Nuremberg's successor, the 1946 International Military Tribunal for the Far East (the "Tokyo Tribunal"), did a better job of addressing sexual violence, but it was still selective in its inclusion of gender-based crimes, ignoring, for instance, the sexual slavery of thousands of "comfort women."[99] Not until the establishment of criminal tribunals for the former Yugoslavia (1993–2014) and Rwanda (1994–2014) was rape treated as a crime in its own right in international criminal trials.[100]

The International Criminal Tribunal for Rwanda (ICTR) did the most to shift the understanding of rape from an inevitable by-product of war to a weapon of war, in part through its redefinition of rape and sexual violence: "The Chamber defines rape as a physical invasion of a sexual nature, committed on a person under circumstances which are coercive. Sexual violence, including rape, is not limited to physical invasion of the human body and may include acts which do not involve penetration or even physical contact. . . . Threats, intimidation, extortion and other forms of duress which prey on fear or desperation may constitute coercion."[101] This innovative definition broadens the focus from rape to sexual violence of any sort. It does not require penetration or even mention body parts but merely speaks of "physical invasion of a sexual nature." It does not even require physical contact, so that sexual violence includes, for example, forcing parents to watch while militiamen gang-rape their daughter. In addition, it says nothing about consent but rather speaks of "coercion" and the context of conflict in which the sexual violence occurred.

However, not until 1998, with the first-ever conviction of genocide by the ICTR, was sexual violence recognized as potentially integral to the destruction of a group. The defendant, Jean-Paul Akayesu, a prominent local official in the Rwandan prefecture of Gitamara, was charged with thirteen counts relating to genocide, crimes against humanity, and war crimes. Akayesu pleaded not guilty to the counts of sexual violence and rape, claiming "that he never heard of them and considers that they never even took place."[102] This was not the most plausible position to take in the wake of the Rwandan genocide, already notorious for vicious and widespread rape. Numerous witnesses contradicted Akayesu. The ICTR concluded that rape and sexual violence are

Figure 7.2. Jean-Paul Akayesu, an official in the Rwandan prefecture of Gitamara, was tried before the ICTR on thirteen counts related to sexual violence. He was convicted of genocide—the first such conviction ever—and of crimes against humanity. His case also established that sexual violence can be "an integral part of the process" of genocide. Associated Press (photo Jean-Marc Bouju). Reprinted with permission.

one of the worst ways of inflicting harm on the victim as he or she suffers both bodily and mental harm. . . . Acts of rape and sexual violence . . . were committed solely against Tutsi women, many of whom were subjected to the worst public humiliation, mutilated, and raped several times, often in public, in the Bureau Communal premises [where Akayesu worked] or in other public places, and often by more than one assailant. These rapes resulted in physical and psychological destruction of Tutsi women, their families and their communities. Sexual violence was an integral part of the process of destruction . . . of the Tutsi group as a whole.[103]

Akayesu was convicted of genocide and crimes against humanity. The *Akayesu* court was able to break so radically with traditional definitions of rape and recognize Tutsi women as the target of genocidal gender violence partly because one of the three judges, Navanethem Pillay, was a feminist.[104]

The feminist legal theorist Catharine MacKinnon suggests that the legal definition of genocide might be revised to add sexual collectivities to the protected groups (national, ethnic, racial, and religious) and sexual violence to its present list of acts (killing members of the group, causing them serious physical or mental harm, and so on).[105] The social historian Daniel Feierstein, without naming women, argues that we *must* revise the UN definition to be fair to all groups that might be victims of genocide. "By focusing on the character of the victims, the 1948 Convention violates the principle of equality before the law, giving human life a relative rather than an absolute value. By restricting genocide to four groups (ethnic, national, racial, or religious), it creates a differentiated (that is, nonegalitarian) law. A planned and ruthless crime is only recognized for what it is if the victims share certain characteristics and not others."[106] In the name of justice, then, the UNCG should be revised to get rid of named categories entirely and redefine genocide as *the execution of a large-scale and systematic plan with the intention of destroying a human group as such in whole or in part*."[107] It might even be good to omit the list of specified *acts* (killing, seriously harming, preventing births, and so on) that can constitute genocide and open the definition to *any* act designed to destroy a group. However, if the list of acts is retained, MacKinnon is certainly right in urging inclusion of "sexual violence" among the acts that constitute genocide.

To ensure more just treatment of genocidal sexual violence, the International Criminal Court (ICC) now has the 2002 Rome Statute, which gives the ICC jurisdiction over genocide, war crimes, and crimes against humanity. For genocide, the statute adopts the UN definition, repeating it word for word with no changes; under "war crimes," it includes rape and other sexual violence during armed conflicts.[108] Its definition of "crimes against humanity" reads as follows:

1. For the purpose of this Statute, "crime against humanity" means any of the following acts when committed as part of a widespread or systematic attack directed against any civilian population, with knowledge of the attack:
   (a) Murder;
   (b) Extermination;

(c) Enslavement;

(d) Deportation or forcible transfer of population;

(e) Imprisonment or other severe deprivation of physical liberty in violation of fundamental rules of international law;

(f) Torture;

(g) Rape, sexual slavery, enforced prostitution, forced pregnancy, enforced sterilization, or any other form of sexual violence of comparable gravity;

(h) Persecution against any identifiable group or collectivity on political, racial, national, ethnic, cultural, religious, gender as defined in paragraph 3, or other grounds that are universally recognized as impermissible under international law, in connection with any act referred to in this paragraph or any crime within the jurisdiction of the Court;

(i) Enforced disappearance of persons;

(j) The crime of apartheid;

(k) Other inhumane acts of a similar character intentionally causing great suffering, or serious injury to body or to mental or physical health.[109]

The definition of "crimes against humanity" in the Rome Statute goes beyond the Genocide Convention by specifying crimes of sexual violence and referring specifically to gender persecution. However—and this is an enormous "however"—it does not define these crimes of sexual violence and gender persecution as genocide. Many onlookers applauded enactment of the Rome Statute, which does indeed give to sexual violence "attention . . . unprecedented in the history of international criminal justice."[110] "The decision of the ICC Statute's drafters to include a specific reference to gender crimes is a defining moment in history," writes the lawyer Mark Ellis, "and an indication of how far the issue of women's human rights has progressed."[111] However, the Rome Statute continues to define rape in terms of penetration, "however slight,"[112] turning its back on the *Akayesu* court's more enlightened concept of sexual violence, which does not require physical contact. And, most importantly, it does not recognize genocidal rape.

Thus, despite tremendous progress, those who drafted the Rome Statute failed to deal with an outstanding issue in genocide prosecutions:

that of genocidal rape. This is not "just" a women's issue; it is a failure to recognize one of the major targets of genocide—and a key means of achieving genocide.[113] Mass rape not only mainly targets women; it debilitates the target group and furthers genocidists' goal of social reorganization. There is only one way to address this problem: rewriting the UN's Genocide Convention so as to erase the language about specific victim groups and leave open the matter of which groups can be targeted for genocide.

* * *

Gender colors the conduct of genocide from start to finish, irrespective of whether the event involves genocidal rape. But how does genocide get to that finish line? How do these events end? This is the fundamental question addressed in chapter 8.

8

How Do Genocides End? Do They End?

The Guatemalan Genocide, 1981–1983

Little research has been done on *how* genocides end or *why*. More time has been spent discussing the moral obligation to stop genocide than on understanding how and when atrocities unwind. Ending genocide through intervention is actually very difficult.[1] Two examples of seemingly effective intervention—the Allies' victory over Germany in World War II and Vietnam's defeat of the Khmer Rouge in 1979—took place against states that were already disintegrating. Moreover, in neither case was the intervention motivated by a high-minded desire to stop genocide; rather, the Allies and Vietnam wanted to topple regimes they opposed.[2] Nor are these cases typical of the endings of genocides in general.

As criminologists know from experience with individual offenders, ethical considerations have little to do with the actualities of desistance from crime. When stickup men give up their careers and juvenile vandals outgrow crime, their reasons have little or nothing to do with morality. Similarly, in analyzing how genocides end, we need to concentrate on the "is," not the "ought"—on how genocides actually deescalate and end, not on the fact that they *should* be terminated.

In addition, we need to be careful with the definitions of "end" and "stop." With genocide, one cannot assume that termination points are easily fixed or mean the same thing to everyone involved. Too often, beliefs about genocide's endings are burdened (as two authorities ruefully observe) "by expectations that all good things go together—concluding conflicts and instability, rescuing civilians and achieving a new, more just dispensation."[3] Just as genocide itself is a process, not an event, so too are its endings processes. In genocide, one can expect, at best, fuzzy endings, ragged conclusions.[4] This becomes obvious when one recalls Daniel Feierstein's analysis of genocide as a technology of power aimed at social reorganization. As he writes, genocide "is a process that starts long before and ends after the actual physical annihilation of the victims, even though the exact moment at which any social practice commences or ceases to play a role in the 'workings' of a society is always uncertain."[5]

A further issue concerns the kind of typology that is most useful and appropriate when analyzing the terminations of genocide and other atrocities. I present two, the first a political typology keyed to perpetrators' experiences, the second a typology of cessation based on my sample and keyed to victims' experiences. Different typologies enable us to address different questions.

In what follows, I discuss these typologies and then turn to the story of the Guatemalan genocide, using the example to show how difficult it can be to fix the endpoint of a genocide. The Guatemalan example also demonstrates—if demonstration be needed—that root social and political causes must be addressed before a genocide can truly be called an event of the past. The chapter's final section, on how genocides reverberate through later generations, identifies ways in which genocides linger on, festering without healing. Here I examine victims' continuing—endless, really—sense of injustice and the personal and political emptiness that genocides leave in their wake.

The Endings of Genocides: Two Typologies

A Political Typology

A team of specialists in international relations—Alex de Waal, Jens Meierhenrich, and Bridget Conley-Zilkic—has proposed a fourfold political typology based on perpetrators' experiences of the terminations of mass atrocities.[6] First, some perpetrators halt their violence when they meet their goals; for example, Suharto ended Indonesia's genocide when he had wiped out the communist opposition. De Waal and his colleagues hold that this kind of ending—goal achievement—is typical of colonial and settler genocides;[7] and they persuasively classify the Guatemalan genocide as (in part) a settler genocide, even though the settlers arrived four centuries earlier.

Second in this typology, perpetrators desist from committing atrocities when they become exhausted or when their campaign is splintered by dissention. Here the analysis by de Waal and his colleagues coincides with that of the historian Christian Gerlach, who offers not a typology but a concept of termination based on his analysis of genocide as conflict among broad coalitions of violent groups, each aimed at a different victim and each multicausal. These coalitions come together, according to Gerlach, and then break apart in kaleidoscopic fashion.[8] De Waal's team illustrates this type of ending with examples of several campaigns, such as a 1992 military campaign in Sudan that ran out of steam due to exhaustion and bickering among the leaders. In criminology, this type of termination is called "aging out"—the offender simply grows too old and tired to commit more crime.

Third in this typology is the ending that occurs when victims flee or otherwise resist the atrocity. A good example is Rwanda, where Paul Kagame's Rwandan Patriotic Front, made up of Tutsi refugees in Uganda, ended the Hutu genocide by invading and marching through the country to its capital city, Kigali. The fourth kind of termination identified by de Waal and his team is that of outside intervention, as when the Allies defeated Nazi Germany and the Vietnamese the Khmer Rouge. But as noted earlier, the main motive of the interveners in these cases was not to stop genocide.[9]

All genocides in my sample fit into one of these categories, indicating that the de Waal typology is fairly comprehensive. The majority fit into the first division, of goal achievement: not only Indonesia and Guatemala but also the genocides of the Herero, the Armenians, and the Poles at Katyn ended when the aggressors had achieved their goals. Only one of the genocides in my sample fits into the second division, that of exhaustion or splintering of the perpetrator regime; Cambodia, having devoured its own resources, in part falls here. (Pol Pot had murdered so many of his top military leaders that the country could not fight off Vietnam. Moreover, having killed off the educated classes and skilled workers, he had destroyed all potential for productivity in his country. Cambodia had "aged out" of genocide.) One example, Rwanda, falls into the third category, that of a genocide that ends because it is stopped by fleeing or resistant victims, and two (Cambodia, again, and the Nazi genocide of the disabled) fall into the final category of outside intervention. That Cambodia fits into two of the de Waal divisions indicates that the categories are not mutually exclusive. Perpetrators end atrocities or succumb to defeat for a variety of political reasons, sometimes several at one time.

One type of ending, genocide by attrition, does not come up either in the de Waal discussion or in my sample. This kind of ending, if one can call it such, is typical of colonial and settler genocides, which stretch over long periods of time and work through slow death and assimilation of the original population. The genocide scholar Helen Fein points out that genocide by attrition also occurs in situations in which a group is stripped of its human rights and gradually disappears through hunger and sickness.[10] Her examples are the Warsaw Ghetto (1939–1943), an atrocity within the Holocaust in which large numbers died of starvation and disease; the Cambodian genocide of 1975–1979 (which also fits into other categories, as discussed earlier); and the decimation of people in South Sudan by war and disease (1983 and following).[11] As a category, genocide by attrition is shaped by sensitivity to the victims' rather than the perpetrators' point of view; it should not be confused with the second category in the de Waal typology, exhaustion and splintering, which refers to desistance on the part of the perpetrators.

With a Bang or a Whimper? Types of Cessation

One purpose of this book is to investigate what genocides look like—whether they follow typical patterns and, if so, what those are. In what follows, using my eight examples, I create a typology of ways in which genocides come to a close.

The genocides in this sample display considerable variety in the processes through which they reached closure. Some knifed off, ending with the proverbial bang; others petered out, ending with a whimper; and one merely dipped below the level of genocide, without a real end to violence.[12]

Five of my eight genocides ended neatly, knifing off with a specific termination date:

- *The Nazi genocide of the disabled.* Due to public outcry against "euthanasia," Hitler issued a stop order in August 1941. However, the genocide went on sub rosa, expanding from the initial children's "euthanasia" through adult "euthanasia" to the 14d13 program in concentration camps.

The program ended with Germany's surrender to the Allies in early May 1945.

- *The Katyn Forest Massacre.* This secret genocide ended with the execution of the last Pole, in May 1940.[13]
- *The Indonesian genocide.* When Suharto took over the country's government in March 1966, establishing his own regime, genocide of the nation's communists (actual and suspected) ended.[14]
- *The Cambodian genocide.* This genocide ended on January 7, 1979, when Vietnam, which Pol Pot had foolishly attacked, invaded Cambodia and defeated the Khmer Rouge.
- *The Rwandan genocide.* Defeat of the Hutu and takeover of the government by the Rwandan Patriotic Force, in mid-July 1994, ended this genocide.

In these five cases, then, the genocides came to a clear, dateable halt, either through victory by invaders or goal achievement by the atrocity's leaders. Sporadic killings often followed the end dates: as if riding an unstoppable train, staff at the German state hospital at Kaufbeuren went right on murdering children for nearly a month after Germany's surrender,[15] and in Rwanda, some Hutu continued killing Tutsi after the Hutu government was overthrown. However, the deaths in such cases were relatively few in number.

Two genocides fit a petering-out model:[16]

- *The Herero genocide.* Even in defeat, this genocide did not come to a sharp end. After losing the decisive Battle of Waterberg, some Herero escaped into the desert, and several thousand managed to reach South Africa or Batswana. Later, von Trotha delivered his extermination order, and later still, when he rescinded it, the remaining Herero (mainly women and children) were moved to Shark Island and other concentration camps. About 50 percent died there before the camps were shut in 1907.[17] Thus, the genocide subsided over a period of three years.
- *The Armenian genocide.* This atrocity played out in successively smaller waves of persecution over a period of years. First came the immense expulsion of 1915 that set Armenians struggling eastward toward the Syrian desert. According to one estimate, no more than 15 percent of the deportees made it to Syria, and many of those died soon thereafter of disease or starvation.[18] A second wave of killings began in 1917, when Armenians

who had taken refuge in Russia were forced by the fall of the Russian government to migrate southward back into Turkey. Another 250,000 Armenians died during this phase of the genocide, many from starvation.[19] Massacres resumed in 1920–1921 as the new Turkish parliament tried to finish what the Unionist government had begun: extermination of all remaining Armenians.[20] Tens of thousands were killed during those years, with more succumbing through persecution and hunger until 1923.

Yet in the politically confused period between the end of World War I in 1918 and establishment of the Republic of Turkey in 1923, the Turks also took steps to indict the Unionists for murdering Armenians. The historian Taner Akçam's research shows that during this period, many Turks condemned the Armenian deportations, at least in hindsight.[21] Thus, Armenian massacres after 1920 did not bear a simple relationship to the massive genocide of 1915. Politically as well as temporally, the Armenian genocide reached a messy conclusion.

My final case, the *Guatemalan genocide*, ended so indecisively that it cannot even qualify for the petering-out category. Data collected by the Catholic Archdiocese of Guatemala show a marked rise and fall in violent crimes just before and after the period 1981–1983—the years of the genocide—and a concentration of this violence in Maya-occupied areas of the country.[22] Ríos Montt, who presided during most of this period, was ousted in August 1983, after which the successor regime reined in the level of violence. In addition, after Ríos Montt's departure, insurgents and counterinsurgents alike deescalated their struggle, although high levels of military violence remained the rule until the peace accords of 1996 formally ended the civil war in which the genocide was embedded. Thus, "sometime in 1983" is the closest one can come to pinpointing the termination of this genocide, which subsided—not to the level of calm seas but from hurricane force to a severe storm.

Even in cases with clear cessation dates, the ending of genocide is never a sudden halt. The Allies' defeat of the Nazis took time, as did the Vietnamese invasion of Cambodia and the Tutsi takeover of Rwanda. Katyn's ending was most "bang"-like in my sample, since it involved nothing more than bulldozing earth over the final burial pit; yet due to the Soviet Union's cover-ups, confusion over the Poles' fate tormented the victims' families and indeed the entire Polish nation for the next fifty years. In Indonesia, descendants of the murdered communists were punished into the third generation. Forgotten land mines killed Cambodians decades after the genocide there ended (indeed, they are still exploding), and for years after the Rwandan genocide, Hutu and Tutsi continued to fight in the Democratic Republic of Congo. The processual character of these events is even more obvious in genocides that peter out and starker still in the case of Guatemala.

Analogously, individuals do not desist from crime quickly. As they contemplate desistance and then struggle through it, individuals and states alike have to plan for a different kind of future, worry about repercussions from those they have harmed, and square their decision to quit with former partners in crime.[23] Like individual criminals, genocide's perpetrators weigh the pros and cons of desistance, considering their reputation (as Germany did when it rescinded the Herero extermination order), seizing an opportunity to at least seemingly reform (as Turks did in the early 1920s), and stalling in order to cover up past crimes (as the Soviets did with Katyn). In these and other cases, genocidal groups have to think about their old and new identities, just as individuals do in the process of desistance.[24] Like organized crime, some genocidal states in effect go underground, expediently lowering their levels of violence (Indonesia, Guatemala)—at least until the storm of criticism blows over. Others stop committing genocide only because they are "caught" (the defeats of the Nazis, Khmer Rouge, and Hutu).

Conversely, impunity serves as a red flag, goading actual or potential genocidal groups to increase their violence. Extermination of the Herero may have encouraged next-generation Germans to employ genocide as a solution to apparent problems. (In fact, the probability of generational transmission can be documented: Heinrich Goring, who had worked in Southwest Africa making land treaties with the Herero, was the father of Hermann Goring, one of Hitler's closest associates; and Eugen Fischer, who studied eugenics in Southwest Africa, passed the doctrine of racial purity on to Hitler. Moreover, the concentration camp, first used by Germans during the Herero genocide, became a major tool of genocide in the Nazis' genocides.) Had Turkey been punished immediately after World War I for what it had already done to the Armenians, it would not have continued to massacre them until 1923. Assured of impunity after the genocide, the Indonesian military continued to commit violent crimes against those whom they considered enemies. Moreover, the Indonesian military's impunity after the 1965–1966 genocide likely encouraged it to commit genocide (or at least genocidal massacres) against East Timor during the period 1975–1999. And in Rwanda, a series of Hutu massacres of Tutsi in the years leading up to the genocide went unpunished. Why should militant Hutu have thought that extermination of *all* Tutsi would have different consequences?

$$* \quad * \quad *$$

The way genocide is evolving makes it necessary to reconceptualize the very idea of endings and closure. Whereas genocide used to be a crime between nation-states or large ethnic groups, today it has evolved into a crime that occurs within weak states, with warring militias and other nonstate actors making raids on helpless civilian populations, striking and then withdrawing. These nonstate actors may be motivated more by personal gain or anger than racial, ethnic, religious, or national ideologies, and they may realign themselves or disappear without settlement of whatever grievances may have motivated them.[25] Political and legal resolutions may be worked out, only to fall apart, as in the case of Darfur, leaving huge numbers of refugees housed in other countries and no real end to the underlying problems. "Endings," in these cases, are equivalent to an assurance of more trouble ahead. In such situations, de Waal and his colleagues observe, "the distinction between peace and war becomes blurred, and 'peace agreements' may not actually lead to an end to violence."[26]

The Guatemalan genocide shows how, like a nightmare that will not stop, genocide can reverberate for decades, making peace impossible for not only individuals but a country itself.

The Guatemalan Genocide, 1981–1983

The roots of Guatemala's genocide lay in conquest: beginning in the sixteenth century, Spain established a colonial system whose legacies were still at issue in the early 1980s, when the genocide began, and continue to trouble the country today. Even after Guatemala became independent of Spain, in 1821, the country was what the historian Greg Grandin describes as merely a state, never truly a nation in which the populace shared a common identity.[27] It was too riven by social class and racial hierarchies to develop a sense of national unity.

These hierarchies formed the macro context in which the genocide took place. Light-skinned descendants of the Spanish owned huge plantations from which they grew rich, while the majority of the population—darker-skinned Mayan descendants of the original Native Americans—lived in poverty as peasants. Exploiting peasant labor, the landowners paid wages that could hardly keep a family alive. A move toward greater equality occurred in the early 1950s with the election as president of Jacobo Árbenz Guzmán, who took land from the United Fruit Company—a US corporation that farmed huge swaths of Guatemala—and redistributed it to peasants. This revolutionary reform (which attracted the twenty-six-year-old Ernesto—"Che"—Guevara, an Argentinian physician who settled in the country) might have led to greater racial and economic integration of Guatemala. However, the Árbenz reforms infuriated the US Central Intelligence Agency, which interpreted them in terms of the Cold War struggle of democracy versus communism. The CIA sponsored a coup that overthrew Árbenz (and, incidentally, drove Che out of the country, to Cuba by way of Mexico).

There followed a thirty-six-year civil war between conservatives, who owned plantations and ruled Guatemala in league with the army, and the leftists who opposed them—including insurgents who took refuge in the mountainous western highlands where the Maya were concentrated. Although the Maya did not necessarily support the insurgents, they were engaged in their own civil-rights struggles with the government, and so the army associated them with the insurgents. In the early 1980s, first under President Romeo Lucas García (1978–1982) and then under President Efraín Ríos Montt (1982–1983), the military decided to sever Mayan ties to the guerrilla insurgents, break the back of Mayan independence, and turn the Maya into Guatemalans by forcing them to speak Spanish and enroll (in the case of men) in paramilitary civil patrols. This reframing of the Maya into political enemies became the meso-level context for the genocide.

With US support, Ríos Montt initiated a scorched-earth policy to cripple the Mayan economy and compulsory civil patrols to militarize the Mayan male population. "Ríos Montt served as Guatemala's head of state for seventeen tumultuous months in 1982–1983," writes the his-

Figure 8.1. These men were shot near Saluciun, in northern Guatemala, in May 1982, during the period of genocidal violence against the Mayan people. The army attempted to blame leftist guerrillas for the killings, but it itself was almost certainly to blame. Associated Press. Reprinted with permission.

torian Virginia Garrard-Burnett, "a period now known in Guatemalan history as *la violencia*, although it was spoken of at the time, if at all, in hushed tones, simply as *la situation*. This sobriquet places Ríos Montt's administration at the core, the bloody nadir, of the nation's thirty-six-year struggle."[28] When Ríos Montt was deposed, anti-Maya violence died down; but the genocide had been accomplished, with 100,000–150,000 Maya killed and at least 150,000 forced to flee to Mexico (some estimates give ten times that figure for internal and external displacements), their villages burned, their culture all but destroyed.[29]

Aftermaths of the Genocide

In late December 1996, peace accords were signed by the military and the National Revolutionary Union of Guatemala (an umbrella group for guerrilla factions), ending the civil war. This concluded a long process of negotiation that had been opposed at every turn by the government but that was pushed forward by the United Nations and a larger movement across Central America to end Cold War struggles and build democracies. After the peace accords were signed, however, the government of Guatemala continued much as it did before, using death squads to silence opponents, thwarting the spread of human rights reforms, and generally operating with its former assurance that violence would have no consequences.

On the other hand, the immediate postwar period saw the publication by the Catholic Archdiocese of Guatemala of the report *Guatemala: Never Again!*, the result of its Recovery of Historical Memory project and a truly remarkable achievement.[30] The report is based on interviews with victims of violence, an approach rooted in the conviction that testimony would not only give victimized people a voice but also confirm their right to *have* a voice, a privilege all but lost over years—centuries, really—of repression.

Guatemala: Never Again! speaks of impunity ("a cause and a consequence of violence, as well as a central obstacle to justice and reconciliation") and of the struggle for memory (which can help dismantle "the mechanisms that made state terrorism possible").[31] In addition to the interviews, from which the report quotes anonymously, the Archdiocese also collected quantitative data on over 14,000 incidents of violence, including murders, rapes, and torture. For the first time, the victims of *la violencia* spoke openly and collectively about the genocide.

When Monsignor Juan José Gerardi Conedera presented the Archdiocese report in Guatemala City's cathedral, in April 1998, he described the work as "an announcement. It is . . . aimed at finding new ways for human beings to live with one another." But he also observed that "people have died for their beliefs."[32] Two days later, in the garage of his parish home, Gerardi was bludgeoned to death with a concrete slab. Three army officers were convicted of his death, and a priest was found guilty as their accomplice. Although the trial set an important precedent for trying military officers in a civilian court, the assassination was a sign of the military's contempt for the peace process. None of the macro factors that had encouraged genocide in the first place had changed.

The depth and longevity of the military's resistance to reform are illustrated by a case that began earlier than the peace accords but was not settled until late 2003: the 1990 murder of the anthropologist Myrna Mack, described by Guatemalan authorities themselves as "one of the paradigmatic cases ensuing from our country's legacy of 36 years of internal warfare."[33] Mack, a Guatemalan of Mayan and Chinese descent, had been working closely with Maya in the country's Ixil Triangle, where they were concentrated, documenting in particular the immense displacement of Maya who had fled to Mexico to escape the army. Although Mack scrupulously reported to the military authorities wherever she did her research, she incurred their wrath by exposing what a witness later called "a reality unknown to Guatemalans who were unaware that almost a million persons had been displaced" by the army's predations.[34] Mack was struck down outside her office in Guatemala City by assailants who stabbed her twenty-seven times.

Over the next thirteen years, Mack's sister, Helen Mack, struggled to bring the state of Guatemala to justice. The obstacles she faced were enormous. No lawyer would take on the case out of fear of reprisals, and so she studied law herself. The detective who identified the chief assailant—and testified that the crime was politically motivated—was murdered. All the witnesses, together with a journalist, a legal assistant, and the detective's supervisor, had to go into exile. Helen Mack and other members of Myrna Mack's family received death threats. The Guatemalan government engaged in legal contortions to protect the higher-ups involved in Mack's assassination, as did the United States, which suppressed information on the killers—with good reason, since it turned out that the death squad that had targeted Mack operated with CIA support.[35]

One perpetrator was sentenced to thirty years in prison but then cleared of all charges by an appeals court. Guatemala continued to place obstacles in Mack's way. Nonetheless, in the end, truth was recovered by the Costa Rican Inter-American Court of Human Rights, to which Helen Mack had carried the case and which decided in her favor. But this was the victory of one individual fighting a corrupt state that refused to change. Most of the circumstances that had primed Guatemala for genocide remained in place.

Figure 8.2. Exhumation in the Ixil Triangle, Guatemala. Since 1997, the Centre of Forensic Anthropology and Applied Sciences has helped families bereaved during the genocide of 1982–1983 identify the remains of those who disappeared. Here Queqchi Mayan people remove remains of family members from an exhumation site for burial. Courtesy of Trocaire, CAFCA archive.

Postwar Violence in Civil Society

Even in peace, Guatemala was one of the most dangerous places on earth. Its weak police force and unscrupulous courts—by-products of the decades-long military dominance of the government and of impunity—proved no match for organized crime and youth gangs. In 2013, its homicide rate was 34 per 100,000 people in the population.[36] (In contrast, the global homicide rate for 2012 was 6 per 100,000 people.)[37] Location further contributes to the country's problems, for proximity to Mexico puts it on the routes of major drug-smuggling cartels. Extortion, kidnapping, and street violence have encouraged nonviolent citizens to arm themselves. To make the country safe would require major reforms and expenditures that a government so long immersed in civil war, and weakened by it, may be powerless to undertake without United Nations help.[38]

The Archdiocese report observes that Guatemala's postwar violence grew out of violence during the civil war. "Militarization has influenced value systems and behavioral patterns and enabled perpetrators to acquire expertise and perpetuate power networks."[39] The report cites, in particular, "pervasive impunity and the profound economic problems assailing many sectors of society" as factors that perpetuate the war's legacy of ongoing violence.[40] Moreover, the war established "clandestine networks that operate in the . . . interests of powerful groups. In the postwar context, these networks have organized into criminal gangs whose object is personal enrichment through drug trafficking, kidnapping, automobile theft, and so forth. . . . These groups cannot be considered in isolation from traditional power structures, including the army."[41] Genocide bleeds into postwar violence, atrocities into street crime.[42]

Reverberations

Even when genocides end in the traditional sense that exterminatory violence comes to a close, they leave in their wake a multitude of problems: economic havoc, homelessness and starvation, physical wounds and broken health, psychological traumas that last decades, constant anxiety and fear, loss of personal and community identity, orphans, refugees, anomie, paralyzing sorrow, cultural destruction, ecological degradation (by, for instance, unexploded munitions and decaying bodies), and an aching sense of injustice. In these ways, genocides last for generations, and the enduring difficulties are not solely problems of the victim group: when the genocide has been internal to a country, genocidists suffer as well.[43]

But truth be told, *individual* genocidists suffer very little, at least in terms of formal punishment. Personal remorse is, of course, another matter, but it is difficult to assess; this is an area in which more research is badly needed. However, anecdotal evidence suggests that, far from feeling shame or grief, genocidists often feel frustrated because their goals of social reorganization were not realized (or not fully realized). Until Rwanda, most low-level genocidists got away with their crimes. Sometimes leaders were condemned: Turkey sentenced the "three pashas" to death, but they fled to Germany before they could be executed. (There, at least two were killed by Armenian avengers.) A number of the doctors who led the German "euthanasia" program were hanged after trials at Nuremberg; others killed themselves, some to escape formal punishment, others apparently because they did not wish to live in a non-Nazi world.[44] But most "mercy killers" evaded capture after World War II; and even those who were tried and sentenced went on, unstigmatized, to practice medicine after brief periods in prison.[45] The Khmer Rouge Tribunal eventually condemned "Comrade Duch" (Kang Kek Iew), the former head of the Tuol Sleng (S-21) torture prison, to life in prison, and it also sentenced two other former high-ranking Khmer Rouge officials to life imprisonment. (A few former midlevel officials went on trial in 2015, but resistance from the current government, which is headed by a former Khmer Rouge member, all but ensured that there would be few, if any, other convictions.)[46] In Guatemala, Ríos Montt was tried, convicted, but then exonerated. "Blue-collar" perpetrators, until recently, suffered no formal consequences whatsoever.[47]

In what follows, I address the aftermaths of genocide from the survivors' point of view, dealing, first, with one of their greatest burdens, the often hopeless struggle for justice, and, second, with their persistent sense of loss. When a group is destroyed, the remnants mourn not only loss of friends and family but also the loss of the culture that gave their lives meaning.

Struggle for Justice

The galling and debilitating sense of injustice confronts victims when they wake in the morning and keeps them awake at night. Those who survive genocide yearn for justice—not necessarily revenge or punishment of the guilty but *some* righting of the wrongs. One of the worst of the enduring aftereffects of genocide is the realization that those who were most harmed will never find justice.[48]

Survivors realize that those who were killed and raped will go unremembered, that the maimed will never heal, and that they themselves will die with their outrage and grief. After a period of time, remnants of the group or descendants may take steps to achieve some small bit of justice, perhaps through erecting a monument (in Guatemala, spontaneous memorials have been assembled at exhumation sites) or winning a court case (as did the family of Myrna Mack); and outside groups may come in to help (for instance, the Guatemalan Forensic Anthropology Foundation, a nongovernmental organization conducts exhumations from clandestine burial sites). But true justice after genocide is never possible.

Perpetrators' denial of genocide hammers home this impossibility, intensifying the pains of injustice. In Guatemala, the continuing impunity of the genocide's guiding hand, former president Ríos Montt, symbolizes this wrong. Equally egregious is Turkey's denial that there ever was an Armenian genocide. Evidence of this genocide is overwhelming—in photographs, Armenian testimonies, and even Turkish newspapers from the time, one of which described the mass violence as "the greatest and most unpardonable act in history."[49] But today the genocide is a taboo topic in Turkish schools, and if someone brings it up in polite conversation, someone else quickly changes the topic. The Turkish government issues so much propaganda to bolster its denials of the Armenian (and Greek) deportations that schoolchildren have come to believe that "Armenian-Greeks killed 3 million Turks"![50] Western countries, reliant on Turkey's strategic location for military operations, hesitate to openly contradict the denials. The year 2007 saw the assassination of Hrant Dink, a Turkish-Armenian journalist, by a Turkish nationalist; 2014 saw threats to the German-Turkish film director Fatih Akin for simply talking to an Armenian weekly about the *possibility* of making a movie about Dink's life. It is difficult for voices of reconciliation to make themselves heard through the barriers of hatred.

Perpetrators' admissions of guilt may bring some comfort to victims, although such confessions are usually forced, grudging, and incomplete. This was true when Russia finally confessed that Stalin had signed the death warrant for the victims of the Katyn Forest Massacre. For decades, Russia had strenuously covered up the genocide: it destroyed the voluminous forensic evidence found on the bodies; and in 1969, it located a war memorial at a village named Khatyn, apparently to throw Polish investigators and mourners off the scent.[51] Even after *glasnost* (the new policy of openness), Mikhail Gorbachev, then president of the Soviet Union, hid the originals of the death orders. But archivists, afraid that the secret police would destroy these documents, cleverly forwarded to Gorbachev stamped and dated copies to prove their existence. After further delays, in the early 1990s, Gorbachev's successor handed over the death order of March 5, 1940, to the Polish government. At last, the Polish people could take some solace in Russia's full confirmation of guilt.[52]

More forthright were apologies made to Rwanda by the United States. At an international gathering, Secretary of State Madeline Albright apologized to African leaders for the United States' failure to prevent the atrocity. In an extraordinary step, Bill Clinton, while he was still US president, traveled to Rwanda to apologize for refusing to intervene and later sending supplies to Hutu killers in refugee camps. Also forthright, if belated, were apologies for the Herero genocide. Germans used the one-hundred-year anniversary of the genocide to apologize, and in 2007, at the invitation of Herero chiefs, descendants of von Trotha's family traveled to Namibia to express shame and dismay over the gross human rights abuses committed a century earlier by their "race warrior" ancestor.

Even hinted admissions of guilt can be comforting. The Australian criminologist John Braithwaite and his team, studying Indonesian peacekeeping, have identified a method whereby perpetrators can indirectly admit and apologize; they call it "non-truth and reconciliation." At reconciliation meetings between previously warring groups,

> sorrow, even remorse, for all the suffering was commonly expressed. . . . Tears flowed, . . . [but] no-one ever . . . admitted . . . to specific atrocities that they or their group perpetrated against the other. . . . A common gesture of practical reconciliation was for a Christian community to start rebuilding a mosque they had burnt down or a Muslim community to start rebuilding a church they had razed. . . . When the cleansed group returned, their former enemies would often organize a moving welcome ceremony for them. . . . When a mosque substantially built by Christian hands was opened, the Christian community would be invited and Christian prayers would sometimes be said inside the mosque.[53]

Although such "non-truth and reconciliation" efforts did not always work, they sometimes facilitated constructive steps that demonstrated goodwill—without requiring an overt apology.

What Is Missing after Genocide?

If injustice is devastating to victims, so too is the sense of emptiness they experience. What is missing when the carnage stops? While the answer may seem to be "everything," it is instructive to look at specific genocides for a clearer and more specific sense of what is lost. Beyond the obvious losses—loved ones, the sense of family, belief in the world as a trustworthy place, social networks, culture—lie other losses.

One is the loss of economic stability. The Herero lost their entire nomadic way of life, which was based on grazing herds of cattle. The Armenians lost everything economically—land, houses, jobs, and productive community life. (Nor was Armenian loss always Ottoman gain. By executing Armenians, the Turks decimated the country's bankers, blacksmiths, carpenters, doctors, lawyers, weavers, and professional tradespeople, collapsing the economy of eastern Turkey.)[54] A similar loss of economic stability—devastating families and weakening nations—occurred after the genocides in the Soviet Union, Indonesia, Cambodia, and Rwanda. As the Katyn massacres began, the Soviets deported the prisoners' families to Siberia or Central Asia, where they had to support themselves without the help of their former breadwinners. Many perished. In Indonesia, Suharto's "Clean Environment" policy, consigning relatives and descendants of former communists to economic marginality, likewise crippled the families of those who had been murdered. The Cambodian genocide, during which Pol Pot took pains to execute everyone with an education or small business, left the country in total economic collapse.

In Rwanda, Philip Gourevitch writes, "When the new government was sworn in [in 1994], there wasn't a dollar or a Rwandan franc left in the treasury; not a clean pad of paper, or a staple, much less a working stapler, left in most government offices. . . . Go to the latrine, it was likely to be stuffed with dead people, and the same went for the well. Electric, phone, and water lines—forget it."[55] Postgenocide, Rwanda was "the poorest country on earth."[56] Although economic chaos may be easier to bear than the loss of parents, a partner, and children, it intensifies the difficulty of recovery.

Another loss after genocide is the traditional patterning of gender relations and roles. In genocides that use mass rape, these patterns are torn apart by sexual violence. Victims are left traumatized, angry, and resentful, feelings exacerbated through postgenocide encounters with their assailants. Genocidal rape makes it difficult or impossible for victims to establish new family relationships, and women may have to endure the wrenching experience of bearing children conceived during rape. Often, victims who have been raped are ostracized by their group and isolate themselves. Genocidal rape vastly reduces the likelihood, in the short run at least, that the group's traditional gender relations can be restored.

Gender is often a major determinant of postgenocidal suffering. If one asks what is lost in genocide, the answer often begins with "men," an absence that leaves women alone, struggling to perform their usual tasks and those of their dead partners as well. In Southwest Africa, the Herero survivors who were herded into concentration camps were mainly women; in Poland, those who were deported to Siberia were women with families. Women formed the majority of those left standing after the Khmer Rouge tsunami passed through Cambodia. In Indonesia, economic marginality and fear of being labeled "communist" made women withdraw from public life—a loss for their country as well as themselves. A decade after the signing of the 1996 peace accords, Guatemalan women experienced a wave of terrifying "feminicide": a sharp spike in the killing of women for which the state, as well as individual offenders, has been held responsible.[57]

Even though loss of traditional gender relations and roles is one way genocide echoes through time, this loss, as shown by Rwanda's example, can be turned into gain. When the slaughter ceased in Rwanda, about 70 percent of the remaining population was female.[58] Many women had been brutalized, and gender subordination worked together with extreme poverty to hobble their recovery. However, President Paul Kagame appointed women to cabinet positions and insisted that reconstruction begin with a critical mass of women in other government posts as well. He appointed a woman to head the *gacaca* court system that helped restore community relations on the local level, and elections of 2013 sent women to 64 percent of the seats in the lower house of parliament. Old laws that forbade women from inheriting property were abolished, and as avenues of opportunity opened, women seized them, rebuilding the country, which today is something of an economic miracle and the envy of other African nations. Rwanda's women did not do this alone—they had help from the otherwise-controversial Kagame, from nongovernmental organizations, and of course from the country's men. But women's hard work helped rebuild a nation in which they formerly had little power.[59] Greater gender equality can rise from the ashes of atrocity.

Yet another loss after genocide is community trust—being able to rely on one's neighbors and feel embedded in a social group. Genocide kills people, but it also kills a group's sense of common humanity. This was one of the greatest tragedies of the Guatemalan genocide: the destruction of Mayan traditions and the Maya's feeling of kinship in their own society.

But even a loss like this can be overcome. In Indonesia, after Suharto's resignation, Putu Oka Sukanta, who had been held without trial for ten years because he had belonged to a "communist" literary and social group, began to talk about the genocide with young people. Putu Oka Sukanta eloquently described his work as "an expression of fighting to become human again."[60] His struggle reflects the effort made by genocide survivors everywhere to belong again to a group that brings meaning to their lives. In some cases, they are able to reconstitute their group and recover lost identities.

In one of genocide's ironies, survivors may feel they have lost everything except the killers, whom they may encounter on a daily basis. One should not overlook the intimacy of postgenocide living conditions. It has been obscured by the Holocaust model, in which after World War II survivors seldom settled down in Germany to live alongside those who tried to exterminate them. In Turkey, too, such intimacy has seldom been a problem because few Armenians attempted to return. But in the majority of genocides in my sample, survivors continued to live near their victimizers.

In Rwanda, men and women doing their marketing brushed elbows with those who gang-raped them; in Cambodia, peasants walked to work past the homes of people who slit their parents' throats; in Guatemala, citizens were asked to vote for the man who engineered the genocide. Such intimacy forces survivors to relive trauma; it revives, sometimes on a daily basis, the shame and helplessness they experienced during the atrocity. Daily encounters with their victimizers make it impossible for genocide to end.

* * *

Genocide keeps on working after the declaration of cease-fires and the signing of peace agreements; it keeps on eating away at the group. I have mentioned just a few of the insidious ways in which the crime reverberates through time—the usually vain but inescapable struggle for justice, the sense of emptiness, economic instability, memories of rape and disruption of traditional gender relations, erosion of community trust and the sense of belonging. These are simply a few examples of how genocides perpetuate themselves, tearing at the already-tattered fabric of communities and at the hearts of individuals.

Analyzing how genocides end through the lens of the typologies discussed here can add substantially to our understanding of the entire process of genocide, over time and across diverse circumstances. Ideally, such analysis can even become part of the effort to intervene in genocide so as to end it sooner. That said, as the Guatemalan example shows, it is not always possible to speak of genocide ending at all. The effects of genocide persist long after the killing stops.

* * *

Chapter 9 returns to the issue of what it means to treat genocide as a crime. How has the criminalization of genocide been furthered in recent decades? What is the nature of this crime—not its legal elements but its profile, its shape, its fundamental character? Is this a crime that can be prevented? Deterred? And how can criminology contribute to our understanding of genocide?

9

Treating Genocide as a Crime

Over the past twenty-five years, enormous progress has been made in treating genocide as a crime. The International Criminal Court (ICC), which became a permanent institution in 2002, formally defined the interrelationships among the three atrocity crimes—genocide, crimes against humanity, and war crimes—thus improving understanding of genocide and easing prosecution.[1] Thanks to the work of the ICC and its predecessor tribunals, mass sexual violence has been recognized as a crime against against humanity and a form of genocide. Moreover, those predecessor tribunals dealt with some of the major crimes committed during the genocides in the former Yugoslavia and Rwanda.

In the period between the establishment of the ICC and 2014, it handled twenty-one other cases. Critics charged that politics helped determine the choice of cases for prosecution. Because the charges that *were* pursued involved violence in eight African countries, some critics complained that Africa itself was put on trial by a racist ICC.[2] However, four of the countries referred themselves to the ICC; two other countries were referred by the UN Security Council and two more by the ICC prosecutor. Thus, the evidence for racist prosecution is far from clear-cut. Of more concern, perhaps, are the cases that the ICC has *not* pursued. It has not charged Syria with genocide or crimes against humanity against its own people despite over 206,000 deaths and well over a million Syrians forced to flee between 2011 and 2014; in this case, Russia and China blocked prosecution. At the end of 2014, the ICC had to drop its long-term efforts to try the president of Sudan, Omar al-Bashir, for war crimes and genocide due to lack of UN support. In early 2015, the United States and other countries tried to thwart Palestinian efforts to use the ICC to prosecute Israel for takeover of its territory and for general military belligerence. As these examples show, politics affect the course of atrocity prosecutions, just as they affected the wording of the UN Genocide Convention in the first place. On the other hand, the ICC has made progress. In addition to the twenty-one African cases, UN tribunals and panels have also investigated serious violence in Cambodia, East Timor, and Lebanon and confirmed genocide as a crime of the utmost magnitude.

The past quarter of a century has seen the flowering of powerful nongovernmental organizations such as Human Rights Watch that monitor violent situations, document genocides, and offer sometimes provocative opinions on pregenocidal and genocidal situations. Research on genocide has exploded in not only legal studies but all social science fields and some of the humanities, and scholars have founded journals and associations dedicated to such research.

Despite this progress, however, we still know very little about the nature of genocide—its typical beginnings and endings and the shapes it traces through time. Next to nothing is known about how to prevent genocide and whether genocide can be deterred. We know more about prosecuting genocide—who to charge, how to deal with conspiracies, how to estimate the length and cost of trials—than about genocide itself.

Therefore, this final chapter addresses three questions. First, what were the typical patterns of twentieth-century genocide? What can criminological research tell us about the prevention and deterrence of genocide? And what can criminology contribute to the theoretical understanding of genocide?

What Does Genocide "Look" Like?

Genocides usually begin with a clear, triggering event: on January 14, 1904, the Herero rebelled against the Germans; on the night of April 24, 1915, the Turks rounded up Armenian leaders and intellectuals in Constantinople; on March 5, 1940, Stalin signed the death order for the Polish prisoners held in the area of Katyn; on September 30, 1965, an attempted coup precipitated the Indonesian genocide; on April 17, 1975, the Khmer Rouge took control of Cambodia; on April 6, 1994, Rwanda's president was assassinated when his plane was shot down. Two of the other genocides in my sample began more gradually: the Nazis' extermination of the disabled and the Guatemalan army's effort to subdue the Maya through terrorism and murder. But more often than not, to judge from my sample, genocide begins with a sudden, dramatic event that either galvanizes perpetrators (as in the case of the downing of Rwanda's president's plane) or marks the first step in execution of a plan (as with the Turks' roundup of Armenian intellectuals).

The twentieth century encompassed at least sixty-five genocides (see appendix A). Uncommon at first, their frequency accelerated in mid-century, peaking during the decades 1961–1980 (see figure 1.1). The midcentury concentration in Europe corresponded to Nazi and Soviet efforts to expand and consolidate their domains. After this peak, the concentration of genocides, fueled by Cold War politics and US interests, swung southwest to Latin America. At the same time, a series of genocides began in Asia, caused in large part by Chinese Communist efforts to consolidate power.[3] (Other international and domestic genocides added to the Asian total.) In Africa, the concentration of genocides in the second half of the twentieth century, due mainly to tribal warfare, in particular clashes between Hutu and Tutsi, subsided slightly toward the century's end.

Genocides (as Christian Gerlach has argued) are generated by multiple players, and they are multicausal events, producing various kinds of violence directed toward various targets.[4] Leaders often create genocidal organizations to carry out the bloodiest part of the work, enhancing their sense of impunity, particularly when they have also established legal states of exception.[5] In the case of both genocidal organizations and legal states of exception, we are usually talking about state-organized crime—a form of organized crime mobilized by the state to help it commit the ultimate organized crime: genocide itself.

Two types of events that presage genocide on the macro level are war and state failure. War greatly increases the likelihood of genocide; the most lethal combination is an external war fought simultaneously with a civil war. State failure is sometimes precipitated by war, at others by a political crisis, but in either case, it leads to massive instability that then cascades through the population, reaping more instability and insecurity and potentially preparing the ground for genocide. Significantly, even though genocide often occurs during a period of war or state failure (or both), its victims and perpetrators may not initially be in direct conflict. Rather, the perpetrator attacks a weak and unprotected victim in the same territory—notably a group that it detests on grounds of race, ethnicity, or ancient rivalry. Often the result is cleansing of some sort—not necessarily ethnic but racial, social class, biological, religious, or political as well.

Some genocidal states accumulate histories of atrocity comparable to the prior records of ordinary offenders, and in these cases, their histories predict reoffending, just as they do for individuals. A quick scan of the list of twentieth-century genocides (appendix A) shows the same offender names popping up time and again: China, the Soviet Union, Turkey (although its multiple genocides occurred almost simultaneously and as part of the same cleansing effort), and the Tutsi. These (perhaps putting Turkey aside) were the twentieth century's most recidivistic nations or groups.

Among groups, the emotional dynamics of genocide involve reframing and stereotyping, identity politics, manipulation of ideologies to create new vocabularies of motives, and often (but not always) dehumanization. The dominant group creates motivational narratives that widen the ever-present emotional spaces between "us" and "them." Demarcation of these divisions is followed by increasingly violent clashes until a dramatic event or marked turning point sets off the genocidal process. Most genocides are "hot," meaning that the emotional temperature of the group runs high and momentum builds to a turning point.[6] This is why, when there is a triggering event such as the downing of the president's plane in Rwanda, the genocide starts immediately; participants are already primed. Although "cold" genocides like Hitler's "euthanasia" program and the Katyn Forest Massacre do occur, they are less common—and more likely to be secret.

The perpetrators of genocide are mostly male, as are most of the victims whom they kill outright. However, genocidal rape constitutes another way of destroying the victim group; it tends to be used when the genocide takes place in the context of state failure—that is, when social control systems have broken down. Symbolically, genocidal rape feminizes the victim group, demonstrating its impotence, while masculinizing the victors.

Some genocides end with a clean break, while others simply peter out or dip below the genocidal level in the intensity of their violence. Some end when perpetrator coalitions break apart, others when they meet their goals or outside forces make them stop. But although genocides end—in the sense that exterminatory violence comes to a close—they leave behind a multitude of troubles, particularly for the women and children who are most likely to survive.[7] The suffering they cause lasts for generations. Insofar as they succeed in reorganizing the society in question, their impact is permanent.

Do genocides follow any particular pattern as they unfold? Gregory H. Stanton, the president of Genocide Watch, an alliance to end genocide, argues that "genocide is a process that develops in eight stages. . . . Logically, later stages must be preceded by earlier stages. But all stages continue to operate throughout the process."[8] Stanton's stages begin with classification and symbolization (the creation of hate signifiers); they continue through dehumanization, organization, and polarization; and they end with preparation, extermination, and denial. Not all of the genocides in my sample went through these stages (dehumanization and denial were missing from several, for example). To the extent that all processes have beginnings, middles, and endings, the genocides in my sample resembled one another, but their patterns and dynamics differed radically.

To what extent do other genocides resemble the Holocaust? This was one of the key questions motivating my study. The genocides in my sample *did* echo the Holocaust in important respects: they occurred during periods of war or extreme upheaval; they involved mobilization of genocidal organizations and creation of legal states of exception; they involved some sort of cleansing; and the genocidists were confident of impunity. To take note of these similarities, however, is very different from holding the Holocaust up as some sort of model or supreme template. Rather, it is to say that genocides, the Holocaust included, have certain common characteristics.

Although generalizations about genocides can be useful, they should not be allowed to obscure the extreme diversity among genocidal events. The problem is that generalizations are based on a median (the middle case in a set) or average (a total divided by the number of items in the set). Neither the median nor an average can convey a sense of the range one finds in genocide: in the numbers killed or raped, in the length of time the genocide took to play out, as well as in the way the process started, the types of weapons used, and the ways of organizing the killing.

How Have Genocides Changed?

A second key question driving this study asked how genocides have evolved over time.

Genocide has changed considerably over time—even over the relatively brief period covered by this study. While all genocides by definition involve an intentional effort to destroy a group (defined by religion, ethnicity, race, or nationality—a list to which specialists now add politics and sometimes culture), genocide as a generic phenomenon changes, sometimes fairly rapidly, in location, size, and scope. In what follows, I identify four ways in which genocide (and awareness of it) changed over the twentieth century and into the twenty-first.

First, colonialism, which often resulted in the elimination of indigenous peoples through death or assimilation, seems to be on the decrease, at least in its grossest forms.[9] Many instances of it occurred during the nineteenth and twentieth centuries, including genocidal massacres and other types of destruction committed over long reaches of time and space, as in the case of indigenous peoples in Australia, Canada, parts of South America, and the United States, although the effects differed for different indigenous groups and there is disagreement about whether such events constituted genocide.[10] But new instances of colonialism have occurred less frequently over time.

Why has colonialism markedly deceased as a macro cause of new genocides? The most obvious explanation is that racism and the drive for new territory have been constrained by changes in world opinion and by UN legislation, including its Genocide Convention. However, this does not mean that racism and greed for resources and territory no longer influence genocide; for example, in Africa, the effects of colonialism continue to determine geographical boundaries that reproduce divisions between Hutu and Tutsi, not to mention the spurious physical and psychological distinctions between the two groups.[11] Moreover, the effects of colonial and settler genocide are by definition ongoing and ineradicable. In Canada, the rate of child removals from indigenous families has actually *increased* since the last residential schools were closed.[12]

In a related change, genocide became less ideological over the twentieth century—less tightly tied to imperialistic visions of race, ethnicity, and nation. To be sure, struggles involving race and ethnicity still drove genocides at the twentieth century's end, but many of these were domestic genocides, occurring within a single country. Like many of the century's worst genocides—including the Nazi genocide of the Jews, the genocidal wars of India and Pakistan in the 1940s, and the genocidal separation of Bangladesh from West Pakistan in 1971—these domestic genocides involved efforts to create racially and ethnically homogeneous nations out of the remains of collapsed empires.[13] Ideology continued to drive genocides, but its reach was now limited to cleansing of a single country and was no longer imperialistic in its ambitions. International genocides fueled by racism, politics, and long-standing rivalries had become less frequent.

Part of the decline in ideological and international genocide corresponds to the ending of the Cold War. During the Cold War, the Soviet Union's drive for expansion, control, and consolidation led to its 1947 genocide against Ukrainians and its 1979 invasion of Afghanistan. On the other side in the Cold War, the United States backed anticommunist genocides in Indonesia (1965–1966), El Salvador (1980), and Guatemala (1981–1983). However, once the Cold War ended and the Soviet Union was dissolved, the United States no longer had as strong a motive for supporting genocidal regimes in other countries.

In a third change, one that carries over into the present, genocide and other atrocity crimes are shrinking and localizing. As Susanne Karstedt points out, many mass killings since the end of World War II have been relatively small events, repeated within a nation-state or beneath the level of nation-states, with perpetrators and victims sometimes changing identities, some groups being repeatedly victimized, or perpetrators targeting successive groups.[14] These atrocities, Karstedt argues, are not so much clearly defined single occurrences as they are moments in the evolution of mass violence. The international pattern of genocide (or at least of genocidal massacres) is getting "stringier"—thinner and with fewer pronounced protuberances on its chain. This change is no doubt partly due to the formation since the 1980s of dozens of small new countries, many of them in the Global South, which are still trying to figure out how to define themselves as nation-states, an effort that can involve ethnic or other types of cleansing and struggles among warring power blocs.[15]

Fourth and finally, from the late twentieth century into the present, awareness has grown of genocide as a crime. Measures intended to eliminate another group and reorganize society have been thoroughly criminalized, thanks to UN prosecutions in the former Yugoslavia, Rwanda, Cambodia, and elsewhere—even when, as in Cambodia, the trials left much to criticize. As a result of these prosecutions, the late twentieth century saw the first challenges to impunity for genocide since Nuremberg, along with recognition of systematic rape as a form of genocide.[16]

Awareness has also been advanced by the transitional justice movement, by media (including movies about genocides such as *Hotel Rwanda*),[17] by creation of memorials to victims, and by a multitude of nongovernmental organizations that monitor atrocities and fill gaps that governments themselves cannot or will not close. Genocide museums have been established in Armenia, Cambodia, the Czech Republic, Israel, Hungary, Rwanda, the United States, and elsewhere. As part of this growth in awareness, some countries that experienced genocide—including Germany, Rwanda, and Cambodia—now encourage genocide tourism. Thus, these countries' own citizens can reflect on their pasts, and visitors from abroad can study genocide in situ. Global awareness of genocide as a crime is growing exponentially.

Genocide Prevention and Deterrence

There are two main strategies to reduce the number of genocides: prevention and deterrence.

Preventing Genocide

The broadest prevention strategy appears in a 2001 document issued by the International Commission on Intervention and State Sovereignty and titled *The Responsibility to Protect*, or R2P. R2P tackled the basic obstacle to any effort to intervene in a developing or ongoing genocide: the ancient doctrine of sovereignty, according to which nations have a right to be free from interference by other states in their affairs. The doctrine of sovereignty—which effectively ruled against intervention, even when a state started committing atrocities on its own people—posed a worldwide dilemma.

The *Responsibility to Protect* project was initiated by the Canadian government in response to a blunt question from the UN secretary general: "If humanitarian intervention is, indeed, an unacceptable assault on sovereignty, how should we respond to a Rwanda, to a Srebrenica—to gross and systematic violations of human rights that affect every precept of our common humanity?"[18] Canada and other members of the R2P working group produced an alternative to the doctrine of sovereignty, *the responsibility to protect*, a doctrine that shifted the emphasis from intervention to protection, refocusing "the international searchlight back where it should always be: on the duty to protect communities from mass killing, women from systematic rape and children from starvation."[19] This change has opened up a new range of possibilities for preventing genocide.

Two core principles govern the R2P doctrine. First, "state sovereignty implies responsibility, and the primary responsibility for the protection of its people lies with the state itself." Second, "Where a population is suffering serious harm, as a result of internal war, insurgency, repression or state failure, and the state in question is unwilling or unable to halt or avert it, the principle of non-intervention [that is, the doctrine of sovereignty] yields to the international responsibility to protect."[20]

The R2P doctrine defines this responsibility not only in terms of *reacting* to human catastrophes but also in terms of *preventing* them and *rebuilding* after such events.[21] Prevention, according to the R2P, includes fighting against poverty, political repression, and uneven distribution of resources. It requires encouraging economic growth, promoting human rights, building democratic institutions, strengthening legal protections, and making sure that vulnerable groups have adequate guardians. The R2P document requires reforming the military in countries that lack effective civilian controls on their armed forces, and it formulates principles for military intervention by other countries as a last resort.

The R2P doctrine was accepted by the UN in 2005;[22] since then, it has been adopted by other governmental bodies such as the European Union, which has repeatedly declared strong support for R2P. (As an EU document points out, this support "is not purely altruistic," for mass atrocities can ruin prospects for development, lead to large flows of refugees, destabilize neighboring countries, and create lasting grievances that can fuel future conflicts.)[23] The US Genocide Prevention Task Force report of 2008 repeated the R2P principles,[24] and the US has taken steps to strengthen genocide prevention, including establishment of an Atrocities Prevention Board and design of military operations to respond to mass atrocities.

But to some degree, the US endorsements were empty gestures. A group of genocide scholars has vigorously criticized the US Atrocities Prevention Board for its "muted response" to a humanitarian crisis that began in 2011 in Sudan's Nuba Mountains.[25] The Atrocities Prevention Board, which was committed to "budget neutrality" (meaning that it was not funded) and which was chaired by the National Security Council (meaning that it lacked independence) had few teeth. Although created by President Barack Obama, it was hamstrung by lack of commitment to the principles of R2P in Washington and around the country.[26]

Another prevention proposal, smaller in scale and thus more practical, comes from the political scientist Ariel Ahram, a specialist in terrorism and political violence who has studied the role of state-sponsored militias in genocide. Ahram argues that "preventing genocide means . . . peeling away militias from the coalition of violence"—stripping the state of support by the types of genocidal organizations analyzed in chapter 6.[27] Ahram recommends international sanctions not only against states that sponsor militias (such as the Interahamwe sponsored by Rwanda's Hutu government before and during the genocide) but also against the militia leaders themselves. Recognizing that these organizations play increasingly important roles in genocides, Ahram advocates a "robust set" of international standards to hold militias—not just the states they work for—responsible for atrocity crimes.[28] Creatively, he also recommends rewarding groups that refuse to join coalitions of violence "with privileged access to international aid, recognition, and immunity from state control."[29] Well-focused proposals such as these stand a better chance of implementation in today's conservative political and fiscal climate than do the more sweeping, idealistic recommendations of R2P. However, as the example of Syria shows, even well-focused efforts to achieve accountability can be next to impossible in the current geopolitical context.

Deterring Genocide

Can deterrence work with genocide? Some scholars say no.[30] It is true that deterrence had little chance to work in the past, when prosecutions were rare and when, in any case, one country's perpetrators might never have learned about the consequences of genocide for perpetrators elsewhere. However, deterrence may work better in a globalized world where even perpetrators in remote locations learn about an International Criminal Court that—sometimes, at least—takes action against genocide seriously.

Until recently, evidence that genocide interventions could have a deterrent effect was mainly anecdotal. Samantha Power, the US ambassador to the United Nations, lists some examples in an article urging Western powers to intervene more frequently in genocidal situations:

- When Ronald Reagan condemned Saddam Hussein's poison-gas attacks against the Kurds, Hussein stopped using gas.
- During the Rwandan genocide, Paul Rusesabagina saved over a thousand Tutsi who had taken refuge inside his hotel, mainly by making phone calls to a US diplomat.
- During the same genocide, 503 UN peacekeepers protected some 25,000 Rwandans.
- The war in Bosnia ended when NATO finally bombed enemy positions, demonstrating determination to intervene.
- NATO bombings in Kosovo in 1999 freed almost two million Albanians from Serb rule.

The problem, Power concludes, is not that deterrent interventions do not work; it is that they are used so infrequently.[31]

But do punishments of genocidists—not just interventions like those cited by Power but the actual sentencing of genocide participants to prison terms—deter would-be genocidists? For conceptual clarity, it is useful to distinguish between two types of deterrence, general and specific. These can be illustrated with the first-ever ICC trial case, of Thomas Lubanga Dyillo of the Democratic Republic of Congo, convicted in 2012 of conscripting child soldiers and sentenced to a total of twelve years in prison. This sentence is likely to have a *specific deterrent* effect, meaning that Lubanga, specifically, is unlikely to conscript child soldiers again. Whether it also has a *general deterrent* effect—meaning an impact on others who in the future might consider conscripting child soldiers—remains to be seen.[32]

There is a third kind of deterrence, *focused deterrence*, which has been developed and put into practice with street gangs. Although it has not been applied in genocidal situations, it might well work in them, too. "Focused deterrence strategies," write Anthony Braga and David Weisburd, criminologists who have evaluated these programs, "honor core deterrence ideas, such as increasing risks faced by offenders, while finding new and creative ways of deploying traditional and nontraditional law enforcement tools . . . such as directly communicating incentives and disincentives to targeted offenders."[33] That is, focused deterrence strategies combine the threats of traditional general deterrence with incentives analogous to those advocated by the R2P doctrine to strengthen at-risk communities. Police working with street offenders offer various opportunities to deflect them from crime, just as UN officials acting on R2P principles might try to build up the economic infrastructure of an at-risk country and reduce political repression.[34]

Focused deterrence, aimed at violent offenders, drug marketers, and recidivist drug users, involves "pulling every lever," as Braga and Weisburd put it—repeatedly assuring members of the targeted group that the police are watching and will use every tool they have to make sure that the next offense leads to speedy arrest and severe punishment.[35] Key to focused deterrence are these efforts to be certain that the targeted audience fully understands the consequences of further offending. But equally important, in Braga and Weisburd's view, are efforts to offer gang members job training, employment, substance-abuse treatment, and other services and opportunities. This dual-pronged approach seems to work to control gang violence, drug markets, and repeat offenders.

How might the focused deterrence approach be applied in the international arena? First, as suggested by the R2P doctrine, UN workers, in tandem with nongovernmental organizations and state officials, would identify groups that pose high risks for genocide—that have a *genocidal propensity*, as defined in chapter 3. These high-risk groups are comparable to the violent gangs targeted by focused deterrence programs. UN officials would let ringleaders of a troublesome group know they are being watched and inform them about what had recently happened to genocidists tried by the ICC and in state-level courts. The officials' work would be analogous to that of "hot spot policing" as defined by the criminologist Larry Sherman.[36] At the same time, UN and other officials would bring in conflict-resolution specialists, create jobs, help residents with medical problems, and take other steps to address the macro- and meso-level factors encouraging genocide in that area.

How could focused deterrence have been used in Rwanda, for example? A series of massacres leading up to the genocide presaged what was to come. UN officials charged with identifying hot spots could have moved in immediately to take action against human rights violations. They could have intervened with the Interahamwe, the militia that was already practicing for the kill; they could have arrested and prosecuted those who refused to lay down their arms and assured others that they would be subjected to the same treatment if they persisted in belligerence. They could have jammed or dismantled the Radio Télévision Libre des Mille Collines station to stop it from broadcasting hate messages against the Tutsi and mobilizing the Hutu for genocide. If no peaceful means of persuasion worked, UN officials could have taken military action. At the same time, they could have started to address underlying problems, such as the lack of jobs and land for young men. Such steps might have stopped the genocide from materializing.

In 2013, when civil war in Syria reached a deadlock, President Bashar al-Assad used chemical weapons to murder his own people. Although this atrocity was well confirmed and well publicized, Assad was not deterred by the bad publicity. What *did* deter him was intervention by Russia's President Vladimir Putin, who told him not only to stop but to destroy the remaining chemical weapons, which Assad did. We do not know what Putin said to Assad, but it was enough to achieve a resolution to a situation that could have blown up into a major disaster and even (had Assad persisted) evolved into a genocide by chemical weapons. In this case, it was not UN officials but the head of another state who provided the focused deterrence.

An emerging theme in the literature on genocide prevention and deterrence is the importance of incentives: offers of help to troublesome groups or states in return for their withdrawal from violence. Earlier I mentioned Ariel Ahram's recommendation that some militias be held responsible for atrocities and others rewarded—with international aid and legitimation of their status, for example—for refusing to join coalitions of violence.[37] (Here is another international analogue to the focused deterrence approach used with street gangs.) Similarly, the criminologist

Laura Dugan and the political scientist Erica Chenoweth, in a study titled "Moving beyond Deterrence," argue that to fight terrorism, the most effective method is not repression but rewards in exchange for abstention from terrorism. "Conciliatory actions," they write, "are generally related to decreases in terror."[38] In these recommendations, prevention and deterrence flow together. They are no longer opposite approaches but partners in peace making.

The Justice Cascade

Ideas about genocide prevention are being rapidly changed by the work of the political scientist Kathryn Sikkink, who identifies a "justice cascade" that seems to be reducing human rights violations the world over. The justice cascade is not a strategy but a worldwide normative change toward holding *individuals* criminally accountable for human rights violations.[39]

Sikkink distinguishes three different models of accountability for human rights violations. Until the 1970s, the immunity, or impunity, model was the norm. It was followed by a state accountability model that held an entire state (but not its individual officials) responsible for genocide and other atrocities. The third, an individual criminal accountability model rooted in the long-ago Nuremberg and Tokyo trials, took hold in the mid-1970s with prosecution of individuals in state courts (Greece, Portugal). Today this third model prevails. "It took a major movement to put these new ideas forward, embed them in law, and put them into practice," write Sikkink and her colleague Hun Joon Kim.[40] Sometimes, when activists were unable to get justice in their own nation's courts, they went to nearby courts with some form of universal jurisdiction; this was the case with the family of Myra Mack (see chapter 8), who thereby contributed, unwittingly, to the normative changes that created the justice cascade.

The justice cascade, Sikkink emphasizes, is a "decentralized but interactive system of accountability" dependent primarily on national courts.[41] While legally it is based on the ICC's Rome Statute, that statute requires that violations be handled primarily in state courts, with the ICC acting only as a backup or last-resort institution. International tribunals such as those used in prosecutions in the former Yugoslavia and

Rwanda are exceptions, not the rule, in this new model of individual accountability.

Sikkink and her colleagues have amassed a large amount of data to support their identification of the justice cascade. Moreover, they are able to describe how it originated and spread. "The justice cascade started in the semiperiphery of global politics and diffused outward and upward through horizontal diffusion from one country to another and then via bottom-up vertical diffusion from individual countries to intergovernmental organizations and international NGOs."[42] Individual activists (such as Myrna Mack's sister) and transnational advocacy networks (such as those that helped bring the former Guatemalan president Ríos Montt to trial, however futilely) pushed along the process through which the justice cascade came into being. It was created by "norm entrepreneurs."[43]

Does the justice cascade make a difference? Has it reduced the number of atrocity crimes across the globe? The answer seems to be yes. Countries that prosecute human rights violations tend subsequently to have lower levels of repression than those that do not. Moreover, "prosecutions of human rights violations have a deterrence effect across borders":[44] even if a transitional country has no prosecutions at all, it will experience a deterrence effect against human rights violations if four or more neighboring states *do* have prosecutions. Deterrence is evidently contagious. Human rights prosecutions, Sikkink has found, also tend to reduce the use of torture—even if the torture case ends in acquittal.[45] It was awareness of torture cases, Sikkink argues, that drove members of the George W. Bush administration to try to shield themselves against torture accusations by generating legal memos on waterboarding.[46]

The work of Sikkink and her colleagues lays to rest older debates about whether prosecutions of atrocity crimes have deterrent effects: they do. These scholars do not argue that prosecution alone can solve the world's most severe problems; very real and difficult structural changes are also needed, as noted earlier in connection with the R2P. But again, a combination of prevention and deterrence seems to hold keys to improving world peace.

Criminology and Genocide

Criminology does not come to genocide with unbloodied hands. The Nazis turned it into a technology of power, merging criminology with eugenics theory to justify extermination of many kinds of "asocials," not only criminals, juvenile delinquents, and prostitutes but also Jews, so-called Gypsies, homosexuals, and other groups that did not meet Nazi ideals. Even earlier, the United States and other countries also developed eugenic criminology into a tool justifying the sterilization of people with mental disabilities and the sentencing of allegedly "feeble-minded" criminals to up-to-life terms.[47] One should always approach criminology and criminal law, fields that can influence decisions about social unfitness and human rights, with skepticism. That said, one can still ask, What can criminology contribute to genocide studies?

To answer this question, I first review previous work and then summarize the criminological findings of this book. I discuss the applicability of several specific criminological theories to the study of genocide and conclude by suggesting ways in which criminology might contribute to genocide study in the future.

Previous Criminological Work on Genocide

Traditionally, criminologists paid little attention to genocide, partly because, defining crime as behavior criminalized by the state, they had trouble thinking of the state itself as criminal in some circumstances. However, a few scholars, especially those involved in analysis of state crime, drew attention to genocide and related atrocities. As early as 1999, Ruth Jamieson, in an article titled "Genocide and the Social Production of Immorality," called attention to ways in which criminology and its subfield of victimology could contribute to understandings of genocide. The next year, L. Edward Day and Margaret Vandiver showed how criminological theory could be applied to genocide and mass killings. The year after *that*, in the magisterial *States of Denial*, Stanley Cohen dissected people's ways of avoiding knowledge about atrocities and suffering, while at the same time Alex Alvarez published a study of governments and genocide. In 2005, Ruth Jamieson and Kieran McEvoy analyzed states' use of "specialist" forces to commit crimes by proxy, thereby protecting themselves from prosecution. Meanwhile, Dawn Rothe and her colleagues kept up a steady stream of analyses of state crime.[48] These were some of criminology's first forays into the study of genocide.

Around 2010, there appeared a spate of game-changing criminological studies of genocide. Most innovative and ambitious of these was *Darfur and the Crime of Genocide* (2009), in which John Hagan and Wenona Rymond-Richmond developed a collective-action theory of genocide. Building a model in which the genocidal state of Sudan emerged from collective action by individuals and groups, Hagan and Rymond-Richmond were able to address genocide at the micro, meso, and macro levels and to specify interactions among them. They also took a "critical collective framing approach," analyzing the atrocities that began in 2003 in Darfur in terms of us-versus-them politics and the racial propaganda that pitted nomadic Arab herders against black African farmers. Further, focusing on rape, Hagan and Rymond-Richmond proved that the Sudanese government supported a policy of raping black women and insisted on the genocidal quality of these rapes. *Darfur and the Crime of Genocide* attracted a great deal of attention, winning prizes and further legitimizing criminological investigations of genocide.

At about the same time, John Braithwaite and his colleagues published *Anomie and Violence* (2010), a work focused not on genocide per se but on widespread violence. It was the first of a projected three-volume series applying the concept of "anomie"—the dissolution of moral standards that leads to social breakdown and a sense of alienation—to the social violence that peaked in Indonesia in the late twentieth and early twenty-first centuries. *Anomie and Violence* develops a restorative justice approach to peace building—"non-truth and reconciliation"—that may become a model for transitional justice in the years ahead.

The outburst of criminological studies of genocide in 2010 further included *Genocidal Crimes* by Alex Alvarez, the first criminological textbook on genocide, and *Crime and Human Rights*, Joachim Savelsberg's criminological study of genocide as a human rights violation. Slightly earlier, in 2009, Daniel Maier-Katkin and his colleagues published an interdisciplinary "theory of social conformity" to explain crimes against humanity, integrating criminological, sociological, and psychological theories in a sequence that, they argue, holds true for many genocides.

More recently, the Minnesota sociologist Christopher Uggen and his colleagues have applied criminology's life-course model to genocide, analyzing commission of the crime in terms of onset, maturation, desistance, and reintegration.[49] Additionally, in an important article, Hollie Nyseth Brehm and her colleagues have analyzed the age and sex of the more than one million defendants in Rwanda's *gacaca* trials, finding that genocidists are like ordinary street offenders in that nearly all were men and that participation declined with age.[50] Although criminology has been aware of these sex and age patterns for over a century, the article indicates that sex/gender and age are even more powerful determinants of criminal behavior than was previously thought, since they so potently shape genocide as well as ordinary offending.

The present book differs from earlier attempts to examine genocide through a criminological lens in several respects. First, by covering eight genocides at once and a full century, it is broader than most in its scope. Second, it seems to be unique in its focus on the nature and shape of genocide—on what genocide "looks" like. Third, it differs from most of the literature in its effort to systematically analyze macro, meso, and micro factors and to specify their interrelationships. Lastly, this work is unusual in its application of criminological reasoning across a number of genocides simultaneously.

Profiling Genocide

Criminologists build profiles of types of crime—who commits them, where, when, why, with what weapons, and with what consequences. But although there are numerous criminological profiles of such crimes as homicide and burglary, at the time I began this study, there was none of genocide. Thus my interest in discovering the size and shape of genocide—in building a profile of this type of crime.

My interest in the patterns associated with genocide as a crime determined my methodological approach—comparisons across events—for that seemed to be the best way to make generalizations. My familiarity with profiles of types of crime sensitized me to the fact that crime is always changing; rates rise and fall, and while some crimes become obsolete (train robbery), new ones appear (identity theft). Thus, I was determined not to draw a static portrait of genocide but to try to remain sensitive to its changes as well—to the ways in which genocide has evolved over time.

Criminologists are, naturally, interested in the causes of crime, and this fundamental type of criminological inquiry also influenced my approach. Today most criminologists acknowledge multicausality, even in the case of minor crimes, and look for structural and intermediate as well as individual-level explanations. My effort to identify various levels of causation in genocide, and to understand their interrelationships, relates to another criminological preoccupation: the relationship of the individual to the group—in, for example, gang offending. In this study, I was particularly interested in the relationship of individual offenders to the group since genocide is by definition a crime by a group against a group. In brief, criminology led me to focus on causes of genocide and to ask the kinds of questions I did about those causes.

I invoke criminological concepts throughout this book, some descriptive, some explanatory. They include the idea of hot spots or concentrations of a specific type of crime; the concept of psychopathy, or remorseless criminality in which the offender evidently lacks all empathy; and the notion of a criminal propensity, which I develop into that of a predisposition to genocide. I borrow liberally from sociocriminological and psychological ideas about dehumanization, about the "seductions" and pleasures of crime,[51] and about moral disengagement and neutralization—the theories offered by Bandura and by Sykes and Matza to explain the cognitive restructuring that is evidently necessary before one can commit crime. I further draw on the literature on desistance and on aging-out of crime—the latter one of the best supported findings in the field. And I draw on routine activity theory, albeit with reservations. Similarly, I have brought to bear a cluster of criminological concepts concerned with punishment or its absence: prevention, deterrence, impunity, recidivism, and retribution.

This book has been further shaped by my own specific criminological interests—long-term concerns that have informed my earlier books as well. One is my abiding interest in marginal and disenfranchised groups and the social psychology of us-them thinking. I have long drawn on the work of Erving Goffman and his followers to explain the framing of outgroups and the social construction of group identities—as I do again here, emphasizing the centrality to genocide of identity issues.

The criminological specialty of gender and crime—an area I helped develop when it was in its infancy—primed me to write chapter 7, on gender and genocide. It led me to the central question of that chapter—in what ways is genocide a gendered event?—and kept me conscious of the centrality of rape in even larger configurations of crime (domestic violence as well as genocide). I came to the topic of genocidal rape already well aware of ways in which gender violence can be used to instill terror and achieve social control.

My earlier work on biological theories of crime led me to observations about the probable role of human evolution and innate traits in genocide. Us-them thinking, as I note in chapter 4, is probably hardwired in the human brain, the evolutionary result of the need to differentiate one's own group from others in order to survive. Thus, the problem is not to overcome the human tendency toward us-them thinking—an impossible task—but to learn how to prevent such distinctions from escalating into genocidal group hatreds. I also draw on evolutionary and social neuroscientific work on empathy (chapters 5 and 7) to explain how genocidists can engage in extreme cruelty and why there are such marked differences between men's and women's rates of engagement in genocide.

Although one goal of this book was to see how criminology might contribute to better understanding of genocide, I found I could make little use of standard criminological theories. Theories that insist on the primacy of individual-level explanations do not work well with genocide. This is especially true of control theories of crime, which explain lawbreaking behavior in terms of individual lack of self-control.[52] Genocide, to repeat, is a crime in which a *group* is the perpetrator; thus, theories that stress the behavior of individuals in isolation from their social contexts seem unpromising—even sterile—when it comes to explaining genocide. Ronald Akers's social-psychological learning theory, which addresses variations in criminal behavior, is less individualistic in that Akers takes social structures and national differences into account; but in its current form, the theory is so very general that is does little to explain genocide in particular, especially its association with relatively sudden changes in the behavior of ordinary people.[53] More promising in explaining genocide is the criminological theory of strain, which Nyseth Brehm is developing into a broad explanation for genocide.[54]

Conflict theory and critical criminology, with their emphasis on the capitalist, authoritarian state, have helped criminologists learn to think of the possibility that the state itself may be criminal—a crucial first step in studying genocide. However, these theories, at least as they have been developed in the United States, seemed too thin to be helpful to me, especially after I adopted Christian Gerlach's view of genocide as an event in which several groups with differing agendas are likely to be in conflict. Finally, while subculture of violence theory has taught criminologists to think in terms of *group* violence, I could not find a way to apply it to the often-fluid, multisourced group violence of genocide. While genocidal violence is often "sub-" to the state, it is not necessarily "sub-" to a specific "culture" within the state.

I initially expected that social disorganization theory, social strain theory, and institutional anomie theory would help explain tensions in periods leading up to genocides. I still do, but the historical data I had to work with made it impossible to separate out the effects anticipated by these three theories. Once I determined that genocide often involves state failure, I combined social disorganization, social strain, and institutional anomie into a single factor—social instability—and called it quits in terms of a finer-grained analysis of pregenocide tensions. The only way to identify the influence of social disorganization, social strain, and institutional anomie on genocide may be through in-depth study of individual genocides, using primary data sources and focusing on these specific issues.

It is worth noting that my methodology—comparisons of eight genocides committed over the course of a century—made my data strongly resistant to most traditional criminological theories simply because the sample involved such disparate events. I wanted this kind of data—comparative but disparate information that would force me to generalize about *all* genocides (at least all in my sample) and protect me against easy generalizations and single-theory analyses. Other scholars have selected genocides to explore a particular theoretical theme—ideology, for instance, which Eric Weitz analyzes in an excellent study of four twentieth-century genocides.[55] However, I wanted the opposite—a data set that would be bullet-proof to any single theme or theoretical interpretation. As noted earlier, criminologists such as Christopher Uggen and Hollie Nyseth Brehm—using different methodological approaches than mine—are doing more than I have to apply traditional theories to genocide, and I expect the literature to develop in this direction in the years ahead.[56] But genocide is such a complex phenomenon that it will probably never be explained by a single theory—from any field.

Areas for Future Development

How can criminology best contribute to genocide studies in the future?

William Schabas, the author of the definitive *Genocide in International Law* (2009), argues that there is a great need for criminologists to have more involvement in difficult issues of international criminal justice, including the politics of prosecutors' choices of cases for prosecution and the rationales for punishment. Moreover, Schabas holds, these choices need to be *evaluated*, which also draws in criminology.[57] The Belgian criminologist Stephan Parmentier seconds these points: "There is a significant need to bring criminological knowledge to the analysis and the evaluation of the many strategies for dealing with international crimes and other legacies of large-scale abuse. Research on policies of repression and prevention, deterrence and rehabilitation, reparation and recovery, retributive and restorative justice, reconciliation and peacebuilding all have a long tradition in criminology."[58] Parmentier lists six ways in which criminology can contribute to international criminology (as Europeans call the study of atrocity crimes). These include

(1) defining and conceptualizing international crimes;
(2) measuring and mapping international crimes;
(3) estimating social costs . . . ;
(4) investigating the causes . . . ;
(5) defining and analyzing ways of dealing with international crimes; and
(6) developing preventive strategies.[59]

That is a close-to-definitive roadmap for criminologists interested in genocide.

Criminologists working on genocide and other types of atrocity need to develop counterfactual thinking, asking "what if" something had happened differently. What if the Herero had not rebelled against the Germans in 1904? Would there have been a genocide in any case at that time?[60] Or what if the German military in Southwest Africa had been less rigid in its reactions to the Herero rebellion? If it had accommodated to some Herero demands and not called in von Trotha, would genocide still have occurred? The answer in this particular case is "probably," but in general, counterfactuals can be used to search for better solutions. Another way to use counterfactuals is to examine situations that seem to have been ripe for genocide but in which genocide did not actually occur.[61] This method can be used to identify preventive factors. Finally, counterfactual thinking can be used to test causal theories. If I assert that *a* caused *b*, you can test my claim by asking "what if": What if *a* had not happened or had happened differently; would *b* have still occurred? I do not use counterfactuals in this book, but Benjamin Valentino uses some in *Final Solutions*, comparing cases in which mass killing did not occur with those in which it did in order to "isolate the specific conditions and intervening factors that increase or decrease the incentives" for mass killing.[62]

In a sense, all genocide studies are victimological, but I would like to see criminology develop a victimology of genocide that would begin with the not-uncomplicated question, Who is the victim? and focus on the victimization of collectivities. It would include systematic, comparative studies of genocide's victims, including those who died, were raped, witnessed violence, and lost family members and those for whom genocide is a memory of a cataclysm that befell their group in an earlier generation. A victimology of genocide might take a rights-based approach, as suggested by the political scientist Robert Elias, and should include study of groups—such as the Herero and, to a lesser extent, the Armenians—that perished in victim-precipitated genocides.[63] Raul Hilberg, whose *The Destruction of the European Jews* helped initiate the study of genocide's victims, insisted, rightly, that "in a destruction process the perpetrators do not play the only role; the process is shaped by the victims too. It is the *interaction* of perpetrators and victims that is 'fate.'"[64] A recent model for what might be done in the victimology of genocide is a dissertation, based on interviews, that compares the narratives of victims of sexual violence in the Armenian and Rwandan genocides not only *across* the two atrocities but also *within* them, gleaning a wealth of information that the author ultimately uses to challenge the UN's definition of genocide and could also guide postgenocidal responses to victims.[65]

Hagan and Rymond-Richmond took an impressive step toward a victimology of genocide in their book on Darfur,[66] but generally, criminologists and scholars in other disciplines have shied away.[67] Perpetrators receive more attention, partly because they most directly create the phenomenon to be explained—genocide—but perhaps also because for researchers, victims constitute a more painful topic. Martin Shaw, in his book on genocide and international relations, calls for a complex victimology that will recognize that "even in the most asymmetrical conflict, victims are also actors. And while *individual* victim-actors are mostly *not* also perpetrators of anti-civilian violence, the larger ethnic and national groups to which they belong—and especially political movements based on them—often include those who are perpetrators, either simultaneously or at a different moment in time. Moreover, even the most asymmetrical conflict is often embedded in a system of conflicts, in which actors from victim-groups are allied to other actors who are perpetrating violence."[68] The day for automatically treating genocide victims—and victim groups—as flat, two-dimensional actors has passed. A victimology of genocide could also raise tough questions about processes aimed at reconciliation and the discovery of "truth," asking whose interests are being served by truth commissions and transitional justice practices.[69]

Genocide intersects with three types of crime—political, organized, and white collar—that criminologists have been studying for decades but seldom in terms of mass violence. All genocides have marked political dimensions, but at the moment, our understanding of the relationship between genocide and political crime is cloudy and confused. Criminology could make a major contribution by theorizing the relationship of genocide as a political crime to political crime as it has traditionally been defined—in terms of acts that threaten the existing government or social stability. In addition, criminology could help sort out the conceptual relationships between genocide and other political crimes, including human rights violations and terrorism. I am calling here for a fundamental reconceptualization of the category of political crime that would include genocide.[70]

Organized crime intersects with genocide in at least two ways: first, when mass killing becomes a means of (or cover for) extracting valuable goods like diamonds or timber from a country or smuggling arms into a country engaged in genocide; and, second, when genocidal regimes mobilize criminal gangs to do the actual killing. "Organized crime" in the first sense refers to centralized, ongoing enterprises engaged in illegal activities; sometimes these enterprises resemble legitimate businesses, while at others they are similar to (or supports for) corrupt political regimes. In the second sense, "organized crime" resembles gangs or militias, the genocidal organizations identified in chapter 6. Both are state-organized crime. The field is wide open for criminology to clarify relationships between genocide and organized crime in both senses.[71]

Traditionally, white-collar offending has been defined as nonviolent, financially motivated crime committed by professionals in business and government. An excellent example is the Reich Committee, the group of well-respected physicians who designed, ran, and professionally profited from Hitler's program for exterminating the disabled. But even groups of soldiers—including soldiers with blue-collar backgrounds—are subject to the same social forces as members of white-collar organizations. In Christopher Browning's history of the police battalion that committed some of the worst atrocities of the Holocaust, he compares the "ordinary men" he studied to ordinary bureaucrats: "Everywhere people seek career advancement. In every modern society, the complexity of life and the resulting bureaucratization and specialization attenuate the sense of personal responsibility of those implementing official policy. Within virtually every social collective, the peer group exerts tremendous pressures on behavior and sets moral norms."[72] These forces shaped the murderous behavior of members of the police battalion as much as they do the behavior of professionals in modern organizations. Clearly, we are here moving away from the original definition of white-collar offending as a financially motivated, nonviolent crime by professionals; and yet, as Browning demonstrates, the concept of white-collar or bureaucratic crime can illuminate diverse phenomena of genocide. Criminology could usefully contribute by developing new theory about the relationships between genocide and white-collar (or professional or occupational) crime.[73]

* * *

No matter what the approach, genocide is a vast, strenuous, and stressful topic to study. Every genocide has its own complexities, including thousands or millions of dead crying out for recognition and explanation. Beyond that, to generalize from even a number of genocides to the phenomenon as a whole is intimidating and fraught, for there are many possibilities for missteps, and generalization itself leaches out the clarity of individual truths. Few topics can be more painful to study. Moreover, no matter how concerted our attempts at explanation, genocides and other atrocities always harbor traces of the inexplicable. When all attempts at interpretation have ended, there is still something mysterious left over, something so dreadful that it cannot be explained.

APPENDIX A

Twentieth-Century Genocides

Area of the world	Victims	Perpetrators	Start date	End date	Estimates of victims (range)
Asia	Filipinos	US gov't	1899	1913	250,000–1,000,000
Australia	Aborigines	White Australians	1910	1970	50,000 "stolen" children
Africa	Herero and Namaqua tribes	German gov't	1904	1907	65,000 Herero (80+% of pop.), 10,000 Namaqua
Middle East	Assyrian Turks	Turkish gov't	1914	1920	275,000–750,000
Middle East	Orthodox Greeks	Turkish gov't	1914	1923	100,000+
Middle East	Armenians	Turkish gov't	1915	1923	500,000–1,500,000
Europe	Don Cossacks	Russian Bolsheviks	1919	1920	10,000–500,000
Europe	Ukrainians	USSR gov't	1932	1933	5,000,000
Europe	Jews, Slavs, Romani, homosexuals, disabled, Jehovah's Witnesses, communists	Nazi German gov't	1939	1945	16,000,000+
Middle East	Alevi Kurds	Turkish gov't	1937	1938	65,000–70,000
Europe	Poles (Katyn Forest Massacre)	USSR gov't	1940	1940	22,000
Europe	Serbs, Jews, Romani	Croatian Ustashe regime	1941	1945	300,000–600,000+
Europe	Croats, Muslims	Serbian gov't	1941	1945	100,000

Area of the world	Victims	Perpetrators	Start date	End date	Estimates of victims (range)
Europe	Chechens, Ingushi, Karachai, Balkars	USSR gov't	1943	1948	170,000–200,000
South America	Yanomami and other indigines	Brazilian settlers, rubber companies	mid-1800s	1993	thousands
Asia	Pakistanis, Indians	Indian gov't, Pakistani gov't	1946	1947	1,000,000+ dead; 75,000+ raped
Asia	Taiwanese	Chinese gov't	1947	1947	10,000–40,000
Africa	Malagasy nationalists	Madagascar gov't	1947	1948	10,000–80,000
Europe	Ukrainian nationalists	USSR gov't	1947	1950	200,000–300,000
Asia	Kuomintang, landlords, rich peasants	Chinese gov't	1950	1951	800,000–3,000,000
Africa	Algerians	French gov't	1954	1962	350,000–1,500,000
Asia	Class enemies (internal genocide)	North Vietnamese gov't	1954	1975	1,000,000
Africa	Nuer, Dinka, Christians, Nuba, southerners (internal genocide)	Sudanese gov't	1956	1972	100,000–600,000
Asia	Chinese (internal genocide)	Chinese gov'ts (successive)	1900	1949	millions
Asia	Chinese	Japanese gov't	1930 (incl. 1937 Rape of Nanking)	1939	4,000,000–6,000,000
Asia	Tibetans	Chinese gov't	1959	2007–present	65,000–1,200,000
South America	Aché Indians	Paraguayan gov't	1959	1978	900

Area of the world	Victims	Perpetrators	Start date	End date	Estimates of victims (range)
Asia	Communists	Laotian gov't	1960	1975	100,000
Africa	Kongo tribe, Assimilados	Angolan gov't	1961	1962	40,000
Africa	Tutsi	Rwandan Hutu	1962	1963	5,000–20,000
Middle East	Kurdish nationalists	Iraqi gov't	1963	1975	10,000–100,000
Africa	Educated Congolese	Congolese People's Republic	1964	1965	1,000–100,000
Asia	Viet Cong	US gov't and South Vietnamese gov't	1965	1975	400,000–500,000
Africa	Hutu	Burundi gov't, Tutsi army	1965	1972	103,000–205,000
Asia	Communists, ethnic Chinese	Indonesian gov't under Sukarno	1965	1966	500,000–1,000,000
Asia	Educated Chinese, traditional culture	Chinese Red Guards under Mao ("Cultural Revolution")	1966	1976	400,000–3,000,000
Africa	Biafrans, Ibos	Nigerian gov't	1970	1970	9,000–3,000,000
Central America	Maya, other political foes	Mexican gov't	1968	1970	2,500–10,000+
Africa	Bubi tribe in Equatorial Guinea	Equatorial Guinean gov't under Francisco Macías; members of Fang tribe	1969	1979	1,000–50,000
Asia	Bengalis and Hindus in East Pakistan (now Bangladesh)	West Pakistani gov't	1971	1971	1,000,000–3,000,000

Area of the world	Victims	Perpetrators	Start date	End date	Estimates of victims (range)
Africa	Various tribal groups, Catholic clergy	Ugandan gov't under Idi Amin	1971	1979	50,000–500,000
Asia	Political foes	Philippines gov't	1972	1976	60,000
Africa	Hutu	Tutsi	1972	1973	5,000–200,000
Asia	Shiites, Baluchi tribe, Christians in West Pakistan	Pakistani gov't	1973	1977	5,000–10,000
South America	Chilean leftists	Chilean gov't under Pinochet	1973	1976	2,000–30,000
Asia	East Timorese	Indonesian gov't	1975	2000	60,000–200,000
Asia	Cambodians (internal genocide), Cham Muslims, Buddhist monks	Cambodian gov't under Pol Pot, Khmer Rouge	1975	1979	800,000–3,500,000 (20%–25% of pop.)
South America	Leftists	Argentinian army ("La Guerra Sucia")	1976	1983	9,000–30,000
Africa	Political foes of Mengistu	Ethiopian gov't (Ethiopian Red Terror)	1977	1978	30,000–200,000
Asia	Muslims, Shan, Karen	Burmese gov't, army	1978	1978	5,000–10,000
Asia	Afghan anticommunists	Soviet invaders of Afghanistan, Mujahidin	1978	1989	90,000–1,800,000 (10% of pop.)
Central America	Leftists	El Salvadoran army backed by USA	1980	1992	20,00–75,000

Area of the world	Victims	Perpetrators	Start date	End date	Estimates of victims (range)
Middle East	Kurds, Sunni Muslims	Syrian army, police	1981	1982	5,000–45,000
Middle East	Kurds, monarchists, Baha'i	Iranian army	1981	1992	10,000–20,000
Central America	Mayan peasants	Guatemalan army	1981	1983	60,000–250,000
Africa	Zaghawa, Fur, Massaleit, and other black Africans	Sudanese gov't and Janjaweed Arab militias	1983	2005	500,00–2,500,000
Africa	Mozambique left-wing gov't	RENAMO (right-wing) insurgents	1987	1992	100,000+
Middle East	Kurds, Marsh Arabs	Iraqi gov't (al Anfal campaign)	1987	1988	50,000–182,000
Africa	Somalis, Isaaq clan	Somalian warlords	1988	1991	15,000–100,000
Africa	Hutu	Burundian Tutsi gov't	1988	1988	5,000–100,000
Asia	Tamils/ Hindus	Sri Lankan Singhalese (Christian) gov't	1989	1990	13,000–30,000
Europe	Bosnian Muslims	Bosnian Serbs	1992	1995	10,000–225,000
Africa	Hutu	Burundi, Tutsi populace	1993	1993	25,000
Africa	Hutu and other tribes in Democratic Republic of Congo	Rwandan army, warlord-led militias	1994	present	800,000–5,400,000; up to 500,000 raped
Africa	Rwandan Tutsi, Hutu moderates	Rwandan Hutu	1994	1994	1,000,000+ dead, 250,000 raped
Europe	Bosnian Muslims	Serbs	1995	1995	8,000+

Area of the world	Victims	Perpetra-tors	Start date	End date	Estimates of victims (range)
Asia	North Korean civilians	North Korean gov't, state-induced famine	1995	1997	1,000,000

Notes: This table was compiled from sources that use different definitions of genocide. The wide ranges in the number of victims indicate that little is known about many of these events. For other listings, in addition to those listed in the sources below, see State Failure Task Force 2000; Krain 1997; and Hitchcock and Koperski 2010.

Sources: Dictionary of Genocide (Totten and Bartrop 2008); Encyclopedia of Genocide (Charney 1999); Encyclopedia of Genocide and Crimes against Humanity (Shelton 2004); Encyclopedia of War Crimes and Genocide (Horvitz and Catherwood 2006); Fein 1993a; Gellately and Kiernan 2003; Genocide Watch 2010; Harff 2003b; Harff 2005; Harff and Gurr 1996; Online Encyclopedia of Mass Violence (Sémelin 2008); Rummel 1997; Straus 2001; US Holocaust Memorial Museum; and Wikipedia entry "Genocides in History" (http://en.wikipedia.org/wiki/Genocides_in_history). These sources do not include cultural genocide—and thus, neither does my chart.

APPENDIX B

Case-Study Questions

STAGE I. PRIOR HISTORY OF TENSION BETWEEN THE
GENOCIDAL AND VICTIM GROUPS
*Key question: Do genocidal and victim groups have a prior history
of conflict?*
1. Was there a prior history of conflict between the perpetrator and
victim groups?
2. If so, what were the causes
   a. from the viewpoint of the perpetrators?
   b. from the viewpoint of the victim group?

STAGE II. SOCIAL INSTABILITY IN THE GENOCIDAL
GROUP OR STATE
*Key question: Are genocides usually preceded by social instability in
the perpetrator group or state?*
3. Was the perpetrator group or state at war or about to go to war? If
so, describe circumstances.
4. Were important groups in the perpetrator state in conflict?
   a. Did the conflicting groups include the victim group and the
      state?
   b. What others groups were in conflict?
5. Was the perpetrator group or state experiencing social disorganization? (defined in terms of apparent or real increases in crime;
lack of adequate housing; beggars; people living on streets; civil
war; high states of anxiety in general population)
6. In the perpetrator group or state, were there signs of social
strain? (defined in terms of imbalances in the social significance
and potency of key institutions: church, economy, police, army,
government)
7. In the perpetrator group or state, were there signs of institutional breakdown? (in church, economy, family, police, army,
government)

STAGE III. DEHUMANIZATION OF THE VICTIM

Key questions: How were victims dehumanized? Is dehumanization of victims universal in genocides?

8. Did the perpetrator attempt to blame its problems on the victim group? If so, how?
9. Was the victim group negatively labeled?
    a. What labels were used?
    b. Were any of the labels based on the victim group's ethnicity, race, religion, language, or other attributes?
    c. Did any of the labels imply that the victims were a source of pollution to the perpetrator group or state? (note especially labels that implied a need for eugenic measures or ethnic cleansing of a territory or population)
    d. Were any of the labels gendered?
10. Were members of the victim group physically stigmatized?
11. If there was negative labeling, how were the labels diffused through the populace of the perpetrator state?
    a. Newspapers and other media?
    b. State-generated propaganda? Give primary examples.
    c. Educational institutions? Give primary examples.
    d. Other means?

STAGE IV. MOBILIZATION FOR GENOCIDE

Key questions: How do perpetrator groups or states mobilize for genocide? Why do they decide that genocide is the best course of action under the circumstances?

12. What groups were mobilized? (army, political leaders, religious leaders, etc.)
13. When and why did the mobilization come to include genocide?
    a. Who made the decision?
    b. What motivated them?
    c. Was a specific document used to authorize the genocide? (If there were several or numerous documents, specify the key documents.)
    d. Why did genocide seem a good decision under the circumstances? (What were the organizational, cultural, and historical circumstances that pushed toward a "final solution"?)

14. Who planned the genocide?
15. Were steps taken to train the mobilized groups in genocidal action?
16. Did the state create a "state of exception" or legal limbo in which its genocidal actions, although against the law, seemed to be legal?

STAGE V. TRIGGERING EVENT AND VICTIM VULNERABILITY

Key questions: How do genocides start? What factors conspire to make victims vulnerable?

17. Was the genocide started by a triggering or catalytic event?
18. If not, how did the genocide start?
19. Was there an absence of a group or groups (e.g., church, UN) that might have served as a "competent guardian" to protect the victim?
20. Did other factors contribute to the victims' vulnerability?
21. Did people or groups inside or outside the perpetrator state attempt to stop its genocidal course?

STAGE VI. EXTERMINATION, NEUTRALIZATION OF GUILT, AND DENIAL

Key questions: How is genocide achieved, physically and psychologically? Do genocidists always experience guilt? Do they always need to "neutralize" their behavior?

22. Through what physical and social means was the genocide achieved?
23. How many were killed? (If possible, estimate their proportion to the total population of the victim group.)
24. Did the perpetrator group or state deliberately encourage rape? If so, did it contribute to destruction of the victim group?
25. Did the genocide involve ethnic cleansing? (efforts to purify a territory or population)
26. How were people killed? What proportion were killed in face-to-face encounters?
27. With reference to the exterminators, what factors enabled them to kill?
    a. Obedience to authority?
    b. Conformity to group norms?
    c. Enjoyment?
    d. Other factors?

28. Is there evidence that the exterminators' actions caused negative reactions in them, such as
    a. A brutalization effect?
    b. Physical or mental deterioration?
    c. Guilt?
    d. Other effects?

29. If the exterminators experienced guilt, did they take steps to neutralize the guilt?
    a. Did they deny that the genocide (or torture or atrocities) had occurred? Under what circumstances?
    b. Did they admit a genocide had occurred but deny responsibility for it?
    c. Did they justify their actions on grounds of the nature or behavior of the victims?

30. Did the genocide involved torture?
    a. What sorts of torture, and how extensively was it used?
    b. Was the torture deliberate or a by-product of other processes (such as being locked in a transport train)?
    c. If the torture was deliberate, what was its purpose? (to gain information? further social control through fear of others in the victim group? enact rituals?)
    d. If the torture was deliberate, what were the positions of those who directed it?

31. Did the genocide involve atrocities other than murder, torture, and rape? (give key examples)

STAGE VII. TERMINATION AND AFTERMATHS
Key questions: How do genocides end? Do they end?

32. When and why did the genocide end?

33. If an order was given to stop the killing, who gave it and why?

34. What were the long-term consequences of the genocide for the perpetrator group or state?

35. Did the perpetrator group or state threaten to renew the violence against the victim group at a later date?

36. What were the long-term consequences of the genocide for the victim group?

NOTES

1. GENOCIDE, CRIMINOLOGY, AND EVOLUTION OF THE "CRIME OF CRIMES"

1. The exact number of executed Poles was 21,857 (Cienciala, Lebedeva, and Materski 2007: 332, reproducing a note from A. Shelepin to N. Khrushchev, March 3, 1959).

2. United Nations 1948.

3. This is the main interpretation of Stalin's motive for the genocide. For others, which the author himself admits are "fantastical," see Levene 2013b: 41–43.

4. Snyder 2010: 89. In quotations throughout the book, I omit internal citations.

5. Snyder 2010: 125.

6. Martin Shaw (2013) makes this point but overstates the case by rejecting comparative genocide studies entirely.

7. Examples of just how productive historical comparisons can be in genocide studies can be found, for example, in Bloxham 2008; Dadrian 2004; Feierstein 2014; Fein 1997; Kiernan 2003; Madley 2004; and Wolfe 2006, among other works.

8. Goldsmith et al. 2013; Hagan and Rymond-Richmond 2008; Harff 2003b; Karstedt 2011a (focused on failed states), 2012a, 2013c; Krain 1997, 2014; Nyseth Brehm 2014a; Straus 2006.

9. For examples of criminological work that *has* addressed genocide, see the sources cited in note 8; Rothe 2009; and Rothe and Mullins 2008, 2010. In chapter 9, I review the criminological literature on genocide to 2013.

10. See, for example, Powell 2007; Woolford 2009; and the essays in Woolford, Benvenuto, and Hinton 2014.

11. Rafter 2008.

12. Rafter 1997.

13. Buck v. Bell, Superintendent, 274 U.S. 200 (1927) (No. 292).

14. Num. 31:15–18 (King James Version).

15. Cienciala, Lebedeva, and Materski 2007: 29, 35, 159.

16. Cienciala, Lebedeva, and Materski 2007: 126, 410.

17. Stanton 1998; Maier-Katkin, Means, and Bernard 2009. Joachim Savelsberg, too, offers a kind of stage model (2010: 84–85).

18. Karstedt 2012b. For a world history of genocide, see Kiernan 2007. In this chapter, I emphasize the evolution of genocide. However, it is also crucial to recognize underlying factors that run through twentieth-century genocides in general; see Kiernan 2003.

19. Wolfe 2006, 2010; Moses and Stone 2007; Shaw 2013; Woolford, Benvenuto, and Hinton 2014.

20. Karstedt 2012b: 795–796, citing Gerlach 2010 for "extremely violent societies." Also see Karstedt 2013b, 2013c; Ahram 2014; and Shaw 2013.

21. The problems involved in calling the Hutu and Tutsi different ethnic groups are reviewed in chapter 7.

22. Uggen, Nyseth Brehm, and McElrath 2014: 16, citing Fujii 2009.

23. Karstedt 2013b; also see my data as shown in figure 1.1 and appendix A. In chapter 9, I discuss the possibility that international ties might work as a genocide preventative; also see Nyseth Brehm 2014b.

24. Shaw 2013.

25. Pinker 2011. For a review of the evidence on the decline of mass violence, see Conley-Zilkic and de Waal 2014: 72.

26. Melson 2011: 279–280.

27. For my data, see appendix A. On militias in weak states, see Ahram 2014.

28. Adolf Hitler, August 22, 1939, as quoted in Bardakjian n.d.

29. A 2010 amendment to the Rome Statute defined the crime of aggression as the planning and execution of military acts that violate the UN Charter. The other three crimes are discussed in chapters 2 and 7.

30. Sikkink and Kim 2013.

31. Hinton 2011; McEvoy and McConnachie 2013; Mersky and Roht-Arriaza 2007; Parmentier 2011.

32. See Michalczyk and Helmick 2013. Some of the earliest films of the concentration and death camps can be seen on YouTube.

33. Brown and Rafter 2013.

34. Young 1993: x.

35. For a condemnation of genocide tourism as simply voyeurism, see Schaller 2007.

36. CBS News 1998.

37. Krain 2014.

38. United Nations 1948.

39. Cienciala, Lebedeva, and Materski 2007.

40. Some of the best-known figures in genocide studies, such as Zygmunt Bauman (1989) and Michael Mann (2005), did not do primary research for these well-known works. Also see Mark Levene 2013a.

41. Straus 2007. There is some debate (according to a personal communication from Andrew Woolford) over what "second generation" means here. Straus himself defines second-generation genocide research as studies that "seek to integrate genocide studies into mainstream research agendas in the social sciences. The aim is to analyze genocide (or mass killing) as one type of outcome and to use the tools of comparative historical analysis to understand why the phenomenon happens" (2007: 478).

42. Klusemann 2010: 277.

43. Arendt 1964; Milgram 1965, 1974.

44. Perry 2012; also see Brannigan 2013.

45. Perry 2012: 10.
46. Fischer 2007; Fox 1999.
47. Yet, at the same time, Gorbachev hid the key document ordering the massacre; it was not given to Poland until 1992 (Zaslavsky 2008: 98). No one was ever brought to trial, and today Russian reactionaries have started denying Stalin's responsibility for Katyn, again reframing the massacre as Germany's responsibility (Fischer 2007). On the backlash, also see Paul 2010: 349–350.
48. Schimmer 2006.
49. See the program's Interactive Geographic Database: http://www.yale.edu/cgp/maplicity.html.
50. Also see Oglesby and Ross 2009.
51. Woolford 2014.
52. Austen 2015, quoting the summary of the report of Canada's Truth and Reconciliation Commission.
53. Woolford 2009: 93.
54. Smeulers and Haveman 2008: 6–7 (emphasis added).
55. The description of criminology as a "rendezvous" field is attributed to the British criminologist David Downes.
56. But see Kiernan 2007.
57. Figure 1.1 shows the locations of only sixty-three genocides because it omits two that started in the nineteenth century.
58. At the time I selected my sample, I was using a somewhat different regional classification of countries than appears on the final version of appendix A. Thus, I sampled from regions that do not precisely correspond to the regions named in appendix A.
59. Friedlander 1995.
60. Baldwin 2004: 18.
61. In terms of the attention that genocide scholars have given various events, Alexander Laban Hinton (2012: 13) has a useful table on "the genocide studies canon" that moves from Prototype (the Holocaust) to Twentieth-Century Core events (e.g., Armenia and, again, the Holocaust) to The Second Circle (e.g., Guatemala and the Herero genocide) and on to The Periphery (e.g., Indonesia). It ends with Forgotten Genocides. My set includes an aspect of the Prototype (Nazi genocide of the disabled); three cases in the Twentieth-Century Core; two cases in The Second Circle; one case in The Periphery; and one case—Katyn—that is among Forgotten Genocides. (Actually, I would put the Nazis' genocide of the disabled in the "forgotten" category as well, but here I am trying to align my cases with Hinton's model.) Thus, to judge from Hinton's table, I have a good spread in terms of the attention given by scholars to my cases.
62. See, generally, the essays in Mahoney and Rueschemeyer 2003.
63. Agamben 2005.
64. Hagan and Morse 2014.
65. On this aim of genocide, see Feierstein 2014.

2. WHAT KIND OF A CRIME IS GENOCIDE?

1. Totten 2012.
2. Powell 2007; Woolford, Benvenuto, and Hinton 2014.
3. I am speaking here of genocidal mass murder that destroys culture, not of cultural genocide per se, which is not illegal, although Lawrence Davidson (2012), among others, argues that it should be.
4. Card 2008: 182.
5. Feierstein 2014.
6. See Karstedt 2014.
7. See DeJong and Long 2014 for the argument that the Ugandan government's attempt, 2009–2012, to require the death penalty as punishment for homosexuality was in effect an attempt at genocide. This is an unusual attempt to use the UN definition of genocide to fight cruel and unusual punishment.
8. Lemkin formally proposed the term in his 1944 book *Axis Rule in Occupied Europe*. Strictly speaking, he coined it in 1943.
9. United Nations 1948: art. 2.
10. Benvenuto, Woolford, and Hinton 2014: 10.
11. United Nations 1946.
12. Kuper 1981: ch. 2.
13. Power 2002: 52.
14. Kuper 1981: ch. 2. As noted earlier, the UN itself had included political groups in its first step toward defining genocide, a 1946 resolution of the General Assembly observing that "many instances of such crimes of genocide have occurred when racial, religious, political, and other groups have been destroyed, entirely or in part" (United Nations 1946).
15. The term "politicide" was coined by the genocide scholars Barbara Harff and Ted Gurr (1988).
16. Some of these definitions are compared in Alvarez 2010: ch. 1; also see Fein 1993b and, for a sociological treatment of definitional issues, Shaw 2010. A particularly thoughtful discussion of these issues appears in Feierstein 2014: ch. 1.
17. On the Yanomami, see Neuman and Diaz 2012; the genocide of the Herero, with whom the Namaqua combined forces, is covered in chapter 3.
18. On inclusion of systematic rape in the definition of genocide, see chapter 7; on cultural genocide, see, e.g., Davidson 2012. Some scholars feel that the destruction of the group must be "substantial" for the event to be called genocide; however, "substantial" is not part of the legal definition.
19. Gamson 1995: 9, 3.
20. Feierstein 2014: 1.
21. Ferrara 2015.
22. Feierstein 2014: 13. Compare Schabas 2009, arguing that the UNCG is sufficiently flexible as it stands.
23. Feierstein 2014: 36.

24. Scheffer 2006: 238.
25. The legal definitions of these crimes appear in United Nations 2002—the Rome Statute of the International Criminal Court.
26. Scheffer 2006: 229.
27. Hull 2003: 162.
28. Madley 2005: 430.
29. Haas 2008: 334; Swan 1991: 54–55; Weikart 2003.
30. Proctor 1988: 209. In addition, records are fragmentary or nonexistent. I have compiled this total from a number of sources including Friedlander 1995; Aly 1994; Burleigh 1994; Evans 2004; Kater 1989; Proctor 1988; Pross 1994; and Torrey and Yolken 2010. Schulze 2012: 25 gives a much lower estimate of 275,000 disabled people murdered by the Nazis.
31. Fischer 2007.
32. Naimark 2010: 92.
33. Colombijn and Lindblad 2002: 8.
34. Cribb 1990b: 23.
35. These figures appear in Hinton 2014; they reflect a recent upward revision in the figures.
36. Garrard-Burnett 2010: 6–7; O'Neill 2005: 333–334; Sanford 2009: 41.
37. Uggen, Nyseth Brehm, and McElrath 2014. Most sources state that 800,000 were killed, but Uggen and his team had access to more recent data generated by Rwanda's *gacaca* courts. As I explain in chapter 7, the genocide probably went on longer that the usually given figure of three months.
38. Gourevitch 1998: 3.
39. "In 1935 Adolf Hitler had told . . . the Reich physician leader . . . that once war began he would implement euthanasia. He kept his word. When war started on 1 September 1939, the machinery to kill the handicapped was in place and the killings began" (Friedlander 1995: 39).
40. Cribb and Coppel 2009: 449.
41. Gerlach 2010: 18; also see Robinson 1995.
42. British Broadcasting Company 2014.
43. State Failure Task Force 2000; Bartov 2003; Kelman 1973; Shaw 2003.
44. Here I am following Straus 2006 in distinguishing between the civil war of 1990–1993 and the one of 1994.
45. Zaslavsky 2008.
46. Some scholars hold that ethnic Chinese were targeted during the Indonesian genocide of 1965–1966; but see Cribb and Coppel 2009.
47. Compare Michael Mann (2005), who does not deny other kinds of cleansing but focuses a lengthy book on ethnic cleansing alone.
48. Also see Karstedt 2011b on the fate of Nazis convicted of genocide of European Jews.
49. Nyseth Brehm, Uggen, and Gasanabo 2014b: 339. United Nations 2013: ch. 8 gives the figure of 1,500,000 cases.

50. Drouin 2010: 93–94
51. As quoted in Zaslavsky 2008: 22.
52. Robinson 1995: 16. Also see Gerlach 2010: 19; and Dwyer and Santikarma 2003: 293.
53. Collins 2008.
54. Collins 2008: 9.
55. Ibarra 2006: 196.
56. However, Scott Straus (2006) found in interviews with Hutu killers that they more commonly described Tutsi as threats and enemies than as insects or animals.
57. Straus 2006: 42.
58. Gourevitch 1998: 150.
59. Cf. Straus 2006: 241, arguing that had the UN responded quickly and decisively when the head of the UN forces in Rwanda first called for help, interventions would have been successful.
60. Akçam 2012: 424.
61. Cohen and Felson 1979: 589.
62. The best demonstration of this point is Andrzej Wajda's monumental film *Katyn*. Also see, e.g., Paul 2010.
63. Gourevitch 1998: 270. By 2015, however, the economy of Rwanda was growing faster than that of other African nations, partly as a result of massive international aid.
64. Valentino 2004; Gerlach 2006, 2010.
65. Valentino 2004: 3.
66. Valentino 2004: 6.
67. Valentino 2004: 11–12.
68. Valentino 2004: 2.
69. For details, see Rafter and Walklate 2012.
70. Cribb 2001a: 230–231.
71. Des Forges 1999: 8.
72. Gerlach 2010: 3.
73. Gerlach 2010: 6.
74. Gerlach 2010: 7; also see Gerlach 2006.
75. The quotations come from Gerlach 2006: 458–467; the Armenian example is mine.
76. Gerlach 2006: 458.
77. Gerlach 2006: 459. Gerlach gives a more succinct definition in his 2006 article: "in extremely violent societies, various population groups become victims of massive physical violence, in which, together with state organs, diverse social groups participate for a multitude of reasons. In other words, there are four characteristics—various victim groups, broad participation, multi-causality, and a great amount of physical violence" (460).
78. Karstedt 2012a, 2013a.
79. Karstedt 2013a: 385.

80. Karstedt 2013a: 393–394.
81. Karstedt 2013a: esp. 386.
82. Karstedt 2013a. On problems with the notion of blameless victims, see McEvoy and McConnachie 2012.
83. Karstedt 2013a: 386.
84. Karstedt 2013a: 388–389.
85. Karstedt 2013a: 389; for the origins of the "hot spot" analysis, see Sherman, Gartin, and Muerger 1989.
86. Karstedt 2013a: 396.
87. Nyseth Brehm, Uggen, and Gasanabo 2014a.
88. Exceptions can be found in "cold" genocides, such as Katyn and the Nazi genocide of the disabled. On "cold" genocides, see chapter 4.
89. On hate speech during genocide, see, especially, Hagan and Rymond-Richmond 2009.
90. Cf. Schabas 2009.
91. Feierstein 2014: 36.

3. THE BIG PICTURE

1. See appendix A for a list of twentieth-century genocides. In fact, "century of genocide" is pretty close to a meaningless term, given how little we know about genocides in earlier centuries; and in any case, there is no reason for a competition. The phrase does serve to underscore the distressingly large number of genocides during the twentieth century, which is why I use it here.
2. It is impossible to feel confident about any estimate of genocide victims due to problems inherent in counting the dead under chaotic conditions. I reached my total of over 50 million by summing the figures in the right-hand column of my appendix A; Mina Cikara and Jay Van Bavel (2014: 245), in contrast, give a total of 200 million for the same period.
3. Agamben 2005 (state of exception).
4. For a somewhat different way of organizing the literature on macro-factors in genocide, see Finkel and Straus 2014.
5. For information on the involvement of the Nama (also known as Namaqua or Hottentots) in the conflict, see Zimmerer 2010.
6. Sarkin 2010: 68, quoting a statement by Samuel Kutako in the *Blue Book*, a 1918 British report on the German colonial period in Namibia. The *Blue Book*, an early record of human rights abuses, was reprinted in 2003, edited by Jeremy Silvester and Jan-Bart Gewald, as *Words Cannot Be Found: German Colonial Rule in Namibia: An Annotated Reprint of the 1918 Blue Book*.
7. Bridgman 1981: 26.
8. Bridgman 1981: 50.
9. Sarkin 2010: 69.
10. Drechsler 1990: 235.
11. Silvester and Gewald 2003: 92.

12. Palmer 1998: 91.
13. Silvester and Gewald 2003: 84–85, reproducing testimony of Herero underchief Daniel Kariko of Omaruru, on the causes of the uprising.
14. Silvester and Gewald 2003: 95.
15. Silvester and Gewald 2003: 95–96.
16. Silvester and Gewald 2003: 94.
17. See Rafter and Walklate 2012 for discussion of victim precipitation in the Armenian genocide.
18. Drechsler 1990: 237–238. Some scholars maintain that the Herero were provoked into revolting by a German officer; see Zimmerer 2010: 332; and the latter part of this chapter.
19. Bridgman 1981: 86.
20. Hull 2003: 146.
21. Sarkin 2010: 15.
22. Madley 2005: 442.
23. Zimmerer 2010: 327.
24. Hull 2005b: 41.
25. Sarkin 2010 argues that the Kaiser himself ordered the genocide. Also see Hull 2005a: esp. ch. 1.
26. Steinmetz 2008: 600.
27. Bridgman 1981: 62–63.
28. Silvester and Gewald 2003: 177.
29. Zimmerer 2010: 325.
30. Hull 2005b.
31. Hull 2003: 162.
32. Madley 2005: 430.
33. Haas 2008; Swan 1991; Weikart 2003.
34. Perraudin and Zimmerer 2011.
35. Schaller 2010a: 300.
36. Zimmerer 2010: 341n23.
37. Hitchcock and Koperski 2010: 577.
38. But see Bloxham and Bartrop 2010 and Kiernan 2007.
39. Schaller 2010b: 349; also see Hull 2005a.
40. Rafter and Walklate 2012. The concept of victim precipitation gained a bad name when it was used to explain rape: women cause their own rape (this argument went) when they dress provocatively or hang out on the streets at night (Amir 1971). However, we should not throw the concept out just because it has been misapplied.
41. Fein 1979, 1993a; Harff 1987, 2003a; Krain 1997; Melson 1992; Nyseth Brehm 2014b; Shaw 2003, 2013; Weitz 2003.
42. Krain 1997: 346.
43. Nyseth Brehm 2014b: 27.
44. Melson 1992: 19.
45. Melson 1992: 170.

46. Shaw 2007: 111 (emphasis in original).
47. Shaw 2007: 112.
48. Shaw 2007: 129–130.
49. Rotberg 2004: 1.
50. Also see Soderlund 2013: 3.
51. Karstedt 2011a: 108–110.
52. Gurr, Marshall, and Harff 2003: v.
53. State Failure Task Force 2000: x; emphasis added. The SFTF—today known as the Political Instability Task Force—is funded by the US government and advises it but is composed of independent scholars.
54. Verwimp 2013 offers an extended analysis of Rwanda's economic and political collapse at the time of the genocide.
55. Sampson 2006; Sampson, Raudenbush, and Earls 1997; Karstedt 2011a: esp. 108; Rotberg 2004: esp. 3.
56. Also see McDoom 2013.
57. Kuper 1981; Fein 1979, 1990, 1993a.
58. Weitz 2003. It is worth noting that Weitz selected his examples just *because* they illustrate the impacts of ideologies of race and nationality. Thus, they do not tell us much about the roles of race and nationalism in genocides more generally.
59. State Failure Task Force 2000: 44.
60. Nyseth Brehm 2014a.
61. Mann 2005; also see Hagan and Rymond-Richmond 2009.
62. The examples comes from Krain 1997: 337n6; Krain is one of the few to acknowledge that Jews were only one of many groups targeted by the Nazis, the others including Jehovah's Witnesses, homosexuals, and the mentally and physically disabled. Shaw's objections appear in his 2007 book.
63. Krain 1997: 355.
64. See Karstedt 2013a: 388–389.
65. Neither race nor ethnicity was important in the Indonesian case. Robert Cribb and Charles Coppel maintain that to use racism to explain the violence in Indonesia in the mid-1960s blinds us analytically "to the real causes of intense violence in Indonesia and other societies. There is growing evidence that one of the most significant elements in outbreaks of violence in Indonesia is the availability of impunity to perpetrators. That is to say, violence may not be motivated by intense hatreds, antagonisms or tensions but rather by the absence or withdrawal of the normal state sanctions of violence" (2009: 460). The same could be said of the Nazi genocide of the disabled, which did not distinguish victims by race or ethnicity, although disabled Jews were probably more vulnerable.
66. Krain 1997; Shaw 2007.
67. Fein 1993c: 798.
68. Fein 1993c: 797. Also see Fein 1993a.
69. Nyseth Brehm 2014b.
70. In a new book, Scott Straus argues that "to explain variation—to explain why

countries with similar crises experience different outcomes—the role of ideology is essential" (2015: x). Straus's book was published too late for me to discuss its argument, but it is noteworthy for its return to the notion that ideology plays a primary role in genocide causation.

71. Pew Center on the States 2011.

72. Kurlychek, Brame, and Bushway 2006.

73. Also see Fein 1993a; Harff 2003b; Nyseth Brehm 2014b.

74. But see Nyseth Brehm 2014a and the Genocide Prevention Project, discussed shortly.

75. State Failure Task Force 2000: x.

76. Kuper 1981; Kiernan 2007; Melson 1992.

77. Genocide Prevention Task Force 2008: 18–19.

78. As of this writing, a few former Cambodian leaders have been convicted. Ríos Montt was convicted—but then pardoned by his allies in Guatemala's courts.

79. Also see Sikkink 2011.

80. E.g., Loeber and Farrington 1998.

81. Farrington and Welsh 2007.

82. International Commission on Intervention and State Sovereignty 2001: 22, sec. 3.12. Also see Genocide Prevention Task Force 2008.

83. State Failure Task Force 2000: 44.

84. Rummel 1983, 1992; also see Finkel and Straus 2014.

85. Also see Gerlach 2006, 2010; Karstedt 2012a, 2013b; Shaw 2013.

86. Mann 2005; also see Karstedt 2011a, 2013b, 2013c; State Failure Task Force 2000; Shaw 2013; cf. Nyseth Brehm 2014b.

87. Mann 2005; also see State Failure Task Force 2000.

88. Weiss-Wendt 2010: 81–82.

89. Krain 1997; cf. State Failure Task Force 2000.

90. Silvester and Gewald 2003: 95.

91. Schaller 2010a: 305.

92. Bridgman 1981: 63–64.

93. Bridgman and Worley 1995: 12, quoting from a letter to Leutwein from Samuel Maherero.

94. Durkheim (1893) 1933, (1897) 2007.

95. Merton 1938.

96. As quoted in Totten, Parsons, and Charny 1995: 34.

97. For a chart of micro, meso, and macro interrelationships in atrocity crimes, see Rothe and Mullins 2009. These authors add a fourth, international level to the other three.

4. THE EMOTIONAL DYNAMICS OF GENOCIDE

1. For moving interviews with remorseful perpetrators, see the award-winning documentary *Enemies of the People* (2009).

2. Fujii 2009: esp. ch. 6.

3. Browning 1992: 184–185.

4. Collins 2008.

5. Hilberg 1985: 133–134.

6. Kühne 2010, writing of Nazi Germany.

7. Fujii 2009.

8. Finkel and Straus 2014: 59.

9. My approach is not entirely new; for instance, Alexander Laban Hinton (2005) examines "the cultural frames through which Khmer Rouge killers interpreted their lethal tasks" (23). However, to my knowledge, other people who have worked on genocide at the meso-level have not concentrated on perpetrator-group emotions.

10. Staub 1989.

11. Goffman (1974) 1986: 10–11, 21.

12. On dehumanization, see Erikson 1996; Gamson 1995; Herrmann 2011; Hinton 2005; Kelman 1973; Levi 1988; Staub 1989; Waller 2007.

13. Collins 2008; Klusemann 2010, 2012; Fujii 2004, 2009, and much of the other recent research on the Rwandan genocide.

14. Fujii 2009.

15. Mann 2005: 490.

16. My analysis generally follows Cribb 2001a, one of the clearest sources on this chaotic and multifaceted genocide.

17. Robinson 1995: 236.

18. Robinson 1995: 239.

19. For details, see Cribb 1990a; Cribb and Coppel 2009; and Robinson 1995.

20. Roosa 2006: 6; Robinson 1995: 282.

21. Cribb 1990b: 15.

22. Gerlach 2010: 65

23. Gerlach 2010: 50.

24. Gerlach 2010: 20.

25. Cribb 2001a: 238n26.

26. Pohlman 2015.

27. Pohlman 2015: 172.

28. Gie 1990: 256.

29. Anonymous 1990: 171.

30. Anonymous 1990: 172.

31. Pohlman 2015.

32. Roosa 2006: 7.

33. Dwyer and Santikarma 2003: 290–291.

34. Anderson and McVey 1971: 114n6; Robinson 1995: 293; Roosa 2006: 29.

35. A. Henry 2014.

36. Roosa 2006: 26.

37. Robinson 1995: 280.

38. Cribb 2001b: 91.

39. Anonymous 1990: 170.

40. Cribb and Coppel 2009.

41. Gerlach 2010: 26.

42. Dwyer and Santikarma 2003: 293.

43. Gerlach 2010: 36.

44. Robinson 1995: 298.

45. Sukarno, as quoted in Roosa 2006: 22, which also describes the genocide as an overreaction.

46. Cribb 1990b: 23.

47. Dwyer and Santikarma 2003: 293.

48. Gerlach 2010: 34.

49. Pohlman 2015.

50. Pohlman 2015: 76, 173.

51. For more detail on this bizarre and wonderful film, see Rafter 2014.

52. Feierstein 2014: 14; emphasis in original.

53. Mills 1940.

54. Komar 2008: 30.

55. Appeal 1990.

56. RTLM 1994.

57. Ruggiero 2010: 716.

58. Cikara and Van Bavel 2014.

59. Fein 1990: 36, citing Fein 1977 as her original use of the term. In an important historical-anthropological analysis, Alexander Laban Hinton (2002) ties this "othering" process to modernity.

60. Erikson 1996: 51, quoting from a manuscript by his father, Erik Erikson.

61. Cienciala, Lebedeva, and Materski 2007: 24.

62. Snow and McAdam 2000: 53; emphasis added.

63. Kelman 1973: 38.

64. Kelman 1973: 50.

65. Kelman 1973: 50.

66. Sereny 1983: 101.

67. Kuper 1981: 92.

68. Fein 1993b: 36.

69. Cf. Smith 2011.

70. Collins 2008.

71. Collins 2008: 8.

72. Collins 2008: 8.

73. Klusemann 2012: 472.

74. Klusemann 2012: esp. 472.

75. Scapegoat theory is not much endorsed these days; but see Verdeja 2002. While scapegoat theory explains much less than does analysis of the antagonists' interactions, as in Collins (2008) and in Klusemann's work (2010, 2012), it does underscore the vulnerability of genocide's victims.

76. Collins 2008: 85.
77. Cribb 2001a; Robinson 1995.
78. Drouin 2010: 93. See chapter 2 for the full account.
79. Collins 2008: 93.
80. Collins 2008: 93.
81. The exception is the Nazi genocide of the disabled.
82. Browning 1992.
83. How the Germans 2003.
84. Mardiganian (1918) 2010: 181.
85. Hatzfeld 2003:16.
86. Hatzfeld 2003: 51.
87. Collins 2008: 94.
88. Katz 1988.
89. Katz 1988: 9.
90. Friedlander 1995: 50.
91. After the war, when testifying before the US Military Tribunal, "Pfannmüller responded to this accusation: 'If he says I tore a poor child out of its bed with my fat hands, I would say in my life I never had fat hands. I certainly never grinned at such a thing. I never laughed." He was actually proud of what he had done (Friedlander 1995: 51).
92. Aly 1994: 31.
93. Cienciala, Lebedeva, and Materski 2007: 124.
94. Dwyer 2004.
95. Ghosts 2004; British Broadcasting Company 2014.
96. Evans 2004: 63–64.
97. Roosa 2006: 25.
98. Gerlach 2010: 85, quoting Robert Elegant of the *Bulletin/Australian Financial Times* (1966).
99. Schonhardt 2012.

5. EXTERMINATION UP CLOSE AND PERSONAL

1. For other micro-level approaches, see Finkel and Straus 2014. I follow some of these later in this chapter.
2. To be clear, the splitting theory that I propose here has nothing in common with Robert Jay Lifton's (1986) psychoanalytic explanation of the behavior of Nazi doctors in terms of "doubling."
3. Collins 2008. On coercion and bribery in (for example) the Rwandan genocide, see Des Forges 1999; Fujii 2009; and Straus 2006. On soldiers' failures to shoot to kill (or kill by other means), see Grossman 1995; de Waal 2009: esp. 218; Straus 2006: esp. 110–121; Verwimp 2005.
4. See chapter 4.
5. Waller 2007: 20.
6. Waller 2007: 22, 91. Also see Staub 1989.

7. Bandura 1990, 1999, 2002.

8. Ervin Staub's *The Roots of Evil* (1989), a well-known and much-admired social psychology of genocide, develops a processual analysis somewhat similar to Bandura's (see, esp., Staub 1989: 21–22), but it relies heavily on the questionable frustration-aggression thesis, according to which hardships and social disorganization create frustrations that cause "the society to turn against a subgroup in it" (4).

9. Bandura 2002.

10. Bandura 2002: 103.

11. Weitz 2003.

12. Bandura 2002: 104.

13. Bandura 2002; also see Milgram 1965, 1974.

14. Conscience 1992.

15. Conscience 1992. It should be noted, however, that authorities may have been monitoring what Nhem En said in the film and that, at the time he took the photographs, he lived in mortal fear of making a mistake.

16. Bandura 2002: 109.

17. Bandura 2002: 110. Criminologists call this process "brutalization." Also see Browning 1992.

18. Maruna and Copes 2005: 224.

19. Sykes and Matza 1957.

20. Specifically, "denial of responsibility" corresponds to Bandura's fourth mechanism, displacement of responsibility. "Denial of injury" overlaps with Bandura's second mechanism, euphemistic language, as well as with his sixth mechanism, disregard or distortion of consequences. "Denial of the victim" is similar to Bandura's seventh mechanism, dehumanization, although far from a perfect fit. "Condemnation of the condemners" corresponds to Bandura's eighth mechanism, attribution of blame; and "appeal to high loyalties" corresponds to Bandura's first mechanism, moral justification. Sykes and Matza have no neutralization technique that corresponds to Bandura's third mechanism, advantageous comparison, although this does relate to condemnation of the condemners. They also have nothing that corresponds to Bandura's fifth mechanism, diffusion of responsibility, although the latter relates closely to their denial of responsibility.

21. Cf. Maruna and Copes 2005.

22. Alvarez 1997; Day and Vandiver 2000; and Cohen 2001.

23. Baron-Cohen 2011: 2.

24. Baron-Cohen 2011: 18.

25. Baron-Cohen 2011: 171.

26. Baron-Cohen 2011: 21,

27. Baron-Cohen 2011: 11.

28. In contrast, Karin Orth (2000), in a study of SS concentration-camp guards, argues that the guards experienced no tension between going to work to kill people and returning home to their lovely *Volkish* villages at night because for them, it was all part of participating in the German *Volk*.

29. Anderson 1999.
30. Anderson 1999: 100.
31. Vann Nath 1998: 62–64.
32. Swidler 1986, 2001; Harding 2007: 346. On the way in which ideas from movies become part of our tool kits, see Rafter 2006.
33. Harding 2007: 346.
34. Sampson and Wilson 1995: 50.
35. Hinton 2005: 86.
36. Singer and Lamm 2009: 81.
37. Singer and Lamm 2009: 84.
38. Singer and Lamm 2009: 84.
39. Singer and Lamm 2009: 89.
40. Singer and Lamm 2009: 91.
41. Also see Vignemont and Singer 2006.
42. de Waal 2009: 208.
43. de Waal 2009: 213.
44. de Waal 2009: 221.
45. de Waal 2009: 214.
46. de Waal 2009: 214.
47. Rueckert and Naybar 2008; but see Hollan 2012: 75–76.
48. Hollan 2012: 74.
49. Baron-Cohen 2011: ch. 3; also see de Waal 2009: esp. 200–201.
50. Hare 1993.
51. Browning 1992: 175–176.
52. Browning 1992: 168.
53. Haney, Banks, and Zimbardo 1973: 69.
54. Milgram 1965, 1974.
55. Perry 2012.
56. One might even relate these variations in willingness to complete the splitting process to the history of slavery in the United States. Slave owners' moral disengagement involved Bandura's first three mechanisms of moral justification: invocation of ideological rationales, euphemistic labeling (use of degrading language to describe the victims), and advantageous comparison (demonstrations of the victims' inferiority). These mechanisms formed the self-serving justifications for slavery throughout the US South; but even in the South, there were individual variations in the ability to complete the splitting process. Some slave owners treated their human property better than others did; a few actually liberated their slaves; and some were so brutally harsh that they destroyed those they owned.
57. Kiernan 1996: 19.
58. Kiernan 1996: 171–177.
59. Hinton 2005: 1.
60. Kiernan 1996: 180.
61. Hinton 2005: 156–157, citing Kiernan 1996: 464.

62. For biographical information on Pol Pot, I have relied mainly on Chandler 1999a and Kiernan 1996.
63. Hinton 2005: 132.
64. Hinton 2005: 128.
65. Hinton 2005: 19.
66. Hinton 2005: 45.
67. Hinton 2005: 91.
68. Kiernan 2002: 486.
69. Kiernan 2002: 486.
70. GSP n.d.; Killing fields n.d.
71. The figure of 12,000 comes from Hinton 2014: 7; it has been revised downward from the previous estimate of 14,000.
72. Chandler 1999b. For more accounts of the guards—and prisoners—see the first-person account by Vann Nath (1998).
73. Chandler 1999a: 147.
74. To identify motives, I have drawn on answers to my case-study questions 8, 9, 10, 27, and 19 (appendix B), looking only at those motives that were in play during the events and excluding ex post facto excuses.
75. The doctors did, however, feel that the disabled were threats to the purity of Aryan "blood" and a drain on national resources.
76. Bridgman 1981: 167.
77. The introduction to Hinton 2005 discusses how ideology interacts with individuals' own cognitive models.
78. Major Ludwig von Estorff objected to the genocide, to von Trotha himself, and later ordered removal of Herero prisoners from Shark Island, where over half had already died. He was reprimanded for removing the prisoners. See Silvester and Gewald 2003: xxi.
79. Friedlander 1995: 57.
80. Evans 2004: 58.
81. Smeulers and Hoex 2010; Straus 2006; Verwimp 2005; Fujii 2009.
82. Fujii 2009: 97.
83. Wirth, as quoted in Evans 2004: 32.
84. Mardiganian (1918) 2010; also see chapter 4.
85. Des Forges 1999; Hatzfeld 2003; Mamdani 2001. For other examples of genocide begin fun, see chapter 4.
86. Hinton 2005.

6. MOBILIZATION FOR DESTRUCTION

1. Michael Burleigh (1994: 202) describes this film, called *Three People*.
2. Akçam 2006; Dadrian 1995.
3. Akçam 2006: 8, 11.
4. Akçam 2006: 44, quoting Sultan Abdul Hamid II.
5. Balakian 2003: 115.

6. Dadrian 1995: 123.
7. Akçam 2006: 43.
8. Naimark 2001: 28.
9. Akçam 2012: xviii.
10. Levene 1998.
11. Akçam 2006: 52.
12. Akçam 2006: 53.
13. Akçam 2004.
14. Bloxham 2003: 184.
15. Akçam 2004.
16. Donald Bloxham analyzes the Ottomans' "desire to create an Ottoman bourgeoisie, which by the beginning of the twentieth century effectively meant creating a Muslim-Turkish middle class as a driver of nationalism and of the Muslim-Turkish 'national economy' at the expense of indigenous Christians" (2010: 327). Also see Üngör 2009; and Üngör and Polatel 2011.
17. Scott 1998.
18. Gerlach 2006, 2010.
19. Akçam 2006; Balakian 2003; Bloxham 2008.
20. For a glimpse of denialists' reasoning, see Erickson 2006.
21. Adolf Hitler, August 22, 1939, as quoted in Robertson 2009: 5.
22. Hitler (1925) 1971: 394.
23. Friedlander 1995: 39.
24. Proctor 1988: 181.
25. Friedlander 1995.
26. The full name was the Reich Committee for the Scientific Registration of Severe Hereditary Ailments. As Henry Friedlander (1995) explains, this was merely a front for the children's "euthanasia" program.
27. Evans 2004: 35–36.
28. Friedlander 1995: 225, 222.
29. Proctor 1988: 68.
30. Rudolf Lonauer n.d.
31. Friedlander 1995: 148.
32. Proctor 1988; Friedlander 1995.
33. On the flexible meanings of "asocials" and the term's criminological implications, see Rafter 2008.
34. Aly 1994: 45; Friedlander 1995: 148.
35. Friedlander 1995: 22.
36. Bauman 1989.
37. Scott 1998: 91.
38. Aly 1994: 22; Evans 2004: 18, 67; Friedlander 1995: 61, 85, 110, 150; Kater 1989: 44; Proctor 1988: 188, 192; Torrey and Yolken 2010: 26. For a lower estimate of 275,000, see Schulze 2012: 25.
39. Tilly 2003.

40. Campbell and Brenner 2002. Moreover, death squads need visibility, not secrecy, to accomplish their work of terror. Also see Hiebert 2008; Sluka 1999; Warren 1999.

41. Alvarez 2006; Ahram 2014.

42. McDoom 2013.

43. Kelman 1973: 29–35. Kelman uses the term to refer to mass violence in which all ordinary human restraints have been dissolved, and that is certainly part of my meaning here.

44. Alvarez 2006: 1. Also see Bloxham 2008.

45. Alvarez 2006: 2.

46. Alvarez 2006: 6.

47. Alvarez 2006: 27.

48. Jamieson and McEvoy 2005.

49. Silvester and Gewald 2003.

50. Akçam 2006: 95 (high-level Unionist officials); Naimark 2001: 28 (hundreds of gangs).

51. Akçam 2006: 132 (worked in secret), 97 (work the government itself could not do). More recently, Akçam (2012: 4) has described the Special Organization as "semi-secret," which seems more accurate for a unit that was formed for other purposes before the genocide started. The Special Organization worked closely with members of local elites (who mobilized "dozens, or in some cases, hundreds of potential killers"; Üngör and Polatel 2011: 166). Altogether, the gangs—the lower level in the two-tiered hierarchy—totaled about 30,000 men, according to Akçam (2006: 136), although other sources give lower figures.

52. Cienciala, Lebedeva, and Materski 2007: 162.

53. The film *The Act of Killing* (2012) shows how this network was formed in one area of Indonesia (Northern Sumatra) and how its parts interacted. On Indonesia's history of mobilizing militias, see Ahram 2014: 8.

54. Smeulers and Hoex 2010; Straus 2006.

55. In this chapter's coverage of Rwanda, I focus on the Interahamwe, but other organizations, including military units and other party militias, also helped lead the genocide.

56. Ariel Ahram calls genocidal militias "state-organized crime" (2014: 2).

57. See Karstedt 2014. Indeed, genocide itself is the supreme form of state-organized crime.

58. See, generally, Huisman 2010.

59. Ahram 2014: 5.

60. Ahram 2014: 6.

61. Ahram 2014: 10.

62. Agamben 2005: 23.

63. Agamben 2005: 50.

64. The Hague Convention of 1899, which Germany had ratified, forbade killing enemies who had surrendered; it also forbade collective punishment. However, Is-

abel Hull (2003: 160) notes that many Europeans did not believe that international law applied in colonies. The settlers' view that German law did not apply to the Herero can be seen in the way they used different standards of proof for violations by the two groups (see chapter 3).

65. Üngör and Polatel 2011; Akçam 2012; Dadrian 1995.
66. Friedlander 1995: 67.
67. Friedlander 1995: 67, quoting Hitler's letter of authorization.
68. Proctor 1988: 193.
69. Burleigh 1994: 112; Friedlander 1995: 67; Proctor 1988: 193.
70. Zaslavsky 2008: 45; Paul 2010: 349; Cienciala, Lebedeva, and Materski 2007: 147.
71. Roosa 2006: 12.
72. Chandler 1999b: 47.
73. Garrard-Burnett 2010: 20.
74. Straus 2006: 93, 137, 173, 221; also see Gourevitch 1998: 96.
75. Nowrojee 1996: 24.

7. GENDER AND GENOCIDE

1. Jones 2004: 3. Jones drew the term "gendercide" from M. Warren 1985.
2. West and Zimmerman 1987: 125, 126.
3. The usual estimate for the number dead in the Rwanda genocide is over 800,000, but new data, derived from testimony before the country's *gacaca* courts, has led to an upward revision to over one million dead. See Uggen, Nyseth Brehm, and McElrath 2014. Nyseth Brehm, Uggen, and Gasanabo (2014b) set the number dead at 1,050,000, or 14 percent of the population.

   As for the genocide's length, Hollie Nyseth Brehm observes that it probably lasted longer than three months, although that is the usually named period. The Rwandan Patriotic Front took over the capital in three months, but, Nyseth Brehm says, "people in many villages told me violence continued after that" (personal communication, December 19, 2014).
4. The figure of 250,000 comes from Uggen, Brehm, and McElrath 2014.
5. McDoom 2013: 28.
6. Justino and Verwimp 2008: 16.
7. Verwimp 2005: 299; Des Forges 1999.
8. Mamdani 2001: 149. On Rwanda's economic problems at the time of the genocide, also see Verwimp 2013: 20, which points out that the country's inability to feed its own people was exacerbated by huge influxes of refugees from conflicts in contiguous states.
9. Nowrojee 1996: 14.
10. Nowrojee 1996: 15.
11. Mamdani 2001. Also see Gourevitch 1998: esp. 55–57.
12. Bell 2014: 114.
13. While the census just preceding the genocide determined that under 10 percent of the population was Tutsi, this group was probably undercounted. Des Forges

(1999: 16–17) discusses problems with determining population percentages at that time. Also see Straus 2006: 19.

14. Gourevitch 1998: 84.
15. Also known as the Rwandan Patriotic Army.
16. Gourevitch 1998: 98–99.
17. Komar 2008: 174.
18. Power 2002: 338–339.
19. Nowrojee 1996: 12–13.
20. Mugesera, as quoted in Power 2002: 339–340.
21. British Broadcasting Corporation 2014.
22. Philip Verwimp (2013: 8) holds that the civil war started in October 1990, when the large massacres of Tutsi began. Scott Straus (2006) holds that there were actually two civil wars, the first running from 1990 until the 1993 Arusha Accords and the second occurring during the genocide, in 1994.
23. Hatzfeld 2003: 36.
24. Nowrojee 1996: 11.
25. Nowrojee 1996: 37.
26. Alison Des Forges (1999: 17–18) discusses the difficulties of getting accurate data on the number of Tutsi killed. Over one million people were killed in the genocide. If we assume that 75 percent of the homicide victims were Tutsi, then Tutsi victims numbered 750,000. But the 75 percent assumption is simply an educated guess, and there is no way to be sure of the Tutsi death count. Similarly, there is no way to be sure of the proportion of Tutsi killed.
27. On the length of the genocide, see note 3.
28. The $1 billion mark was reached in 2007; it represented costs over the previous thirteen years, including salaries for 1,000 workers and airplane tickets for fugitives and others flown in from abroad.
29. The figure comes from Nyseth Brehm, Uggen, and Gasanabo 2014b.
30. Nyseth Brehm, Uggen, and Gasanabo 2014b.
31. In addition to the three court processes described here, a fourth—trials in European and North American countries, under the principle of universal jurisdiction—tried about a dozen people. See Bouwknegt 2014.
32. Straus 2006: 51–52, drawing on Des Forges 1999, gives figures ranging from 25,000 to 60,000 for the number of Hutu killed by the RPF.
33. Also see Carpenter 2002.
34. Jones 2004.
35. Jones 2002: 66.
36. Jones 2002: 69.
37. Prunier 1997: 231–232, as quoted in Jones 2002: 68.
38. British Broadcasting Corporation 2014.
39. Hatzfeld 2003: 47–48.
40. Straus 2006: 100.
41. Hollie Nyseth Brehm, personal communication, December 19, 2014.

42. Verwimp 2005: 306.

43. This figure refers to the number of first trials, but the actual number of cases heard by the *gacaca* courts was 1.9 million. The latter figure includes appeals and trials conducted in absentia.

44. Nyseth Brehm, Uggen, and Gasanabo 2014a, 2014b.

45. Bell 2014: 96.

46. Bell 2014: 96.

47. Bell 2014: 104.

48. Bell 2014: 101.

49. Bell 2014: 92.

50. Britton 2011: 102–107, discussing the characteristics of "rape-prone societies."

51. Two of these lewd propaganda drawings can be seen in Taylor 1999.

52. Nowrojee 1996: 14.

53. Nowrojee 1996: 14. Also see Hagan and Rymond-Richmond 2009 for use of racial epithets during Janjaweed genocidal massacres in Darfur.

54. Lee Ann Fujii writes that "rapes were part of the practices of killing, and not the act of individuals going off on their own" (2009: 174).

55. Rape as an instrument of power has been an analytical theme in the literature on rape from Susan Brownmiller ([1975] 1993) through Peggy Reeves Sanday (2007) and Dana Britton (2011).

56. Fujii (2009: esp. 177–178) is particularly illuminating on this point with regard to Interahamwe rapists.

57. Nowrojee 1996: 2.

58. Feierstein 2014. However, although "ordinary" rape is less physically destructive of individuals and groups, it too serves the purpose of configuring neighborhoods into safe and unsafe areas for girls and women—and thus, ultimately, of male social control of females. See Miller 2008.

59. Nowrojee 1996: 4.

60. Nowrojee 1996: 4.

61. Fein 1999: 44.

62. Kaiser and Hagan 2015: 3.

63. Hull 2003: 146. Also see Hull 2005b.

64. Bell 2014: 119.

65. Bell 2014.

66. Koonz 1988.

67. Burleigh 1994: 101.

68. Friedlander, 1995: 218; emphasis in original. A few "euthanasia" nurses were prosecuted after the war. Irmgard Huber, the chief nurse at the Hademar killing center, was sentenced, initially, to twenty-five years in prison for selecting patients for murder, falsifying death certificates, and supplying doctors with drugs. Later, in another trial, she was sentenced to eight additional years as an accomplice to at least 120 murders. However, Huber was released from prison in 1952 and granted a new lease on life, as were many convicted war criminals in the postwar period.

69. Pohlman 2015: 85, citing Komnas Perempuan, an Indonesian book published in Jakarta in 2007. Pohlman's excellent study of sexual violence in the Indonesian genocide was published too late for me to incorporate its analyses here, although I do draw on earlier parts of the manuscript that she shared with me.

70. Wieringa 2003: 72; also see Dwyer 2004.

71. Garrard-Burnett 2010: 209n41.

72. REMHI 1999: 37.

73. Chandler 1999b: 26.

74. Also see notes 90 and 91.

75. Also see von Joeden-Forgey 2012.

76. The belief in female inferiority was evident even during the Katyn Forest Massacre, in which all participants—victims as well as perpetrators—were men aside from one woman, Janina Antonina Lewandowska, who had joined the Polish air force reserves. Women were barred from the military, although an exception had been made in this case, perhaps because Lewandowska was the daughter of a general. Cienciala, Lebedeva, and Materski 2007: 398.

77. I say "often" because this was not the case in the Nazi genocide of disabled people, Katyn Forest Massacre, or Cambodian genocide. The Nazi genocide of the disabled was organized in terms of gender roles, but the violence was not aimed specifically against females. In the Katyn Forest Massacre, all but one of the victims was male, and there was no recorded sexual violence. During the Cambodian genocide, the target again was not defined in terms of gender; but there was extensive forced marriage by a state that assumed its right to control everyone in the country, and there may have been extensive rape as well—ongoing investigations may shed light on that matter.

78. Sjoberg 2013. Also see Hagan and Rymond-Richmond 2009.

79. West and Zimmerman 1987.

80. Chakrabarti and Baron-Cohen 2006; Rueckert and Naybar 2008; Singer and Lamm 2009; de Waal 2009; Baron-Cohen 2011.

81. All items in this list except the last, which I added, are drawn from Chakrabarti and Baron-Cohen 2006.

82. Singer and Lamm 2009: 91.

83. Singer and Lamm 2009: 90.

84. Anderson 1999: 36.

85. United Nations 1948.

86. On February 2, 2015, the International Court of Justice (ICJ)—not the International Criminal Court but a body that settles international disputes—ruled that neither Croatia nor Serbia had committed genocide during the breakup of the former Yugoslavia in the early 1990s. However, in 2007, the ICJ upheld the judgment of the International Criminal Tribunal for the Former Yugoslavia (ICTY) that the 1995 Srebrenica massacre was genocide against Bosnian Muslims; seven men were convicted of genocide in that event. The ICTY decided that mass rapes

of Bosniak and other women by Serbs during the same period constituted not
genocide but crimes against humanity.

87. Hagan and Morse 2014.

88. Sjoberg 2013.

89. Jeremy Silvester and Jan-Bart Gewald comment on sexual abuse by German
    soldiers: "There are numerous references in the Blue Book [testimonies on the
    genocide] to allegations of sexual abuse in the prison camps" (2003: 177n165).

90. Of course, one might say rape is relevant in these two cases through its absence.
    The disabled victims of the Nazis were probably considered too unattractive to
    rape, while to rape the Polish prisoners would have violated the Russian soldiers'
    sense of manliness.

91. Studzinsky 2013: 181. Studzinsky found evidence of rapes at detention centers in
    addition to S-21, but the Extraordinary Chambers in the Courts of Cambodia
    refused to hear the evidence. She cites one unpublished study of rape during the
    Khmer Rouge regime, and two others are cited on Google Scholar; but none of
    those yields usable citations. Thus, I was unable to get further information on this
    point.

92. In 2010, the Extraordinary Chambers in the Courts of Cambodia convicted
    "Duch," the head of the S-21 prison, of rape, among other crimes. See Askin 2013:
    51; and Studzinsky 2013. On gender-based violence in general under the Khmer
    Rouge, see the Gender-Based Violence under the Khmer Rouge Regime website:
    http://gbvkr.org/.

93. The use of rape by Serbs in the 1990s wars in the former Yugoslavia has received
    considerable—and lively—attention from scholars contrasting it in particular
    with its use by Hutu in Rwanda. See, especially, Card 2008; and Weitsman 2008.

94. Rafter and Bell 2013.

95. Futter and Mebane 2001.

96. Futter and Mebane 2001; Caringella 2009.

97. Full details can be found in Askin 2013.

98. Karstedt 2010: 13.

99. Cole 2010; Ellis 2007: 228.

100. N. Henry 2011.

101. ICTR 1998: para. 38.

102. ICTR 1998: para. 11.

103. ICTR 1998: para. 51.

104. In 2008, the UN Security Council "noted" that sexual violence is a "constitu-
     tive act with respect to genocide" (UN Security Council Resolution 1820, sec. 4
     [2008]). This constituted international recognition of sexual violence as a form of
     genocide; it was, however, simply a "note."

105. MacKinnon 2006: 232.

106. Feierstein 2014: 17.

107. Feierstein 2014: 36; emphasis in original.

108. United Nations 2002: arts. 6, 8.
109. United Nations 2002: art. 7.
110. N. Henry 2011: 97.
111. Ellis 2007: 238.
112. United Nations 2002: art. 7 (1) (g)-1 ("Elements of Crimes").
113. Also see Kaiser and Hagan 2015.

8. HOW DO GENOCIDES END? DO THEY END?

1. Also see Conley-Zilkic and de Waal 2014: 61, 70; and Krain 2014.
2. De Waal, Meierhenrich, and Conley-Zilkic 2012.
3. Conley-Zilkic and de Waal 2014: 57.
4. Also see Schneiderhan 2013: esp. 289 ("a continual process with no real beginning or end, no specific, concrete end toward which one moves by deploying particular means").
5. Feierstein 2014: 12.
6. De Waal, Meierhenrich, and Conley-Zilkic 2012.
7. De Waal and his colleagues recognize the problem involved in holding that colonial and settler genocides actually end when "for the victims/survivors and their descendants, the injustice remains very much alive as they seek recognition, compensation, and reparation. In many cases, the remnant indigenous people retain a tenacious hold of their experience as victims of genocide" (2012: 20). Writing of settler colonialism, in which the settlers' object is land, Patrick Wolfe develops the concept of "structure" to indicate ways in which traces of the original group persist: "The native repressed continues to structure settler-colonial society. It is both as complex social formation and as continuity through time that I term settler colonization a structure rather than an event" (2006: 390).
8. Gerlach 2006: 466. Also see Gerlach 2010.
9. For two other—quite similar but less developed—typologies, see Verdeja 2002; and Krain 2014.
10. Fein 1997: 10–13.
11. Also see Totten 2012.
12. The phrase "not with a bang but a whimper" comes from T. S. Eliot's poem "The Hollow Men" (1925), forecasting how the world will end.
13. According to Allen Paul (2010: 103), the precise start and finish dates of the Katyn genocide are April 3–May 13, 1940.
14. Gerlach 2010: 67; cf. Pohlman 2015: 10.
15. Friedlander 1995: 162–163.
16. The Indonesian genocide, too, may have petered out, as new evidence suggests; but until revisionist historians tell the full story of this atrocity, the best policy is to stick with the traditional endpoint, defined by Suharto's assumption of power, of 1966.
17. Haas 2008: 333.
18. Naimark 2001: 12.
19. Naimark 2001: 39.

20. Akçam 2006: 325.
21. Akçam 2004, 2006.
22. REMHI 1999: 302–303.
23. Maruna 2001.
24. Paternoster and Bushway 2011: 190; Maruna 2001.
25. Ahram 2011, 2014.
26. De Waal, Meierhenrich, and Conley-Zilkic 2012: 28.
27. Grandin 2000: 221.
28. Garrard-Burnett 2010: 3. Descriptions of the army's violence against the Maya appear in chapters 2, 4, 5, and 7 of this book.
29. See Garrard-Burnett 2010: 6–7; O'Neill 2005: 333–334; and Sanford 2009: 41. Victoria Sanford reports that according to the Guatemalan Truth Commission, "Army massacres destroyed 626 villages, more than 200,000 people were killed or disappeared, 1.5 million were displaced by the violence, and more than 150,000 were driven to seek refuge in Mexico. The state was responsible for 93 percent of the violent acts" (n.d.: 1). It is difficult to state precise numbers of Mayan dead because historians tend to count the total number killed in Guatemala's civil war, which included targets in addition to the Maya. For figures covering a sample of the massacres, see REMHI 1999.
30. REMHI 1999. This is an English-language condensation of the original four-volume report of the same title.
31. REMHI 1999: xxxiii.
32. Speech by Monsignor Juan Gerardi, in REMHI 1999: xxiii.
33. Inter-American Court of Human Rights 2003: 13.
34. Inter-American Court of Human Rights 2003: 29 (testimony of Clara Arenas Bianchi).
35. Inter-American Court of Human Rights 2003: 48.
36. International Crisis Group 2014: 2.
37. United Nations Office on Drugs and Crime 2013: 12.
38. But see International Crisis Group 2014, detailing progress in Guatemala.
39. REMHI 1999: 176.
40. REMHI 1999: 176.
41. REMHI 1999: 176.
42. Also see Archibold 2012.
43. See, too, McEvoy and McConnachie 2012.
44. Mildt 1996. That Rudolph Lonauer, chief of Austria's Hartheim extermination center, killed not only himself but also his family hints that his dreams for a Nazified world had been crushed.
45. Evans 2004; Karstedt 2011b.
46. On the Cambodian trials, see Scheffer 2015.
47. Chrisje Brants (2007: 310) uses the term "blue-collar" to refer to those genocidists who actually do the killing.
48. See, especially, Sanford 2009 and the entire book in which this article was published: Hinton and O'Neill 2009.

49. Akçam 2006: 247.
50. Armenian Genocide 2006.
51. Fischer 2007.
52. Zaslavsky 2008; Cienciala, Lebedeva, and Materski 2007: 118–120 ("Beria Memo-randum to Joseph Stalin Proposing the Execution of the Police Officers . . . , Accepted by the Politburo 5 March 1940, Moscow"). Another factor that helped force the Russian leaders to tell the truth was the courageous act of Natalia S. Leb-edeva, a Russian historian, who in 1990 published "The Katyn Tragedy," an article consisting of an interview and documents, without first obtaining government permission. This article too let the cat out of the bag (Cienciala, Lebedeva, and Materski 2007: 252).
53. Braithwaite, Braithwaite, Cookson, and Dunn 2010: 43.
54. Committee on Armenian Atrocities 1915: 24.
55. Gourevitch 1998: 229.
56. Gourevitch 1998: 270.
57. Sanford and Lincoln 2011.
58. Nowrojee 1996: 3.
59. Hunt 2014.
60. Schonhardt 2012.

9. TREATING GENOCIDE AS A CRIME

1. United Nations 2002: arts. 5–8.
2. E.g., Hoile 2014.
3. Shaw 2013: esp. 102–106.
4. Gerlach 2006, 2010.
5. Agamben 2005.
6. Collins 2008.
7. Advocates of the concept of colonial and settler genocide argue that these do not end at all; see Blackstock 2007; and Woolford, Benvenuto, and Hinton 2014.
8. Stanton 1998.
9. On settler colonialism, see especially Patrick Wolfe, who argues that "settler colo-nialism is inherently eliminatory but not invariably genocidal" (2006: 387). Wolfe defines settler colonialism as a kind of "structural genocide" (2006: 403; cf. Shaw 2013: 54) and sees Israel's colonization of the West Bank and Gaza as a possibly pregenocidal situation (2006: 404).
10. Alvarez 2014; Woolford, Benvenuto, and Hinton 2014.
11. Wolfe 2006: 394.
12. Blackstock 2007.
13. Levene 2013a, 2013b; Mann 2005; Shaw 2013.
14. Karstedt 2012a, 2013a; ICISS 2001: esp. 16.
15. Mann 2005; Shaw 2013: esp. ch. 8.
16. United Nations 2008.
17. Brown and Rafter 2013.

18. ICISS 2001: 2.
19. ICISS 2001: 19.
20. ICISS 2001: 4.
21. ICISS 2001: 20.
22. United Nations 2005: paras. 138, 139.
23. Budapest Centre 2013: 8, 29.
24. Genocide Prevention Task Force 2008.
25. Totten 2012.
26. Norris and Malknecht 2013.
27. Ahram 2014: 497.
28. Ahram 2014: 497.
29. Ahram 2014: 498. For a similar argument, see Dugan and Chenoweth 2012.
30. This literature is reviewed in Sikkink and Kim 2013. Also see Wippman 1999; and Mennecke 2007.
31. For another example, see Mennecke 2007: 324.
32. This distinction between general and specific deterrence, as Stafford and Warr 1993 point out, has fuzzy edges.
33. Braga and Weisburd 2012: 325.
34. Karstedt (2013a: 395–396) makes similar points under the headings of "protective deterrence" and "selective deterrence."
35. Braga and Weisburd 2012: 326.
36. Sherman, Gartin, and Muerger 1989; also see Karstedt 2013a.
37. Ahram 2014.
38. Dugan and Chenoweth 2012: 597.
39. Sikkink 2011; Sikkink and Kim 2013.
40. Sikkink and Kim 2013: 271.
41. Sikkink 2011: 18.
42. Sikkink and Kim 2013: 278.
43. Sikkink and Kim 2013: 276.
44. Sikkink and Kim 2013: 281.
45. Sikkink and Kim 2013; Sikkink 2011.
46. Sikkink 2011.
47. Rafter 1997, 2008.
48. Rothe 2009; Rothe and Mullins 2008, 2009, 2010.
49. Uggen, Nyseth Brehm, and McElrath 2014. Personally, I hesitate to apply the life-course model to phenomena other than individual offending as it can lead to false analogies between human development and the evolution of other phenomena (such as criminology itself; see Laub 2004). However, the parallels between individual and genocidal crimes in terms of life course can certainly lead to useful generalizations about the nature of crime itself, as they do here.
50. Nyseth Brehm, Uggen and Gasanabo 2014a.
51. See, especially, Katz 1988.

52. Gottfredson and Hirschi 1990; Britt and Gottfredson 2003; cf. Brannigan and Hardwick 2003.

53. Akers 2009; Akers and Jensen 2010; also see Sampson 1999 for a critique of social learning theory. Maier-Katkin, Mears, and Bernard reject social learning theory as an explanation for genocide because it "does not accord with the theoretic accounts, in other disciplines, of crimes against humanity, which associate genocide with sudden changes in the behavior of ordinary people" (2009: 238).

54. Nyseth Brehm 2014a, 2014b. On strain theory itself, see Agnew 1992; Agnew and Brezina 2010.

55. Weitz 2003.

56. Uggen, Nyseth Brehm, and McElrath 2014; Nyseth Brehm 2014a, 2014b.

57. Schabas 2011.

58. Parmentier 2011: 388.

59. Parmentier 2011: 387, drawing on Smeulers 2006. Parmentier goes on to make yet further recommendations.

60. Indeed, the Herero seem to have posed this counterfactual to themselves at the time and to have decided that, with or without a rebellion, their tribal way of life would disappear.

61. This method is used in Straus 2015, which was published just as the present book went to press.

62. Valentino 2004: 7.

63. Elias 1986; Rafter and Walklate 2012.

64. Hilberg 1985: 293.

65. Bell 2014.

66. Hagan and Rymond-Richmond 2009.

67. But see Bartov 1998; Bell 2014; the essays in Letschert, Haveman, de Brouwer, and Pemberton 2011; and Rafter and Walklate 2012.

68. Shaw 2013: 35.

69. McGarry and Walklate 2015.

70. We need a new understanding of political crime such as that provided long ago by Austin Turk (1982). Also see Straus 2012.

71. Following the historian Charles Tilly (1985), we can also think of some genocidal states as themselves examples of organized crime, maintained partly or mainly to collect protection money. The idea of the state as organized crime bleeds into the idea of the state as a white-collar-crime enterprise, organized during genocides to kill bureaucratically.

72. Browning 1992: 189.

73. A good start has been made by Chrisje Brants (2007).

REFERENCES

The Act of Killing. 2012. Dir. Joshua Oppenheimer. Film.

Agamben, Giorgio. 2005. State of Exception. Chicago: University of Chicago Press.

Agnew, Robert. 1992. Foundation for a general strain theory of crime and delinquency. Criminology 30/1: 47–87.

Agnew, Robert, and Timothy Brezina. 2010. Strain theories. Ch. 5 (pp. 96–113) in Eugene McLaughlin and Tim Newburn, eds., The Sage Handbook of Criminological Theory. Los Angeles: Sage.

Ahram, Ariel I. 2011. Proxy Warriors: The Rise and Fall of State-Sponsored Militias. Stanford, CA: Stanford University Press.

Ahram, Ariel I. 2014. The role of state-sponsored militias in genocide. Terrorism and Political Violence 26/3: 488–503.

Akçam, Taner. 2004. From Empire to Republic: Turkish Nationalism and the Armenian Genocide. London: Zed Books.

Akçam, Taner. 2006. A Shameful Act: The Armenian Genocide and the Questions of Turkish Responsibility. New York: Metropolitan Books.

Akçam, Taner. 2012. The Young Turks' Crime against Humanity: The Armenian Genocide and Ethnic Cleansing in the Ottoman Empire. Princeton, NJ: Princeton University Press.

Akers, Ronald L. 2009. Social Learning and Social Structure: A General Theory of Crime and Deviance. New Brunswick, NJ: Transaction.

Akers, Ronald L., and Gary F. Jensen. 2010. Social learning theory: Process and structure in criminal and deviant behavior. Ch. 3 (pp. 56–71) in Eugene McLaughlin and Tim Newburn, eds., The Sage Handbook of Criminological Theory. Los Angeles: Sage.

Alvarez, Alex. 1997. Adjusting to genocide: The techniques of neutralization and the Holocaust. Social Science History 21:139–178.

Alvarez, Alex. 2001. Governments, Citizens, and Genocide: A Comparative and Interdisciplinary Approach. Bloomington: Indiana University Press.

Alvarez, Alex. 2006. Militias and genocide. War Crimes Genocide & Crimes against Humanity 2:1–33.

Alvarez, Alex. 2010. Genocidal Crimes. London: Routledge.

Alvarez, Alex. 2014. Native America and the Question of Genocide. Lanham, MD: Rowman and Littlefield.

Aly, Götz. 1994. Medicine against the useless. Ch. 2 (pp. 22–98) in Götz Aly, Peter

Chroust, and Christian Pross, eds., Cleansing the Fatherland. Baltimore: Johns Hopkins University Press.

Amir, Menachem. 1971. Patterns in Forcible Rape. Chicago: University of Chicago Press.

Anderson, Benedict R., and Ruth T. McVey, with Frederick P. Bunnell. 1971. A Preliminary Analysis of the October 1, 1965, Coup in Indonesia. Singapore: Equinox. Originally published by Modern Indonesia Project, 1965.

Anderson, Elijah. 1999. Code of the Street: Decency, Violence, and the Moral Life of the Inner City. Chicago: University of Chicago Press.

Anonymous. 1990. Additional data on counter-revolutionary cruelty in Indonesia, especially in East Java. Ch. 7 (pp. 169–176) in Robert Cribb, ed., The Indonesian Killings of 1965–1966: Studies from Java and Bali. Clayton, Australia: Monash University Center of Southeast Asian Studies.

Appeal to the Bahutu Conscience (with the Hutu Ten Commandments). 1990. *Kangura* 6 (December): 2–3. Available at Rwanda File, http://www.rwandafile.com/Kangura/k06a.html.

Archibold, Randal C. 2012. Guatemala shooting raises concerns about military's expanded role. New York Times International, October 21: 9.

Arendt, Hannah. 1964. Eichmann in Jerusalem: A Report on the Banality of Evil. 2d ed. New York: Viking.

The Armenian Genocide. 2006. Two Cats Productions. PBS. Film.

Askin, Kelly. 2013. Treatment of sexual violence in armed conflicts: A historical perspective and the way forward. Ch. 2 in Anne-Marie de Brouwer, Charlotte Ku, Renée Romkens, and Larissa van den Herik, eds., Sexual Violence as an International Crime: Interdisciplinary Approaches. Antwerp, Belgium: Intersentia.

Austen, Ian. 2015. Report details "cultural genocide" at schools for aboriginal Canadians. New York Times International, June 3: A7.

Balakian, Peter. 2003. The Burning Tigris: The Armenian Genocide and America's Response. New York: HarperCollins.

Baldwin, Peter. 2004. Comparing and generalizing: Why all history is comparative, yet no history is sociology. Ch. 1 (pp. 1–22) in Deborah Cohen and Maura O'Connor, eds., Comparison and History: Europe in Cross-National Perspective. New York: Routledge.

Bandura, Albert. 1990. Selective activation and disengagement of moral control. Journal of Social Issues 46:27–46.

Bandura, Albert. 1999. Moral disengagement in the perpetration of inhumanities. Personality and Social Psychology Review 3/3: 193–209.

Bandura, Albert. 2002. Selective moral disengagement in the exercise of moral agency. Journal of Moral Education 31/2: 101–119.

Bardakjian, Keork B. n.d. Hitler and the Armenian genocide. http://www.armenian-genocide.org/hitler.html. Accessed August 8, 2013.

Baron-Cohen, Simon. 2011. The Science of Evil: On Empathy and the Origins of Cruelty. New York: Basic Books.

Bartov, Omer. 1998. Defining enemies, making victims: Germans, Jew, and the Holocaust. American Historical Review 103:771–816.

Bartov, Omer. 2003. Seeking the roots of modern genocide. Ch. 4 (pp. 75–96) in Robert Gellately and Ben Kiernan, eds., The Specter of Genocide: Mass Murder in Historical Perspective. Cambridge: Cambridge University Press.

Bartrop, Paul R., and Samuel Totten, eds. 2007. Dictionary of Genocide. Vol. 2. Westport, CT: Greenwood.

The Battle of Algiers. 1966. Dir. Gillo Pontecorvo. Film.

Bauman, Zygmunt. 1989. Modernity and the Holocaust. Ithaca, NY: Cornell University Press.

Bell, Kristin A. 2014. Victims' voices: Sexual violence in the Armenian and Rwandan genocides. Criminology and Justice Policy Dissertations 22. https://repository.library.northeastern.edu/files/neu.336397.

Benvenuto, Jeff, Andrew Woolford, and Alexander Laban Hinton. 2014. Colonial genocide in Indigenous North America. Introduction. In Andrew Woolford, Jeff Benvenuto, and Alexander Laban Hinton, eds., Colonial Genocide in Indigenous North America. Durham, NC: Duke University Press.

Blackstock, Cindy. 2007. Residential schools: Did they really close or just morph into child welfare? Indigenous Law Journal 6/1: 71–78.

Bloxham, Donald. 2003. The Armenian genocide of 1915–1916: Cumulative radicalization and the development of a destruction policy. Past & Present 181 (November): 141–191.

Bloxham, Donald. 2008. Organized mass murder: Structure, participation, and motivation in comparative perspective. Holocaust and Genocide Studies 22/2: 203–245.

Bloxham, Donald. 2010. Internal colonization, inter-imperial conflict and the Armenian genocide. Ch. 14 (pp. 325–342) in A. Dirk Moses, ed., Empire, Colony, Genocide: Conquest, Occupation, and Subaltern Resistance in World History. New York: Berghahn Books.

Bloxham, Donald, and Paul R. Bartrop, eds. 2010. The Oxford Handbook of Genocide Studies. Oxford: Oxford University Press.

Bouwknegt, Thijs. 2014. Dutch extraditions to Kigali underway. Supranational Criminology Newsletter on Criminology and International Crimes 9/1: 7–8.

Braga, Anthony A., and David L. Weisburd. 2012. The effects of focused deterrence strategies on crime: A systematic review and meta-analysis of the empirical evidence. Journal of Research in Crime and Delinquency 49/3: 323–358.

Braithwaite, John, Valerie Braithwaite, Michael Cookson, and Leah Dunn. 2010. Anomie and Violence: Non-truth and Reconciliation in Indonesian Peacebuilding. Canberra, Australia: ANU E Press.

Brannigan, Augustine. 2013. Beyond the Banality of Evil: Criminology and Genocide. Oxford: Oxford University Press.

Brannigan, Augustine, and Kelly H. Hardwick. 2003. Genocide and general theory. Ch. 6 (pp. 109–131) in Chester L. Britt and Michael R. Gottfredson, eds., Control Theories in Crime and Delinquency. New Brunswick, NJ: Transaction.

Brants, Chrisje. 2007. Gold-collar crime: The peculiar complexities and ambiguities of war crimes, crimes against humanity, and genocide. Ch. 1 (pp. 309–326) in Henry N. Pontell and Gilbert L. Geis, eds., International Handbook of White-Collar and Corporate Crime. New York: Springer.

Bridgman, Jon M. 1981. The Revolt of the Hereros. Berkeley: University of California Press.

Bridgman, Jon M., and Leslie J. Worley. 1995. Genocide of the Hereros. Ch. 1 (pp. 3–48) in Samuel Totten, William S. Parsons, and Israel W. Charny, eds., Genocide in the Twentieth Century: Critical Essays and Eyewitness Accounts. New York: Garland.

British Broadcasting Corporation. 2014. Rwanda's untold story. Vimeo.com/107867605. Video.

Britt, Chester L., and Michael R. Gottfredson, eds. 2003. Control Theories of Crime and Delinquency. New Brunswick, NJ: Transaction.

Britton, Dana. 2011. The Gender of Crime. Lanham, MD: Rowman and Littlefield.

Brown, Michelle, and Nicole Rafter. 2013. Genocide films, public criminology, collective memory. British Journal of Criminology 53:1017–1032.

Browning, Christopher R. 1992. Ordinary Men: Police Battalion 101 and the Final Solution in Poland. 2d ed. New York: HarperCollins.

Brownmiller, Susan. (1975) 1993. Against Our Will: Men, Women, and Rape. New York: Ballantine Books.

Budapest Centre for the International Prevention of Genocide and Mass Atrocities. 2013. The EU and the Prevention of Mass Atrocities: An Assessment of Strengths and Weaknesses. Budapest: Foundation for the International Prevention of Genocide and Mass Atrocities.

Burleigh, Michael. 1994. Death and Deliverance: "Euthanasia" in Germany, 1900–1945. Cambridge: Cambridge University Press.

Campbell, Bruce B., and Arthur D. Brenner, eds. 2002. Death Squads in Global Perspective. New York: Palgrave Macmillan.

Card, Claudia. 2008. The paradox of genocidal rape aimed at enforced pregnancy. Southern Journal of Philosophy 46:176–189.

Caringella, Susan. 2009. Addressing Rape Reform in Law and Practice. New York: Columbia University Press.

Carpenter, R. C. 2002. Beyond "gendercide": Incorporating gender into comparative genocide studies. International Journal of Human Rights 6/4: 77–101.

CBS News. 1998. Text of Clinton's Rwanda speech. March 25. http://cbsnews.com/news/text-of-clintons-rwanda-speech.

Chakrabarti, Bhismadev, and Simon Baron-Cohen. 2006. Empathizing: Neurocognitive developmental mechanisms and individual differences. Progress in Brain Research 156:403–417.

Chandler, David P. 1999a. Brother Number One: A Political Biography of Pol Pot. Rev ed. Boulder, CO: Westview.

Chandler, David P. 1999b. Voices from S-21: Terror and History in Pol Pot's Secret Prison. Berkeley: University of California Press, 1999.

Charney, Israel W., ed. 1999. Encyclopedia of Genocide. 2 vols. Santa Barbara, CA: ABC-CLIO.

Cienciala, Anna M., Natalia S. Lebedeva, and Wojciech Materski, eds. 2007. Katyn: A Crime without Punishment. New Haven, CT: Yale University Press.

Cikara, Mina, and Jay J. Van Bavel. 2014. The neuroscience of intergroup relations: An integrative review. Perspectives on Psychological Science 9/3: 245–274.

Cohen, Laurence E., and Marcus Felson. 1979. Social change and crime rate trends: A routine activity approach. American Sociological Review 44:588–608.

Cohen, Stanley. 2001. States of Denial: Knowing about Atrocities and Suffering. Cambridge, UK: Polity.

Cole, Alison. 2010. International criminal law and sexual violence: An overview. Ch. 3 (pp. 47–60) in Clare McGlynn and Vanessa E. Munro, eds., Rethinking Rape Law: International and Comparative Perspectives. New York: GlassHouse/Routledge.

Collins, Randall. 2008. Violence. Princeton, NJ: Princeton University Press.

Colombijn, Freek, and J. Thomas Lindblad. 2002. Introduction. In Freek Colombijn and J. Thomas Lindblad, eds., Roots of Violence in Indonesia: Contemporary Violence in Historical Perspective. Leiden, Netherlands: KITLV.

Committee on Armenian Atrocities. 1915. Report of Committee on Armenian Atrocities. 4 October. Reprinted in Ara Sarafian and Eric Avebury, British Parliamentary Debates on the Armenian Genocide, 1915–1918. Princeton, NJ: Gomidas Institute, 2003.

Conley-Zilkic, Bridget, and Alex de Waal. 2014. Setting the agenda for evidence-based research on ending mass atrocities. Journal of Genocide Research 16/1: 55–76.

The Conscience of Nhem En. 1992. Dir. Steven Okazaki. HBO Documentary Films. Film.

Cribb, Robert, ed. 1990a. The Indonesian Killings of 1965–1966: Studies from Java and Bali. Clayton, Australia: Monash University Center of Southeast Asian Studies.

Cribb, Robert. 1990b. Introduction: Problems in the historiography of the killings in Indonesia. Ch. 1 (pp. 1–43) in Robert Cribb, ed., The Indonesian Killings of 1965–1966: Studies from Java and Bali. Clayton, Australia: Monash University Center of Southeast Asian Studies.

Cribb, Robert. 2001a. Genocide in Indonesia, 1965–66. Journal of Genocide Research 3/2: 219–239.

Cribb, Robert. 2001b. How many deaths? Problems in the statistics of massacre in Indonesia (1965–1966) and East Timor (1975–1980). Pp. 82–98 in Ingrid Wessel and Georgia Wimhöfer, eds., Violence in Indonesia. Hamburg, Germany: Abera.

Cribb, Robert, and Charles A. Coppel. 2009. A genocide that never was: Explaining the myth of anti-Chinese massacres in Indonesia, 1965–66. Journal of Genocide Research 11/4: 447–465.

Dadrian, Vahakn N. 1995. The History of the Armenian Genocide. Providence, RI: Berghahn Books.

Dadrian, Vahakn N. 2004. Patterns of twentieth century genocides: The Armenian, Jewish, and Rwandan cases. Journal of Genocide Research 6/4: 487–522.

Davidson, Lawrence. 2012. Cultural Genocide. New Brunswick, NJ: Rutgers University Press.

Day, Edward L., and Margaret Vandiver. 2000. Criminology and genocide studies: Notes on what might have been and what still could be. Crime, Law and Social Change 34:43–59.

DeJong, Christina, and Eric Long. 2014. The death penalty as genocide: The persecution of "homosexuals" in Uganda. Ch. 16 (pp. 339–362) in Dana Peterson and Vanessa R. Panfil, eds., Handbook of LGBT Communities, Crime, and Justice. New York: Springer.

Des Forges, Alison. 1999. "Leave None to Tell the Story": Genocide in Rwanda. New York: Human Rights Watch, 1999. http://www.hrw.org/legacy/reports/1999/rwanda/rwanda0399.htm.

de Waal, Alex, J. Meierhenrich, and Bridget Conley-Zilkic. 2012. How mass atrocities end: An evidence-based counter-narrative. Fletcher Forum on World Affairs 36/1: 15–31.

de Waal, Frans. 2009. The Age of Empathy: Nature's Lessons for a Kinder Society. New York: Three Rivers.

Drechsler, Horst. 1990. The Herero uprising. Pp. 231–248 in Frank Chalk and Kurt Jonassohn, eds., The History and Sociology of Genocide: Analyses and Case Studies. New Haven, CT: Yale University Press.

Drouin, Marc. 2010. Understanding the 1982 Guatemalan genocide. Ch. 4 (pp. 81–103) in Marcia Esparza, Henry Huttenbach, and Daniel Feierstein, eds., State Violence and Genocide in Latin America: The Cold War Years. New York: Routledge.

Dugan, Laura, and Erica Chenoweth. 2012. Moving beyond deterrence: The effectiveness of raising the expected utility of abstaining from terrorism in Israel. American Sociological Review 77/4: 597–624.

Durkheim, Emile. (1893) 1933. The Division of Labor in Society. Trans. George Simpson. New York: Macmillan.

Durkheim, Emile. (1897) 2007. On Suicide. New York: Penguin.

Dwyer, Leslie. 2004. The intimacy of terror: Gender and the violence of 1965–66 in Bali. Intersections: Gender, History, and Culture in the Asian Context 10/2. http://intersections.anu.edu.au/issue10/dwyer.html.

Dwyer, Leslie, and Degung Santikarma. 2003. "When the world turned to chaos": 1965 and its aftermath in Bali, Indonesia. Ch. 13 (pp. 289–306) in Robert Gellately and Ben Kiernan, eds., The Specter of Genocide: Mass Murder in Historical Perspective. Cambridge: Cambridge University Press.

Elias, Robert. 1986. The Politics of Victimization: Victims, Victimology, and Human Rights. Oxford: Oxford University Press.

Ellis, Mark. 2007. Breaking the silence: Rape as an international crime. Case Western Reserve Journal of International Law 38:225–247.

Enemies of the People: A Personal Journey into the Heart of the Killing Fields. 2012. Dir. Thet Sambath and Rob Lemkin. Old Street Films. Film.

Erickson, Edward J. 2006. Reexamining history: Armenian massacres: New records undercut old blame. Middle East Quarterly 13/3: 67–75.

Erikson, Kai. 1996. On pseudospeciation and social speciation. Ch. 5 (pp. 51–57) in Charles B. Strozier and Michael Flynn, eds., Genocide, War, and Human Survival. Lanham, MD: Rowman and Littlefield.

Evans, Suzanne E. 2004. Forgotten Crimes: The Holocaust and People with Disabilities. Chicago: Ivan R. Dee.

Farrington, David P., and Brandon C. Welsh. 2007. Saving Children from a Life of Crime. Oxford: Oxford University Press.

Feierstein, Daniel. 2014. Genocide as Social Practice: Reorganizing Society under the Nazis and Argentina's Military Juntas. New Brunswick, NJ: Rutgers University Press.

Fein, Helen. 1977. Imperial Crime and Punishment: The Massacre at Jallianwala Bagh and British Judgment, 1919–1920. Honolulu: University Press of Hawaii.

Fein, Helen. 1979. Accounting for Genocide: National Response and Jewish Victimization during the Holocaust. New York: Free Press.

Fein, Helen. 1990. Genocide: A sociological perspective. Current Sociology 38:1–126.

Fein, Helen. 1993a. Accounting for genocide after 1945: Theories and some findings. International Journal on Group Rights 1:79–106.

Fein, Helen. 1993b. Genocide: A Sociological Perspective. London: Sage.

Fein, Helen. 1993c. Revolutionary and antirevolutionary genocides: A comparison of state murders in Democratic Kampuchea, 1975 to 1979, and in Indonesia, 1965 to 1966. Comparative Studies in Society and History 35:796–823.

Fein, Helen. 1997. Genocide by attrition 1939–1993: The Warsaw Ghetto, Cambodia, and Sudan: Links between human rights, health, and mass death. Health and Human Rights 2/2: 10–45.

Fein, Helen. 1999. Gender and genocide: The uses of women and group destiny. Journal of Genocide Research 1:43–63.

Ferrara, Antonio. 2015. Beyond genocide and ethnic cleansing: Demographic surgery as a new way to understand mass violence. Journal of Genocide Research 17/1: 1–20.

Finkel, Evgeny, and Scott Straus. 2014. Macro, meso, and micro research on genocide: Gains, shortcomings, and future areas of inquiry. Genocide Studies and Prevention 7/1: 56–67.

Fischer, Benjamin B. 2007. The Katyn controversy: Stalin's killing field. Studies in Intelligence, Winter. Available at https://www.cia.gov/library/center-for-the-study-of-intelligence/csi-publications/csi-studies/studies/winter99-00/art6.html.

Fox, Frank. 1999. God's Eye: Aerial Photography and the Katyn Forest Massacre. West Chester, PA: West Chester University Press.

Friedlander, Henry. 1995. The Origins of Nazi Genocide: From Euthanasia to the Final Solution. Chapel Hill: University of North Carolina Press.

Fujii, Lee Ann. 2004. Transforming the moral landscape: The diffusion of a genocidal norm in Rwanda. Journal of Genocide Research 6/1: 99–114.

Fujii, Lee Ann. 2009. Killing Neighbors: Webs of Violence in Rwanda. Ithaca, NY: Cornell University Press.

Futter, Stacy, and Walter R. Mebane, Jr. 2001. The effects of rape law reform on rape case processing. Berkeley Women's Law Journal 16:72–139.

Gamson, William. 1995. Hiroshima, the Holocaust, and the politics of exclusion. American Sociological Review 60:1–20.

Garrard-Burnett, Virginia. 2010. Terror in the Land of the Holy Spirit: Guatemala under General Efraín Ríos Montt 1982–1983. Oxford: Oxford University Press.

Gellately, Robert, and Ben Kiernan, eds. 2003. The Specter of Genocide: Mass Murder in Historical Perspective. Cambridge: Cambridge University Press.

Genocide Prevention Task Force. 2008. Preventing Genocide: A Blueprint for US Policymakers. Executive Summary. US Institute of Peace. http://media.usip.org/reports/genocide_taskforc_rep.

Genocide Watch. 2010. Genocides, politicides, and other mass murders since 1945. Unpublished list. Courtesy of Genocide Watch.

Gerlach, Christian. 2006. Extremely violent societies: An alternative to the concept of genocide. Journal of Genocide Research 8/4: 455–471.

Gerlach, Christian. 2010. Extremely Violent Societies: Mass Violence in the Twentieth-Century World. Cambridge: Cambridge University Press.

Ghosts of Rwanda. 2004. Dir. Greg Barker. PBS/Frontline. Film.

Gie, Soe Hok. 1990. The mass killing in Bali. Pp. 252–258 in Robert Cribb, ed., The Indonesian Killings 1965–1966: Studies from Java and Bali. Monash Papers on Southeast Asia 21. Clayton, Australia: Centre of Southeast Asian Studies, Monash University.

Goffman, Erving. (1974) 1986. Frame Analysis: An Essay on the Organization of Experience. Boston: Northeastern University Press.

Goldsmith, Benjamin E., Charles R. Butcher, Dimitri Semonovich, and Arcot Sowmya. 2013. Forecasting the onset of genocide and politicide: Annual out-of-sample forecasts on a global dataset, 1988–2003. Journal of Peace Research 50/4: 437–452.

Gottfredson, Michael R., and Travis Hirschi. 1990. A General Theory of Crime. Stanford, CA: Stanford University Press.

Gourevitch, Philip. 1998. We Wish to Inform You That Tomorrow We Will Be Killed with Our Families: Stories from Rwanda. New York: Farrar, Straus, and Giroux.

Grandin, Greg. 2000. The Blood of Guatemala. Durham, NC: Duke University Press.

Grossman, Dave. 1995. On Killing: The Psychological Cost of Learning to Kill in War and Society. Boston: Little, Brown.

GSP (Genocide Studies Program, Yale University). n.d. Cambodian Genocide Program: The CGP, 1994–2015. http://www.yale.edu/cgp/.

Gurr, Ted Robert, Monty G. Marshall, and Barbara Harff. 2003. State Failure Task Force Report: Phase II Findings. College Park: University of Maryland, Center for International Development and Conflict Management.

Haas, Francois. 2008. German science and black racism: Roots of the Nazi Holocaust. FASEB Journal 22/2: 332–337.

Hagan, John, and Jaimie Morse. 2014. State rape and the crime of genocide. Pp.

690–707 in Rosemary Gartner and Bill McCarthy, eds., The Oxford Handbook on Gender, Sex, and Crime: An Interdisciplinary Review of Research and Theory. New York: Oxford University Press.

Hagan, John, and Wenona Rymond-Richmond. 2008. The collective dynamics of racial dehumanization and genocidal victimization in Darfur. American Sociological Review 73:875–902.

Hagan, John, and Wenona Rymond-Richmond. 2009. Darfur and the Crime of Genocide. New York: Cambridge University Press.

Haney, Craig, W. Curtis Banks, and Philip G. Zimbardo. 1973. Interpersonal dynamics in a simulated prison. International Journal of Criminology and Penology 1:69–97.

Harding, David J. 2007. Cultural context, sexual behavior, and romantic relationships in disadvantaged neighborhoods. American Sociology Review 72/3: 341–346.

Hare, Robert D. 1993. Without Conscience: The Disturbing World of the Psychopaths among Us. New York: Guilford.

Harff, Barbara. 1987. The etiology of genocide. Ch. 3 (pp. 41–59) in Isidor Walliman and Michael N. Dobkowski, eds., Genocide and the Modern Age: Etiology and Case Studies. New York: Greenwood.

Harff, Barbara. 2003a. Early Warning of Communal Conflict and Genocide: Linking Empirical Research to International Responses. Boulder, CO: Westview.

Harff, Barbara. 2003b. No lessons learned from the Holocaust? Assessing risks of genocide and political mass murder since 1955. American Political Science Review 97/1: 57–73.

Harff, Barbara. 2005. Assessing risks of genocide and politicide. In Ted Robert Gurr and Monty G. Marshall, eds., Peace and Conflict. College Park: University of Maryland, Center for International Development.

Harff, Barbara, and Ted R. Gurr. 1988. Toward empirical theory of genocides and politicides: Identification and measurement of cases since 1945. International Studies Quarterly 32:359–371.

Harff, Barbara, and Ted R. Gurr. 1996. Victims of the state: Genocides, politicides, and group repression from 1945 to 1995. Ch. 3 (pp. 33–58) in A. J. Jongman, ed., Contemporary Genocides: Causes, Cases, Consequences. Leiden, Netherlands: University of Leiden, Interdisciplinary Research Programme on Root Causes of Human Rights Violations.

Hatzfeld, Jean. 2003. Machete Season: The Killers in Rwanda Speak. New York: Picador.

Henry, Adam Hughes. 2014. Polluting the waters. Genocide Studies International 8/2: 153–175.

Henry, Nicola. 2011. War and Rape: Law, Memory and Justice. London: Routledge.

Herrmann, Steffen K. 2011. Social exclusion: Practices of misrecognition. Ch. 10 (pp. 133–150) in Paulus Kaufmann, Hannes Kuch, Christian Neuhäuser, and Elaine Webster, eds., Humiliation, Degradation, Dehumanization: Human Dignity Violated. New York: Springer.

Hiebert, Maureen S. 2008. Theorizing destruction: Reflections on the state of comparative genocide theory. Genocide Studies and Prevention 3/3: 309–339.

Hilberg, Raul. 1985. The Destruction of the European Jews. New York: Holmes and Meier.

Hinton, Alexander Laban. 2002. The dark side of modernity. Ch. 1 (pp. 1–40) in Alexander Laban Hinton, ed., Annihilating Difference: The Anthropology of Genocide. Berkeley: University of California Press.

Hinton, Alexander Laban. 2005. Why Did They Kill? Cambodia in the Shadow of Genocide. Berkeley: University of California Press.

Hinton, Alexander Laban, ed. 2011. Transitional Justice: Global Mechanisms and Local Realities after Genocide and Mass Violence. New Brunswick, NJ: Rutgers University Press.

Hinton, Alexander Laban. 2012. Critical genocide studies. Genocide Studies and Prevention 7/1: 4–15.

Hinton, Alexander Laban. 2014. Justice and time at the Khmer Rouge Tribunal: In memory of Vann Nath, painter and S-21 survivor. Genocide Studies and Prevention 8/2: 6–17.

Hinton, Alexander Laban, and Kevin Lewis O'Neill, eds. 2009. Genocide: Truth, Memory, and Representation. Durham, NC: Duke University Press.

Hirschi, Travis. 1969. Causes of Delinquency. Berkeley: University of California Press.

Hitchcock, Robert K., and Thomas E. Koperski. 2010. Genocides of indigenous people. Ch. 22 (pp. 577–617) in Dan Stone, ed., The Historiography of Genocide. New York: Palgrave Macmillan.

Hitler, Adolf. (1925) 1971. Mein Kampf. Trans. Ralph Manheim. Boston: Houghton Mifflin.

Hoile, David. 2014. Justice Denied: The Reality of the International Criminal Court. London: Africa Research Center. Available at http://www.africaresearchcentre.org.

Hollan, Douglas. 2012. Emerging issues in the cross-cultural study of empathy. Emotion Review 4:70–78. http://emr.sagepub.com/content/4/1/70.

Horvitz, Leslie Ann, and Christopher Catherwood, eds. 2006. Encyclopedia of War Crimes and Genocide. New York: Facts on File Infobase.

How the Germans exterminated the Hereros. 2003. New African 418 (May): 62–67.

Huisman, Wim. 2010. Business as Usual? Corporate Involvement in International Crimes. The Hague, Netherlands: Eleven International.

Hull, Isabel V. 2003. Military culture and the production of "final solutions" in the colonies: The example of Wilhelminian Germany. Ch. 7 (pp. 141–162) in Robert Gellately and Ben Kiernan, eds., The Specter of Genocide. Cambridge: Cambridge University Press.

Hull, Isabel V. 2005a. Absolute Destruction: Military Culture and the Practices of War in Imperial Germany. Ithaca, NY: Cornell University Press.

Hull, Isabel V. 2005b. The military campaign in German Southwest Africa, 1904–1907. Bulletin of the German Historical Institute 37:39–49.

Hunt, Swanee. 2014. The rise of Rwanda's women. Foreign Affairs 93/3: 150–156.

Ibarra, Carlos F. 2006. The culture of terror and the Cold War in Guatemala. Journal of Genocide Research 8/2: 191–208.

ICISS (International Commission on Intervention and State Sovereignty). 2001. The

Responsibility to Protect. Ottawa, ON: International Development Research Centre, December. http://responsibilitytoprotect.org/ICISS%20Report.pdf.

ICTR (International Criminal Tribunal for Rwanda). 1998. Jean-Paul Akayesu, Summary of the Judgment. ICTR-96–4-T, September 2.

Inter-American Court of Human Rights. 2003. Case of Myrna Mack Chang v. Guatemala, Judgment of November 25. Available at http://www.corteidh.or.cr/docs/casos/articulos/seriec_101_ing.pdf.

International Court of Justice. 2015. Case Concerning Application of the Convention on the Prevention and Punishment of the Crime of Genocide (Croatia and Serbia). February 3. General List No. 118.

International Crisis Group. 2014. CrisisWatch 2014 Latin America, Report No. 52, June 4. http://www.crisisgroup.org/en/regions/latin-america.

Jamieson, Ruth. 1999. Genocide and the social production of immorality. Theoretical Criminology 3/2: 131–146.

Jamieson, Ruth, and Kieran McEvoy. 2005. State crime by proxy and juridical othering. British Journal of Criminology 45:504–527.

Jones, Adam. 2002. Gender and genocide in Rwanda. Journal of Genocide Research 4/1: 65–94.

Jones, Adam. 2004. Gendercide and genocide. Ch. 1 (pp. 1–38) in Adam Jones, ed., Gendercide and Genocide. Nashville, TN: Vanderbilt University Press.

Justino, Patricia, and Philip Verwimp. 2008. Poverty dynamics, violent conflict and convergence in Rwanda. MICROCON Research Working Paper 4. University of Sussex, UK: MICROCON.

Kaiser, Joshua, and John Hagan. 2015. Gendered genocide: The socially destructive process of genocidal rape, killing, and displacement in Darfur. Law & Society Review 49/1: 69–107.

Karstedt, Susanne. 2010. From absence to presence, from silence to voice: Victims in international and transitional justice since the Nuremberg trials. International Review of Victimology 17:9–30.

Karstedt, Susanne. 2011a. Exit: The state: Globalisation, state failure and crime. Ch. 6 (pp. 107–124) in David Nelken, ed., Comparative Criminal Justice and Globalization. Burlington, VT: Ashgate.

Karstedt, Susanne. 2011b. Life after punishment for Nazi war criminals: Reputation, careers and normative climate in post-war Germany. In Stephen Farrall, Mike Hough, Shadd Maruna, and Richard Sparks, eds., Escape Routes: Contemporary Perspectives on Life after Punishment. Oxford: Oxford University Press.

Karstedt, Susanne. 2012a. Contextualising mass atrocity crimes: The dynamics of "extremely violent societies." In International crimes and transitional justice, special issue, European Journal of Criminology 9/5: 499–513.

Karstedt, Susanne. 2012b. Genocide. Pp. 793–796 in George Ritzer, ed., The Wiley-Blackwell Encyclopedia of Globalisation, vol. 2. Oxford, UK: Blackwell.

Karstedt, Susanne. 2013a. Contextualizing mass atrocity crimes: Moving towards a relational approach. Annual Review of Law and Social Sciences 2013:383–404.

Karstedt, Susanne. 2013b. The emotion [sic] dynamics of mass atrocities: Doing violence. Paper presented at the Emotions and Violence in 20th Century Europe: Historical Perspectives on Violence Prevention conference, Max Planck Institute for Human Development, Berlin, June 26–28.

Karstedt, Susanne. 2013c. Globalisation, mass atrocities and genocide. Ch. 10 (pp. 146–164) in Francis Pakes, ed., Globalisation and the Challenge to Criminology. London: Routledge.

Karstedt, Susanne. 2014. Organizing crime: The state as agent. In Letizia Paoli, ed., The Oxford Handbook of Organized Crime. doi:10.1093/oxfordhb/9780199730445.013.031.

Kater, Michael H. 1989. Doctors under Hitler. Chapel Hill: University of North Carolina Press.

Katyn. 2007. Dir. Andrzej Wajda. Film.

Katz, Jack. 1988. Seductions of Crime: Moral and Sensual Attractions in Doing Evil. New York: Basic Books.

Kelman, Herbert C. 1973. Violence without moral restraint: Reflections on the dehumanization of victims and victimizers. Journal of Social Issues 29:25–61.

Kiernan, Ben. 1996. The Pol Pot Regime: Race, Power, and Genocide in Cambodia under the Khmer Rouge, 1975–79. 3d ed. New Haven, CT: Yale University Press.

Kiernan, Ben. 2002. Conflict in Cambodia, 1945–2002. Critical Asian Studies 34/4: 483–495.

Kiernan, Ben. 2003. Twentieth-century genocides: Underlying ideological themes from Armenia to East Timor. Ch. 2 (pp. 29–52) in Robert Gellately and Ben Kiernan, eds., The Specter of Genocide: Mass Murder in Historical Perspective. Cambridge: Cambridge University Press.

Kiernan, Ben. 2007. Blood and Soil: A World History of Genocide and Extermination from Sparta to Darfur. New Haven, CT: Yale University Press.

Killing fields. n.d. Wikipedia. https://en.wikipedia.org/wiki/Killing_Fields. Accessed April 24, 2012.

Klusemann, Stefan. 2010. Micro-situational antecedents of violent atrocity. Sociological Forum 25:272–294.

Klusemann, Stefan. 2012. Massacres as process: A micro-sociological theory of internal patterns of mass atrocities. European Journal of Criminology 9/5: 468–480.

Komar, Debra A. 2008. Variables influencing victim selection in genocide. Journal of Forensic Sciences 53/1: 172–177.

Koonz, Claudia. 1988. Mothers in the Fatherland: Women, the Family and Nazi Politics. New York: St. Martin's Griffin / Macmillan.

Krain, Matthew. 1997. State-sponsored mass murder: The onset and severity of genocides and politicides. Journal of Conflict Resolution 41/3: 331–360.

Krain, Matthew. 2014. The effects of diplomatic sanctions and engagement on the severity of ongoing genocides or politicides. Journal of Genocide Research 16/1: 25–53.

Kühne, Thomas. 2010. Belonging and Genocide. New Haven, CT: Yale University Press.

Kuper, Leo. 1981. Genocide: Its Political Use in the Twentieth Century. New Haven, CT: Yale University Press.

Kurlychek, Megan C., Robert Brame, and Shawn D. Bushway. 2006. Scarlet letters and recidivism: Does an old criminal record predict future offending? Criminology and Public Policy 5/3: 483–504.

Laub, John H. 2004. The life course of criminology in the United States. Criminology 42/1: 1–26.

Lebedeva, Nataliya. 1990. The Katyn tragedy. International Affairs 6/36: 98–144.

Lemkin, Raphael. 1944. Axis Rule in Occupied Europe. Washington, DC: Carnegie Endowment.

Letschert, Rianne, Roelof Haveman, Anne-Marie de Brouwer, and Antony Pemberton, eds. 2011. Victimological Approaches to International Crimes: Africa. Cambridge, UK: Intersentia.

Levene, Mark. 1998. Creating a modern "zone of genocide": The impact of nation- and state-formation on Eastern Anatolia, 1878–1923. Holocaust and Genocide Studies 12/3: 393–433.

Levene, Mark. 2013a. The Crisis of Genocide v. 1: Devastation: The European Rimlands 1912–1938. Oxford: Oxford University Press.

Levene, Mark. 2013b. The Crisis of Genocide, v. 2: Annihilation: The European Rimlands 1939–1953. Oxford: Oxford University Press.

Levi, Primo. 1988. The gray zone. Ch. 2 (pp. 36–69) in The Drowned and the Saved. Trans. Raymond Rosenthal. New York: Summit Books.

Lifton, Robert Jay. 1986. The Nazi Doctors: Medical Killing and the Psychology of Genocide. New York: Basic Books.

Loeber, Rolf, and David P. Farrington, eds. 1998. Serious and Violent Juvenile Offenders: Risk Factors and Successful Interventions. London: Sage.

MacKinnon, Catharine A. 2006. Genocide's sexuality. Ch. 22 (pp. 208–233) in Are Women Human? And Other International Dialogues. Cambridge, MA: Harvard University Press.

Madley, Benjamin. 2004. Patterns of frontier genocide 1803–1910: The Aboriginal Tasmanians, the Uki of California, and the Herero of Namibia. Journal of Genocide Research 6/2: 167–192.

Madley, Benjamin. 2005. From Africa to Auschwitz: How German South West Africa incubated ideas and methods adopted and developed by the Nazis in eastern Europe. European History Quarterly 35/3: 429–464.

Mahoney, James, and Dietrich Rueschemeyer, eds. 2003. Comparative Historical Analysis in the Social Sciences. Cambridge: Cambridge University Press.

Maier-Katkin, Daniel, Daniel P. Means, and Thomas J. Bernard. 2009. Towards a criminology of crimes against humanity. Theoretical Criminology 13:227–255.

Mamdani, Mahmood. 2001. When Victims Become Killers: Colonialism, Nativism, and the Genocide in Rwanda. Princeton, NJ: Princeton University Press.

Mann, Michael. 2005. The Dark Side of Democracy: Explaining Ethnic Cleansing. New York: Cambridge University Press.

Mardiganian, Aurora. (1918) 2010. Ravished Armenia: The Story of Aurora Mardiganian, the Christian Girl Who Lived through the Great Massacres. Charleston, SC: Nabu.

Maruna, Shadd. 2001. Making Good: How Ex-Convicts Reform and Rebuild Their Lives. Washington, DC: American Psychological Association.

Maruna, Shadd, and Heith Copes. 2005. What have we learned from five decades of neutralization research? Crime and Justice: A Review of Research 32:221–320.

McDoom, Omar Shahubudin. 2013. Antisocial capital: A profile of Rwandan genocide perpetrators' social networks. Journal of Conflict Resolution 58:865–893.

McEvoy, Kieran, and Kristen McConnachie. 2012. Victimology in transitional justice: Victimhood, innocence and hierarchy. European Journal of Criminology 9/5: 527–538.

McEvoy, Kieran, and Kirsten McConnachie. 2013. Victims and transitional justice: Voice, agency and blame. Social and Legal Studies 22/4: 489–513.

McGarry, Ross, and Sandra Walklate. 2015. Victims: Trauma, Testimony, Justice. London: Routledge.

Melson, Robert. 1992. Revolution and Genocide: On the Origins of the Armenian Genocide and the Holocaust. Chicago: University of Chicago Press.

Melson, Robert. 2011. Critique of current genocide studies. Genocide Studies and Prevention 6/3: 279–286.

Mennecke, Martin. 2007. Punishing genocidaires: A deterrent effect or not? Human Rights Review 8/4: 319–339.

Mersky, Marcie, and Naomi Roht-Arriaza. 2007. Guatemala. Ch. 1 (pp. 7–32) in Victims Unsilenced: The Inter-American Human Rights System and Transitional Justice in Latin America. Washington, DC: Due Process of Law Foundation.

Merton, Robert K. 1938. Social structure and anomie. American Sociological Review 3:672–682.

Michalczyk, John J., and Raymond G. Helmick, eds. Through a Lens Darkly: Films of Genocide, Ethnic Cleansing, and Atrocities. New York: Peter Lang.

Mildt, Dick de. 1996. In the Name of the People: Perpetrators of Genocide in the Reflection of Their Post-war Prosecution in West Germany: The "Euthanasia" and "Aktion Reinhard" Trial Cases. The Hague, Netherlands: Martinus Hijhoff.

Milgram, Stanley. 1965. Some conditions of obedience and disobedience to authority. Human Relations 18/1: 57–75.

Milgram, Stanley. 1974. Obedience to Authority: An Experimental View. New York: Harper and Row.

Miller, Jody. 2008. Getting Played: African American Girls, Urban Inequality, and Gendered Violence. New York: NYU Press.

Mills, C. Wright. 1940. Situated actions and vocabularies of motives. American Sociological Review 5:904–913.

Moses, A. Dirk, and Dan Stone. 2007. Colonialism and Genocide. New York: Routledge.

Naimark, Norman M. 2001. Fires of Hatred: Ethnic Cleansing in Twentieth-Century Europe. Cambridge, MA: Harvard University Press.

Naimark, Norman M. 2010. Stalin's Genocides. Princeton, NJ: Princeton University Press.

Neuman, William, and Maria Eugenia Diaz. 2012. Venezuela to investigate report that Brazilian miners massacred Indian village. New York Times International, August 31: A7.

Night and Fog. 1955. Dir. Alain Resnais. Film.

Norris, John, and Annie Malknecht. 2013. Atrocities Prevention Board: Background, performance, and options. Center for American Progress, June 13. http://www.americanprogress.org/issues/security/report/2013.

Nowrojee, Binaifor. 1996. Shattered Lives: Sexual Violence during the Rwandan Genocide and Its Aftermath. New York: Human Rights Watch.

Nyseth Brehm, Hollie. 2014a. Assessing risk factors of modern genocide. Unpublished paper.

Nyseth Brehm, Hollie. 2014b. Rethinking risk factors of modern genocide. Ph.D. dissertation, Department of Sociology, University of Minnesota.

Nyseth Brehm, Hollie, Christopher Uggen, and Jean-Damascène Gasanabo. 2014a. Age, sex, and the crime of crimes: Toward a life-course theory of genocide participation. Unpublished paper.

Nyseth Brehm, Hollie, Christopher Uggen, and Jean-Damascène Gasanabo. 2014b. Genocide, justice, and Rwanda's *gacaca* courts. Journal of Contemporary Criminal Justice 30/3: 333–352.

Oglesby, Elizabeth, and Amy Ross. 2009. Guatemala's genocide determination and the spatial politics of justice. Space and Polity 13/1: 21–39.

O'Neill, Kevin L. 2005. Writing Guatemala's genocide: Truth and reconciliation commission reports and Christianity. Journal of Genocide Research 7/3: 331–349.

Orth, Karin. 2000. The concentration camp SS as a functional elite. Ch. 11 (pp. 306–336) in Ulrich Herbert, ed., National Socialist Extermination Policies: Contemporary German Perspectives and Controversies. New York: Berghahn.

Palmer, Alison. 1998. Colonial and modern genocide: Explanations and categories. Ethnic and Racial Studies 21/1: 89–115.

Parmentier, Stephan. 2011. The missing link: Criminological perspectives on transitional justice and international crimes. Ch. 25 (pp. 380–392) in Mary Bosworth and Carolyn Hoyle, eds., What Is Criminology? Oxford: Oxford University Press.

Paternoster, Raymond, and Shawn Bushway. 2011. Studying desistance from crime: Where quantitative meets qualitative methods. Ch. 12 (pp. 183–197) in Mary Bosworth and Carolyn Holye, eds., What Is Criminology? Oxford: Oxford University Press.

Paul, Allen. 2010. Katy: Stalin's Massacre and the Triumph of Truth. DeKalb: Northern Illinois University Press.

Perraudin, Michael, and Jürgen Zimmerer, eds. 2011. German Colonialism and National Identity. New York: Routledge.

Perry, Gina. 2012. Behind the Shock Machine: The Untold Story of the Notorious Milgram Psychology Experiments. Melbourne, Australia: Scribe.

Pew Center on the States. 2011. State of Recidivism: The Revolving Door of America's Prisons. Washington, DC: Pew Charitable Trust.

Pinker, Steven. 2011. The Better Angels of Our Nature: Why Violence Has Declined. New York: Viking Books.

Pohlman, Annie. 2015. Women, Sexual Violence and the Indonesian Killings of 1965–1966. London: Routledge.

Powell, Christopher. 2007. What do genocides kill? A relational conception of genocide. Journal of Genocide Research 9/4: 527–547.

Power, Samantha. 2002. A Problem from Hell: America and the Age of Genocide. New York: HarperCollins.

Proctor, Robert N. 1988. Racial Hygiene: Medicine under the Nazis. Cambridge, MA: Harvard University Press.

Pross, Christian. 1994. Introduction. Pp. 1–21 in Götz Aly, Peter Chroust, and Christian Pross, eds., Cleansing the Fatherland. Baltimore: Johns Hopkins University Press.

Prunier, Gerard. 1997. The Rwanda Crisis: History of a Genocide. New York: Columbia University Press.

Rafter, Nicole. 1997. Creating Born Criminals. Urbana: University of Illinois Press.

Rafter, Nicole. 2006. Shots in the Mirror: Crime Films and Society. 2d ed. New York: Oxford University Press.

Rafter, Nicole. 2008. Criminology's darkest hour: Biocriminology in Nazi Germany. Australian and New Zealand Journal of Criminology 41/2: 287–306.

Rafter, Nicole. 2014. Film review: The Act of Killing. Theoretical Criminology 18/2: 257–260.

Rafter, Nicole, and Kristin Bell. 2013. Gender and genocide. Paper presented at the American Society of Criminology, Presidential Panel Sessions of 2013. https://asc41.com/Annual_Meeting/2013/Presidential%20Papers/Rafter,%20Nicole-Bell,%20Kristin.pdf.

Rafter, Nicole, and Sandra Walklate. 2012. Genocide and the dynamics of victimization: Some observations on Armenia. European Journal of Criminology 9/5: 514–526.

REMHI (Recovery of Historical Memory Project, Archdiocese of Guatemala). 1999. Guatemala: Never Again. Maryknoll, NY: Orbis Books.

Robertson, Geoffrey. 2009. Was There an Armenian Genocide? Geoffrey Robertson QC's Opinion. Policy Memorandum, Foreign & Commonwealth Office to the Minister, Her Majesty's Government. London: Doughty Street Chambers, April 12. Available at http://groong.usc.edu/Geoffrey-Robertson-QC-Genocide.pdf.

Robinson, Geoffrey. 1995. The Dark Side of Paradise: Political Violence in Bali. Ithaca, NY: Cornell University Press.

Roosa, John. 2006. Pretext for Mass Murder: The September 30th Movement and Suharto's Coup d'État in Indonesia. Madison: University of Wisconsin Press.

Rotberg, Robert I. 2004. The failure and collapse of nation-states: Breakdown, prevention, and repair. Ch. 1 (pp. 1–50) in Robert I. Rotberg, ed., When States Fail: Causes and Consequences. Princeton, NJ: Princeton University Press.

Rothe, Dawn L. 2009. State Criminality: The Crime of All Crimes. Lanham, MD: Lexington Books.

Rothe, Dawn L., and Christopher W. Mullins. 2008. Genocide, war crimes and crimes against humanity in Central Africa. Ch. 6 (pp. 135–158) in Alette Smeulers and Roelof Haveman, eds., Supranational Criminology: Towards a Criminology of International Crimes. Antwerp, Belgium: Intersentia.

Rothe, Dawn L., and Christopher W. Mullins. 2009. Toward a criminology of international criminal law: An integrated theory of international criminal violations. International Journal of Comparative and Applied Criminal Justice 33/1: 97–118.

Rothe, Dawn L., and Christopher W. Mullins, eds. 2010. State Crime: Current Perspectives. New Brunswick, NJ: Rutgers University Press.

RTLM (Radio Télévision Libre des Mille Collines). 1994. Transmission of July 3. Transcription available at Rwanda File, Tape 0037: Side B, http://rwandafile.com/rtlm/rtlm0037.html.

Rudolf Lonauer. n.d. Wikipedia. https://de.wikipedia.org/wiki/Rudolf_Lonauer. Accessed July 7, 2012.

Rueckert, Linda, and Nicolette Naybar. 2008. Gender differences in empathy: The role of the right hemisphere. Brain and Cognition 67:162–167.

Ruggiero, Vincenzo. 2010. Armed struggle in Italy: The limits to criminology in the analysis of political violence. British Journal of Criminology 50:708–724.

Rummel, Rudolph J. 1983. Libertarianism and international violence. Journal of Conflict Resolution 27:27–71.

Rummel, Rudolph J. 1992. Democide: Nazi Genocide and Mass Murder. New Brunswick, NJ: Transaction.

Rummel, Rudolph J. 1997. Statistics of Democide: Genocide and Mass Murder since 1900. Charlottesville: Center for National Security Law, University of Virginia.

Sampson, Robert J. 1999. Techniques of research neutralization. Theoretical Criminology 3–4:438–451.

Sampson, Robert J. 2006. Collective efficacy theory: Lessons learned and directions for future inquiry. Ch. 5 (pp. 149–167) in Frank T. Cullen, John Paul Wright, and Kristie R. Blevins, eds., Taking Stock: The Status of Criminological Theory. New Brunswick, NJ: Transaction.

Sampson, Robert J., Stephen W. Raudenbush, and Felton Earls. 1997. Neighborhoods and violent crime: A multi-level study of collective efficacy. Science 277:918–924.

Sampson, Robert J., and William Julius Wilson. 1995. Toward a theory of race, crime, and urban inequality. Ch. 2 (pp. 37–54) in John Hagan and Ruth D. Peterson, eds., Crime and Inequality. Stanford, CA: Stanford University Press.

Sanday, Peggy Reeves. 2007. Fraternity Gang Rape: Sex, Brotherhood, and Privilege on Campus. 2d ed. New York: NYU Press.

Sanford, Victoria. 2009. What is an anthropology of genocide? Reflections on field research with Maya survivors in Guatemala. Ch. 1 (pp. 29–53) in Alexander Laban Hinton and Kevin Lewis O'Neill, eds., Genocide: Truth, Memory, and Representation. Durham, NC: Duke University Press.

Sanford, Victoria. n.d. Violence and genocide in Guatemala. New Haven, CT: Yale University Genocide Studies Program. http://gsp.yale.edu/case-studies/guatemala/violence-and-genocide-guatemala (accessed August 27, 2012).

Sanford, Victoria, and Martha Lincoln. 2011. Body of evidence: Feminicide, local justice, and rule of law in "peacetime" Guatemala. Ch. 3 (pp. 67–91) in Alexander Laban Hinton, ed., Transitional Justice: Global Mechanisms and Local Realities after Genocide and Mass Violence. New Brunswick, NJ: Rutgers University Press.

Sarkin, Jeremy. 2010. Germany's Genocide of the Herero: Why Kaiser Wilhelm II Gave the Order. Cape Town, South Africa: UCT Press.

Savelsberg, Joachim J. 2010. Crime and Human Rights: Criminology of Genocide and Atrocities. London: Sage.

Schabas, William A. 2009. Genocide in International Law: The Crime of Crimes. Cambridge: Cambridge University Press.

Schabas, William A. 2011. Criminology, accountability, and international justice. Ch. 23 (pp. 346–358) in Mary Bosworth and Carolyn Hoyle, eds., What Is Criminology? Oxford: Oxford University Press.

Schaller, Dominik J. 2007. From the editors: Genocide tourism—educational value or voyeurism? Journal of Genocide Research 9/4: 513–515.

Schaller, Dominik J. 2010a. From conquest to genocide: Colonial rule in German Southwest Africa and German East Africa. Ch. 13 (pp. 296–324) in A. Dirk Moses, ed., Empire, Colony, Genocide: Conquest, Occupation, and Subaltern Resistance in World History. New York: Berghahn Books.

Schaller, Dominik J. 2010b. Genocide and mass violence in the "heart of darkness": Africa in the colonial period. Ch. 17 (pp. 345–364) in Donald Bloxham and A. Dirk Moses, eds., The Oxford Handbook of Genocide Studies. Oxford: Oxford University Press.

Scheffer, David. 2006. Genocide and atrocity crimes. Genocide Studies and Prevention 1/3: 229–250.

Scheffer, David. 2015. What has been "extraordinary" about international justice in Cambodia? Address delivered at William and Mary Law School, February 25. Available at http://www.cambodiatribunal.org/2015/02/25/speech-by-un-special-expert-david-scheffer.

Schimmer, Russell. 2006. Indications of genocide in the Bisesero Hills, Rwanda, 1994. Working Paper 32. New Haven, CT: Yale University Genocide Studies Program.

Schirmer, Jennifer. 1998. The Guatemalan Military Project: A Violence Called Democracy. Philadelphia: University of Pennsylvania Press.

Schneiderhan, Erik. 2013. Genocide reconsidered: A pragmatist approach. Journal for the Theory of Social Behaviour 43/3: 280–300.

Schonhardt, Sara. 2012. Indonesia chips away at the enforced silence around a dark history. New York Times, January 19: A9.

Schulze, Rainer. 2012. "Life unworthy of life": From coerced sterilization to Action T4—stepping stones to genocide. Pp. 13–28 in Rainer Schulze, ed., The Holocaust in History and Memory, Vol. 5: Euthanasia Killings: The Treatment of Disabled People in Nazi Germany and Disability since 1945. Essex, UK: University of Essex, Department of History.

Scott, James C. 1998. Seeing like a State. New Haven, CT: Yale University Press.

Sémelin, Jacques, ed. 2008. Online Encyclopedia of Mass Violence. Paris: Center for International Studies and Research. http://www.massviolence.org/.

Sereny, Gitta. 1983. Into That Darkness: An Examination of Conscience. New York: Vintage Books.

Shaw, Martin. 2003. War and Genocide: Organised Killing in Modern Society. Cambridge, UK: Polity.

Shaw, Martin. 2007. What Is Genocide? Cambridge, UK: Polity.

Shaw, Martin. 2010. Sociology and genocide. Ch. 7 (pp. 142–162) in Donald Bloxham and A. Dirk Moses, eds., The Oxford Handbook of Genocide Studies. Oxford: Oxford University Press.

Shaw, Martin. 2013. Genocide and International Relations: Changing Patterns in the Transitions of the Late Modern World. Cambridge: Cambridge University Press.

Shelton, Dinah, ed. 2004. Encyclopedia of Genocide and Crimes against Humanity. 3 vols. New York: Macmillan.

Sherman, Larry W., Patrick R. Gartin, and Michael E. Muerger. 1989. Hot spots of predatory crime: Routine activities and the criminology of place. Criminology 27/1: 27–55.

Sikkink, Kathryn. 2011. The Justice Cascade: How Human Rights Prosecutions Are Changing World Politics. New York: Norton.

Sikkink, Kathryn, and Hun Joon Kim. 2013. The justice cascade: The origins and effectiveness of prosecutions of human rights violations. Annual Review of Law and Social Science 9:269–285.

Silvester, Jeremy, and Jan-Bart Gewald, eds. 2003. Words Cannot Be Found: German Colonial Rule in Namibia: An Annotated Reprint of the 1918 Blue Book. Leiden, Netherlands: Brill.

Singer, Tania, and Claus Lamm. 2009. The social neuroscience of empathy. Annals of the New York Academy of Sciences 1156:81–96.

Sjoberg, Laura. 2013. Gendering Global Conflict: Toward a Feminist Theory of War. New York: Columbia University Press.

Sluka, Jeffrey A., ed. 1999. Death Squad: The Anthropology of State Terror. Philadelphia: University of Pennsylvania Press.

Smeulers, Alette. 2006. Toward a criminology of international crimes. Criminology and International Crimes Newsletter 1/1: 2–3. http://www.supernationalcriminology.org.

Smeulers, Alette, and Roelof Haveman. 2008. Introduction. In Alette Smeulers and Roelof Haveman, eds., Supranational Criminology: Toward a Criminology of International Crimes. Antwerp, Belgium: Intersentia.

Smeulers, Alette, and Lotte Hoex. 2010. Studying the microdynamics of the Rwandan genocide. British Journal of Criminology 50:435–454.

Smith, David Livingstone. 2011. Less than Human: Why We Demean, Enslave, and Exterminate Others. New York: St. Martin's.

Snow, David A., and Doug McAdam. 2000. Identity work in the context of social movements: Clarifying the identity/movement nexus. Ch. 2 (pp. 41–67) in Sheldon Stryker, Timothy J. Owens, and Robert W. White, eds., Self, Identity, and Social Movements. Minneapolis: University of Minnesota Press.

Snyder, Timothy. 2010. Bloodlands: Europe between Hitler and Stalin. New York: Basic Books.

Soderlund, Walter. 2013. The responsibility to prevent: From identification to implementation. Paper presented at the annual conference of the Canadian Political Science Association, June 4–6. http://www.cpsa-acsp.ca/papers-2013.

Stafford, Mark C., and Mark Warr. 1993. A reconceptualization of general and specific deterrence. Journal of Research in Crime and Delinquency 30/2: 123–135.

Stanton, Gregory. 1998. The 8 Stages of Genocide. Genocide Watch. http://www.genocidewatch.org/aboutgenocide/8stagesofgenocide.html.

State Failure Task Force. 2000. Report: Phase III Findings. McLean, VA: Science Applications International.

Staub, Ervin. 1989. The Roots of Evil: The Origins of Genocide and Other Group Violence. Cambridge: Cambridge University Press.

Steinmetz, George. 2008. The colonial state as a social field: Ethnographic capital and native policy in the German overseas empire before 1914. American Sociological Review 73:589–612.

Straus, Scott. 2001. Contested meanings and conflicting imperatives: A conceptual analysis of genocide. Journal of Genocide Research 3/3: 349–375.

Straus, Scott. 2006. The Order of Genocide: Race, Power, and War in Rwanda. Ithaca, NY: Cornell University Press.

Straus, Scott. 2007. Second generation comparative research on genocide. World Politics 59:476–501.

Straus, Scott. 2012. "Destroy them to save us": Theories of genocide and the logic of political violence. Terrorism and Political Violence 24/4: 544–560.

Straus, Scott. 2015. Making and Unmaking Nations: War, Leadership, and Genocide in Modern Africa. Ithaca, NY: Cornell University Press.

Studzinsky, Silke. 2013. Victims of sexual and gender-based crimes before the Extraordinary Chambers in the Courts of Cambodia: Challenges of rights to participation and protection. Ch. 9 in Anne-Marie de Brouwer, Charlotte Ku, Renée Romkens, and Larissa van den Herik, eds., Sexual Violence as an International Crime: Interdisciplinary Approaches. Antwerp, Belgium: Intersentia.

Swan, Jon. 1991. The final solution in South West Africa. Military History Quarterly 3:36–55.

Swidler, Ann. 1986. Culture in action: Symbols and strategies. American Sociological Review 51:273–286.

Swidler, Ann. 2001. Talk of Love. Chicago: University of Chicago Press.

Sykes, Gresham M., and David Matza. 1957. Techniques of neutralization: A theory of delinquency. American Sociological Review 22/6: 664–670.

Taylor, Christopher C. 1999. Sacrifice as Terror: The Rwandan Genocide of 1994. Oxford, UK: Berg.

Tilly, Charles. 1985. War making and state making as organized crime. Ch. 5 (pp. 169–186) in Peter B. Evans, Dietrich Rueschemeyer, and Theda Skocpol, eds., Bringing the State Back In. Cambridge: Cambridge University Press.

Tilly, Charles. 2003. The Politics of Collective Violence. Cambridge: Cambridge University Press.

Torrey, E. Fuller, and Robert H. Yolken. 2010. Psychiatric genocide: Nazi attempts to eradicate schizophrenia. Schizophrenia Bulletin 36/1: 26–32.

Totten, Samuel. 2012. Genocide by Attrition: The Nuba Mountains of Sudan. New Brunswick, NJ: Transaction.

Totten, Samuel, and Paul R. Bartrop, eds. 2008. Dictionary of Genocide. Vol. 1 Westport, CT: Greenwood.

Totten, Samuel, William S. Parsons, and Israel W. Charny. 1995. Introduction. In Samuel Totten, William S. Parsons, and Israel W. Charny, eds., Genocide in the Twentieth Century: Critical Essays and Eyewitness Accounts. New York: Garland.

Turk, Austin. 1982. Political Criminality. Thousand Oaks, CA: Sage.

Uggen, Christopher, Hollie Nyseth Brehm, and Suzy McElrath. 2014. A dynamic life-course approach to genocide. American Society of Criminology, Presidential Panel Sessions of 2013. https://asc41.com/Annual_Meeting/2013/Presidential%20Papers/Uggen_Nyseth_Brehm_McElrathGenocide.pdf.

Üngör, Ugur Ümit. 2009. Seeing like a nation-state: Young Turk social engineering in eastern Turkey, 1913–50. Ch. 2 (pp. 9–33) in Dominik J. Schaller and Jürgen Zimmerer, eds., Late Ottoman Genocides: The Dissolution of the Ottoman Empire and Young Turkish Population and Extermination Policies. New York: Routledge.

Üngör, Ugur Ümit, and Mehmet Polatel. 2011. Confiscation and Destruction: The Young Turk Seizure of Armenian Property. New York: Continuum.

United Nations. 1946. General Assembly Resolution 96/1: The Crime of Genocide. December 11.

United Nations. 1948. Convention on the Prevention and Punishment of the Crime of Genocide. December. http://www.hrweb.org/legal/genocide.html.

United Nations. 2002. Rome Statute of the International Criminal Court, UN Doc. 2187 U.N.T.S. 90. Entered into force July 1.

United Nations. 2005. General Assembly Resolution 60/1.

United Nations. 2008. Security Council Resolution 1820.

United Nations. 2013. Background Information on the Justice and Reconciliation Process in Rwanda. http://www.un.org/en/preventgenocide/rwanda/al.

United Nations Office on Drugs and Crime. 2013. Global Study on Homicide 2013. Vienna: United Nations Office on Drugs and Crime.

Valentino, Benjamin A. 2004. Final Solutions: Mass Killing and Genocide in the 20th Century. Ithaca, NY: Cornell University Press.

Vann Nath. 1998. A Cambodian Prison Portrait: One Year in the Khmer Rouge's S-21. Bangkok: White Lotus.

Verdeja, Ernesto. 2002. On genocide: Five contributing factors. Contemporary Politics 8/1: 37–54.

Verwimp, Philip. 2005. An economic profile of peasant perpetrators of genocide: Micro-level evidence from Rwanda. Journal of Development Economics 77:297–323.

Verwimp, Philip. 2013. Peasants in Power: The Political Economy of Development and Genocide in Rwanda. New York: Springer.

Vignemont, Frederique de, and Tania Singer. 2006. The empathic brain: How, when and why? Trends in Cognitive Sciences 10/10: 435–441.

von Joeden-Forgey, Elisa. 2012. Genocidal masculinity. Ch. 5 (pp. 76–94) in Adam Jones, ed., New Directions in Genocide Research. London: Routledge.

Waller, James. 2007. Becoming Evil: How Ordinary People Commit Genocide and Mass Killing. 2d ed. New York: Oxford University Press.

Warren, Kay. 1999. Death squads and wider complicities: Dilemmas for an anthropology of violence. In Jeffrey A. Sluka, ed., Death Squad: The Anthropology of State Terror. Philadelphia: University of Pennsylvania Press.

Warren, Mary Anne. 1985. Gendercide: The Implications of Sex Selection. Totowa, NJ: Rowman and Allanheld.

Weikart, Richard. 2003. Progress through racial extermination: Social Darwinism, eugenics, and pacifism in Germany, 1860–1918. German Studies Review 26:273–294.

Weiss-Wendt, Anton. 2010. The state and genocide. Ch. 4 (pp. 81–101) in Donald Bloxham and A. Dirk Moses, eds., The Oxford Handbook of Genocide Studies. Oxford: Oxford University Press.

Weitsman, Patricia A. 2008. The politics of identity and sexual violence: A review of Bosnia and Rwanda. Human Rights Quarterly 30/3: 561–578.

Weitz, Eric D. 2003. A Century of Genocide: Utopias of Race and Nation. Princeton, NJ: Princeton University Press.

West, Candace, and Don H. Zimmerman. 1987. Doing gender. Gender and Society 1/2: 125–151.

Wieringa, Saskia. 2003. The birth of the New Order state in Indonesia: Sexual politics and nationalism. Journal of Women's History 15/1: 70–91.

Wippman, David. 1999. Atrocities, deterrence, and the limits of international justice. Fordham International Law Journal 23:473–488.

Wolfe, Patrick. 2006. Settler colonialism and the elimination of the native. Journal of Genocide Research 8/4: 387–409.

Wolfe, Patrick. 2010. Structure and event: Settler colonialism, time, and the question of genocide. Ch. 4 (pp. 102–132) in Dirk A. Moses, ed., Empire, Colony, Genocide: Conquest, Occupation, and Subaltern Resistance in World History. New York: Berghahn Books.

Woolford, Andrew. 2009. Ontological destruction: Genocide and Canadian Aboriginal peoples. Genocide Studies and Prevention 4/1: 81–97.

Woolford, Andrew. 2014. Discipline, territory, and the colonial mesh: Indigenous boarding schools in the United States and Canada. Ch. 1 (pp. 29–48) in Andrew Woolford, Jeff Benvenuto, and Alexander Laban Hinton, eds., Colonial Genocide in Indigenous North America. Durham, NC: Duke University Press.

Woolford, Andrew, Jeff Benvenuto, and Alexander Laban Hinton, eds. 2014. Colonial Genocide in Indigenous North America. Durham, NC: Duke University Press.

Young, James E. 1993. The Texture of Memory: Holocaust Memorials and Meaning. New Haven, CT: Yale University Press.

Zaslavsky, Victor. 2008. Class Cleansing: The Katyn Massacre. New York: Telos.

Zimmerer, Jürgen. 2010. Colonial genocide: The Herero and Nama war (1904–8) in German South West Africa and its significance. Ch. 12 (pp. 323–343) in Dan Stone, ed., The Historiography of Genocide. New York: Palgrave Macmillan.

INDEX

ABOUT THE AUTHOR

Nicole Rafter is Professor Emerita of Criminology and Criminal Justice at Northeastern University, where she taught from 1977 until 2015. She is the author of *Partial Justice: Women, State Prisons, and Social Control*; *Creating Born Criminals*; *Shots in the Mirror: Crime Films and Society*; *The Criminal Brain*; and (with Michelle Brown) *Criminology Goes to the Movies*. She has also translated (with Mary Gibson) the major criminological works of Cesare Lombroso and published over fifty journal articles and chapters. In 2009, she received the American Society of Criminology's Sutherland Award; other honors include a Fulbright Fellowship and several fellowships to Oxford University.